THE
BANK MANAGER
AND THE
HOLY GRAIL

BYRON ROGERS is the author of *An Audience with an Elephant* ('Very funny but also beautiful and moving' – *New Statesman*), *The Green Lane to Nowhere* ('The most beautiful book in recent memory about the Midlands' – *Daily Express*), *The Last Englishman: The Life of J.L. Carr*, acclaimed by Simon Jenkins in *The Times* as 'a miniature masterpiece of social history', and *The Last Human Cannonball* ('Another Rogers masterpiece' – *Western Mail*). All are published by Aurum. He lives in Northamptonshire.

'A great journalist from the older school' – *Guardian*

'A wonderful writer: droll, poignant and dreamy' – *New Statesman*

THE
BANK MANAGER
AND THE
HOLY GRAIL

TRAVELS IN WALES, WITH SNAPSHOTS

BYRON ROGERS

'What ish my nation? Who talks of my nation ish a villain,
and a bastard, and a knave, and a rascal.'
Henry V, Act III, scene ii.

To Bethan Gwenllian

who spent her early childhood in England introducing
herself as Bethan Getting-on Rogers.

First published in Great Britain
2003 by Aurum Press Ltd
25 Bedford Avenue, London WC1B 3AT

Reprinted twice

This paperback edition first published 2005

Many of the pieces in this book first appeared in earlier versions in the *Daily Telegraph* Magazine, *Sunday Telegraph*, *Guardian*, *International Herald Tribune* and *Saga Magazine*.
Every effort has been made to trace the copyright holders of material quoted in this book.
If application is made in writing to the publisher, any omissions will be included in
future editions.

A catalogue record for this book is available from the British Library.

ISBN 1 84513 050 2

1 3 5 7 9 10 8 6 4 2
2005 2007 2009 2008 2006

Designed in 11 on 14pt Bulmer by Geoff Green Book Design
Printed by Bookmarque, Croydon, Surrey

CONTENTS

FOREWORD

Most of what follows was written from exile, or England as some call it. This meant I could aspire to the detachment of an observer, something that horrified my mother. '*Cas yw'r gwr na charo'r wlad a'i maco.*' The man is despicable who does not love the land which bred him. When she was not saying that, she was assuring me she would never again dare show her face in this world, or at least not in the town of Carmarthen, which in her case was more or less the same thing. The Welsh have never liked detachment, or observers.

Daw Saeson fel gwibed… 'Englishmen in the shape of Editors, Newspaper Correspondents, Government Commissioners and such like are crossing Offa's Dyke like flies,' thundered an 1847 editorial in *Y Diwygiwr* (The Reformer). They came because industrial and agrarian unrest in Wales had forcibly reminded the English of their first colony, and this had puzzled them.

'These wily knaves, in the fullness of their official dignity, look us up and down, and take upon themselves to understand everything about our numbers, morals, religion and fashions, and then, knowing no more about us than moles about the sun, return whence they came, concocting their stories and fashioning far-fetched, absurd and baseless fables about us.'

The English attitude to the Welsh had its origins in worry ('Be ware of Wales, Christ Jesus must us keep / That it make not our child's child to weep'). Military conquest removed that worry at great financial cost (the expense of one military expedition, wrote Giraldus Cambrensis in the twelfth century, was as much as the taxes that could be levied on the Welsh 'over a whole series of years'). The inevitable sense of anticlimax brought the irritated condescension that survives today, through which at times there surfaces the question Butch Cassidy asked the Sundance Kid: 'Who are these guys?'

It is still being asked today. While I was in the process of compiling this book I heard it twice in four weeks on, of all things, the Radio 4 programme *The News Quiz*. One speaker said he could understand why Africans, say, hated the English, but the Welsh... what had the English ever done to the Welsh? Conquest, ethnic cleansing, then colonisation with the attitudes that bred in coloniser and colonised, that is all. Only the English have forgotten this, just as they have forgotten that the first Prince of Wales was not an Englishman; the Welsh, as George Borrow wrote, will never forget.

But in the 1840s the question was being asked with some urgency, the 1831 Merthyr Rising and the 1839 Chartist March on Newport having alerted the English Government to a society in which, because of the way industrialisation had torn into Wales, villages had become towns virtually overnight, only these were towns without a middle class or gentry, where anything could happen. And it was not just industrial Wales; in the same decade the Rebecca Riots broke out in the agrarian west. At such moments English politicians could only shakily echo what a nineteenth-century bishop had told a vicar just appointed to a Welsh parish, 'I leave you as a missionary in the heart of Africa.' So, after the troops (the last cavalry charge on the British mainland took place in a Carmarthen street in 1843, when the 4th Light Dragoons charged the Rebecca Rioters), over the border like flies ('*fel gwibed*') they came, the correspondents and the commissions of inquiry. And to what?

It is 1957, and on a beautiful October morning I am travelling westward from Carmarthen in a van with my father and his workmate Ifor Phillips, Ifor Pencraig, it being the Welsh custom to call a man after his small-holding or farm. Both these men are carpenters, and the van smells of planed wood and cement dust – odd, cold smells. I am a boy of fifteen off school with flu, who has just come along for the ride, but I have not forgotten that morning: across forty-six years it has become a moment of social history.

At the time I was conscious only of irritation, for every 15 minutes or so Ifor would turn to me and ask, 'Happy?' Now I was fond of Ifor, but I was in my first term in the Lower Sixth, and full of myself, as anyone might be, who in purple ink and three different handwriting styles had just completed an essay on the Prioress's Tale from Chaucer. And here I had as travelling companion a man never out of the British Isles, who in the middle of the twentieth century *was unable to frame a single English sentence*. Yet between the 'Happy's', he and my father talked. That is to say, they talked in Welsh.

What would you expect two workmen to have talked about? People they knew? Yes, they did that. Sport? No. Neither of them had ever watched a game of organised sport, and had probably never taken part in one. What these two talked about for the most part was sermons they had heard.

I record this now with bewilderment, for that October morning I might have been on the road with two Cromwellian troopers. But it was not theology that interested them, it was the word play of the old preachers they could quote by the yard, for their oral memories were not of the late twentieth century at all. I listened as they roared with laughter at the metaphors and the rhetoric, listening with the condescension of someone who was about to turn his back on the world of which they, and all my ancestors, were part. The amazing thing is that they would not have borne me any ill will for this. The education of which they approved underwrote such a process: to get on, which was what it was all about, meant leaving behind their culture and the Welsh language. In 1957 we were still a colonial people.

'What will you be studying at Oxford?' asked Percy Mott, who kept a sweet shop in Carmarthen. English, I said. 'So what will you become?' An Englishman, I said. Mr Mott nodded.

I am the first one in my family to make a living from the English language: nothing remarkable in that, it is the experience of most writers. *But I am also the first generation of my family to speak it as a first language.* When I told people this at Oxford, they did not believe me. It had never occurred to them that 150 miles down the A40 there was a way of life so different, it could be that of another country. The English had forgotten who the Welsh were.

All this was our island, we were the British.

The first English immigrants, staring at us across the wreckage of the Roman Empire, called us that, when they weren't calling us the 'weallas', the Welsh, the strangers. And what happened after, in those 200 lost years between 400 and 600, is still a mystery. Had things followed the pattern they took in the other provinces of the Western Empire, in France, Italy and Spain, where the host populations, as in Britain, vastly outnumbered the barbarian immigrants, you would today be speaking a form of Latinised Welsh. The mystery lies in the fact that you are not.

My father could speak English but was not comfortable in it, being capable of such antique lurches as when, in a temper, he said of one man, 'Him? He's nothing but a whoremaster.' His father, it was thought, could speak it but never did, though he read the whole of the *Western Mail* every day. But before that, my people, farm labourer after farm labourer disappearing into the poverty and the lime-washed cottages of west Wales, were monoglot Welsh. That is to say, all the generations before me, before television and for the most part before radio, were part of a culture that owed nothing at all to England: they sang none of its popular songs, and, being countrymen, played no sport. They took little interest in English politics, except in the career of Lloyd George, one of their own who had brought in the old age pension. Now this was not the experience of most Welshmen: it was not the experience of industrial South Wales, or that of the people of the Borders or the cities, but mine was pura Wallia, the shrinking agricultural Welsh-speaking west. My cousin Felicity, looking back on her experience of being evacuated there as a child from London during the war, said it was like turning up in southern Spain. But it was a small world.

I was born three miles from the town of Carmarthen, near the village of Bancyfelin, my father in a small-holding 300 yards beyond that, my mother in a farm a mile and a half away. When my mother's funeral cortege left Carmarthen for the crematorium in Narberth, it passed in less than five minutes through her whole world, past places where she had been born, married, given birth, lived and died. Yet here there were cultivated men.

My grandfather's job was to lead shire stallions – huge, terrifying creatures – from farm to farm, so had you met him you would have assumed you were meeting someone whose main interest was in anything that ate oats and farted. Not so. My grandfather's main interest was poetry, which he wrote in the old, elaborate metres of the Middle Ages, and where in England would you encounter such a figure? His very existence would be a shock to you, except he was cultivated behind the escarpment of the Welsh language, where few English scholars have gone.

In 1846 among the flies coming over the Border were three English barristers, hired by the Government to inquire into the state of Welsh education. These men duly published a report that is one of the most extraordinary documents ever compiled on anything. The fact that most of the people they were investigating could not speak English did not faze them in the least: they just concluded they were illiterate, and went further. The Welsh language, they wrote, contributed to crime. The fact that prison figures did not bear this out was breezily brushed aside as being due to the sneakiness of the Welsh, or, as they wrote, 'to the extreme shrewdness and caution of the people'.

That absurdity has gone but the ignorance persists. When the poet R.S. Thomas, on a writers' tour sponsored by the Arts Council, was asked in Bury St Edmunds as to who had had the most influence on him, the questioner expected him to name a writer in English. Instead he said Sion Cent, a fifteenth-century misanthrope after his own heart. Thomas told me he had done this out of mischief, to see the reaction of his audience but also to rub their noses in the fact that there was a great lyric tradition in their island of which they knew absolutely nothing. When did you see a translation of Welsh verse in any English bookshop, the oldest vernacular literature in Europe? But then how many Welshmen know it to be so?

I started to leave the world of my ancestors at the age of five, when my parents moved to Carmarthen. This, though it had a much earlier Roman past and was the oldest continually inhabited town in Wales, was, like all old Welsh towns, still an English colonial outpost. Eight centuries after its Norman foundation, there was probably nowhere on earth such a distinction as there was here between town and country. It was a source of pride to its inhabitants that they could not talk Welsh, for this was the language of the country people to whom they felt as superior as any settlers. I saw the last of this garrison mentality, just as I was old enough to see the Welsh squires pass.

A small boy, I was asked to a Coronation party by our doctor, who owned a television set. The adult guests were what passed for a middle class in a small Welsh town, but amongst them was an old couple of whom the assembled doctors and vets seemed in awe. Both were very tall and very gaunt, and both were very smashed before the Queen even got to the Abbey. I followed them around all day, fascinated by their upper-class English accents, also in the hope they would fall over. Later I was told that these were the last of the squires, members of a family the origins of which were lost in ballads and folklore. English public schools had made a nonsense of these origins; death duties and a hereditary talent for ruin did the rest.

It was the new bilingual employment policies of the local council at the end of the twentieth century which were to do for the garrison mentality of Carmarthen. The ambitious parents of my time who brought their children up not to speak Welsh have given way to others, even more ambitious, who have enrolled their children in Welsh language schools, which is almost as bizarre. For, as I asked a Welsh Nationalist whose dream in this respect had been realised, 'What do they speak when they get outside school?' He said sadly, 'I think you know the answer to that.'

I saw the start of this process when the novelist Islwyn Ffowc Elis, whom you will encounter in these pages, wrote an open letter in the local paper. The post of Secretary to the Welsh Joint Education Council had just become vacant, and Ffowc Ellis addressed the parents of Carmarthen. 'This job requires a knowledge of Welsh. See to it now that your children one day may qualify…'. With some of my friends I wrote to the paper in response, protesting against such blackmail. But the tide was turning for us.

We made jokes, like the one about the lifeguard seen watching a man drown off the coast at Llansteffan. Asked why he did not try to rescue him, the lifeguard said he couldn't swim. 'There were six of us on the short list. Five had reached Olympic standards in swimming, but not one of them could speak Welsh. Isn't that terrible?' Such policies exclude the vast majority of the Welsh who are not fluent in the language, perhaps as much as 85 per cent, from all senior bureaucratic and teaching jobs, just as once a similar majority would have been excluded for a lack of fluency in English. Dispossession in our own country is for us a very old experience, it is just that in its time it has taken many forms.

So why do I keep returning? Many of my generation never do, but the answer is that I never really went away. Even now I can go back and within a few hours take on the accent, the language and the folklore of a place I left in 1945. The other selves, expensively educated, honed on the English class system, fall away, and I walk through the graveyards at Cana, near Bancyfelin, remembering from my father's stories the people who lie beneath those stones, the farmers, the lorry driver to whose deathbed I was taken aged four; the lady called Alsace, born amidst the headlines of World War I in which he fought, the great flying hero buried just across the road. Here is the lane from which my grandmother's illegitimate child whistled to check whether her husband, my grandfather, was at home, and here the house where every night an old lady put milk out for the fairies: that house has solar panels now.

Besides, I was never that good as an Englishman. What had I found hardest to adapt to, asked the elderly Lady Megan Lloyd George on the one occasion I met her. 'The English middle class,' I said. 'Ah yes, I never got used to them,' she said. 'All those rules.'

So over the Border I kept coming, like a fly. *Fel gwibedyn*. In these pages you will meet the people I met and those whom time prevented my meeting. You will meet racehorse trainers and boxers, drunks and writers, a coracleman and a collider with every form of authority he has ever encountered. You will meet Great War flying aces, and Victorian convicts, and princes, for the Welsh past is never more than a few fingertips away. You will walk through the landscape and encounter the Welsh language in which there is no word for orgasm. My quest for the Holy Grail allows me to record the strangest dialogue I have ever had with another human being, and *Behemoth Called, With Roses* the strangest incident I ever read about in a newspaper. The sections are self-explanatory; the shorter snapshots with which they start are an attempt to encapsulate them in a person, a moment or an event.

The single exception is the one cause I have taken up, that of the people in Pembroke accused of being part of a paedophile ring employing satanic rituals. You heard a lot about such things in the 1990s, though not now. Yet this one case, one alone, made the criminal courts, though few of you will have heard of the greatest miscarriage of justice in my time.

I use the term for a reason those with no experience of life in a small Welsh town may find naïve: I did not *believe* any of it. But then, unlike the other flies, 'Editors, Newspaper Correspondents, Government Commissioners and such like', I come from a society in which keeping an eye on the neighbours is the most important leisure pursuit. Compared with the mothers of west Wales, the most implacable intelligence gathering set-up ever known, the members of the old KGB were amateurs, so the accused could not have done what they were charged with for one simple reason: someone, somewhere, sometime, would have seen them doing it. The watchers and the watched, and all the others you will meet in these pages, are my people.

Carmarthen, 2003

PART ONE
INTRODUCTIONS

AT THE GRAVE OF
EVAN GRIFFITHS,
AN ILLEGITIMATE

CANA, 1999

You whistled from the lane
outside your mother's house,
    you, her shame, asking
    to be let in
to family and home.
I hear your nails upon the window pane.

No need to whistle now.
You lie beside her,
she under marble, you,
more discreet in death,
your earth grave level with the earth,
so no one knows your secret except us.

You, the man outside,
unmarried, drunk,
a hired hand on farms,
your name not written
in the fading Bible ink.
And we are here to give you back your name.
We, the relatives you never knew, have come,
after seventy years, to ask you in.

THE HOUSE

The house, like Jerusalem, stood at the centre of all things. A lane ran by it and where that turned was the edge of the known world, marked by a grove of trees beyond which one did not go, for these were on a steep bank, their roots writhing in and out of each other like serpents. Our one neighbour, who lived beside this, sold butter and eggs and each night put out a saucer of milk to appease the fairies – just as her mother had done and her mother before her. And each morning the milk had been drunk. All this I know for certain truth.

The house seemed taller than the Empire State building, its gates greater than those of Babylon, which no one man might open, and beside it a dark pool I knew to be bottomless, with water so poisonous it ate through shoes and could dissolve bone. I slipped in once and for days sat quietly in corners checking my toes. Here I was born, in the house called Cowin Villa.

I called again some years ago. It was a warm day but the fire in the kitchen range was blazing, and the old lady who had bought the house from us was crouched before this, prodding it vigorously with a poker. As she straightened up, I saw her hair was a wild blonde colour. Good for her, I thought, for she was almost into her nineties.

'How did you manage with this thing?' she said in Welsh, as though I had just popped out for a walk in the intervening years.

Before I could answer, the fire coughed, and for a few seconds her head and shoulders actually disappeared from view. It was then that I realised her hair colour did not come from a bottle at all. 'Forty years I've been trying to stop this smoking,' she said. 'What did you do?'

'I was four,' I said, 'you don't notice things like that when you're four.'

But other things you do, and the years just etch them deeper and deeper in the memory, for there is no present to blur their effect, only a past that becomes more and more vivid, like a Victorian photograph. I can close my eyes and walk round the house and its gardens now, and the only shock on opening the gates is the knowledge that the house is *not* taller than the Empire State, its gates not greater than those of Babylon.

The people who lived in your house before you are mysterious figures, for it is hard to believe in them, but the ones who come afterwards are a nuisance: you walk through rooms you no longer recognise, so it is hard to believe in your own memories. Did I really live here? Did all those things happen?

The extraordinary thing about Cowin Villa is that nothing at all has changed. It was bought from us as a retirement home by a farmer and his sister, and now that the Chinese have broken up the lamaseries of Tibet, the most conservative people on Earth are Welsh farmers in retirement: they altered nothing. The pebble dash is still there, the gates are those my father put up, and there has been no change of any kind except that, the old couple being dead, the house was bought at auction two years ago by a lottery winner who has still to move in. The result is that, with the garden having run wild, Cowin Villa will soon look like something out of time, which explorers could stumble on in the rain forests of South America. Yet I was born there.

My father was a carpenter (when I became speech writer to the Prince of Wales, there was a small headline, 'Charles to take on son of carpenter', which my wife said made it sound as though the Second Coming was at hand). He made gates, doors, chairs, wheels for our neighbours' carts and also their coffins. And he made toys.

These were the war years when nobody had toys, but he must have had a contract with a shop in the town, for, without telling me, he kept one of everything he made. On Christmas Day 1945 my parents drew back the curtains and as far as I could see there were tanks, gypsy caravans, lorries, trains and a pedal car. I was three – and an only child.

And if the house was at the centre of all things, I was at the centre of the house. It contained four adults, my parents and my mother's parents, also retired farmers. I would walk the lane with my grandfather, whose company allowed me to brave the grove of trees, gravely discussing with him the weather and the possibility of a good hay harvest. On the rare occasions I met other children, I was stunned to learn they were not interested in such things.

I took my responsibilities seriously, especially those relating to the bantam chickens someone must have told me to guard, which was a big mistake: whenever one of my visiting cousins wandered up the garden in their direction, I bit him or her. It was when I bit an adult neighbour and then tried to finish her off with my father's heavy wooden train that it had to be explained to me that there were limits to my guardianship. I can remember that scene now around the rain barrel on which, in a preserving jar, my mother had put an 18-inch tapeworm I had passed.

We were remote from all public events, even the war, for there were no rations in the country, a pig being quietly slaughtered whenever there was need. I once saw a stabbed pig rise from a bench, scattering the men, a knife in its throat, before I was hurried away. I knew there had to be a world outside the lane, for cousins materialised from this and occasionally my father would disappear into something called the Home Guard. I stole his bayonet, because I associated this with his absences, and buried it among the potato rows. Nobody noticed it had gone until the Victory Parade.

In Europe, German generals were denying all knowledge of war crimes, as in the west of Wales a small boy said he had seen a cat called Micky making off with the bayonet. They found it in the autumn, a rusted relic from what could have been the Bronze Age.

Because I had no friends of my own age, the games I played were very strange. My favourite, played on Sunday nights when my mother had gone to chapel, was to get my father to produce the boxes of cutlery and spoons they had been given as wedding presents. I would open them one by one, marvelling at the blue gathered silk and the glittering metal, and, with all this treasure on the table between us, my father would tell me stories. Grown-ups told stories then, sitting round the fire that smoked, though I didn't notice, with shadows racing up the wall, for there was no electric light.

We lived there for almost five years, during which time I did not hear a word of English spoken. We then moved to Carmarthen, and more children than I had ever seen in one place crowded around the van. They stared at me, and I, who had not a syllable of speech in common with them, stared back.

1993

THE TOWN

In the west of Wales, in the late twentieth century, there is a town under a permanent state of siege from its inhabitants. In the last twenty years they have pulled down its old alleys, demolished the narrow street that was all that remained of a town gate and driven a four-lane bypass between it and the one reason for its existence: the River Towy. The town centre has become a light industrial slum.

The man who designed much of it is in Europe, sought by the police forces of South Wales who are eager to discuss his vision with them, and, as I write, ninety of its inhabitants are recovering from a gas, as yet unidentified, that laid them out in rows in the biggest supermarket in the town centre. Most things that happen in my town are a black comedy.

Last year the district council began to build what it said was to be a 'suite' for its chairman. Only when the suite was found to be 30 feet underground did they admit that they were building a bomb shelter.

It would have cost £30,000; protests, injunctions and legal fees have now made that £300,000, and all that exists is a large hole. When a great obelisk in memory of General Thomas Picton, who died at Waterloo, was found to be unsafe, the council at first thought of demolishing it. The outcry that this prompted outside the town, especially among senior army officers and the Duke of Wellington, made them change their minds. So they cut the thing in half, saying they were taking the stones into care. They have now replaced them, only the wrong mortar was used and the long white stains make it look as though the old memorial has been sick all over itself.

At the eastern end there was once the Old Oak, familiar to millions from postcards and even a folk song. A long fingernail of dead wood, it stood in concrete, and the council routed the road around it because of a prophecy, associated with the magician Merlin, that when the Old Oak fell, so would the town, supposedly by flood. It fell late one Saturday night when three drunks climbed it with a hacksaw, falling on the head of one who was convinced he heard great waters. Afterwards they were contrite, but for four days nobody even noticed it had gone and the town did not fall, or if it did, nobody was aware of the fact.

For Carmarthen is the only place on Earth inhabited not by two races but by two distinct species of humans, something that has not happened since the dawn when Neanderthal man and Homo sapiens coexisted. The Homo sapiens are an emerging Welsh middle class – most of them bureaucrats. More than 50 per cent of the people of Carmarthen are employed by the state, the town being the centre of administration for West Wales. Such wary figures do not complain about anything, and the other species just does not notice anything.

These are a lost race of behemoths, men of startling size – 18, 19, even 20 stone – and they are children of history. When the Normans conquered Wales, they built castles and then towns around the castles, to which they attracted colonial settlers with the usual promises of economic exploitation. Only they could hold markets, and whenever there were markets, the pubs were open. There are markets now on four days of every week in Carmarthen, sometimes five.

So the pubs were open all day, which of course they are everywhere now, but when I was a boy it was amazing. From 11.00 in the morning to 11.00 at night they were open, with the exception of two pubs that opened at 9.30, 'so the farmers could wash their hands'. And it was known that the only things that closed at 11.00 in Carmarthen were the curtains in the pubs.

Where were the six-bottle men, sighed the old Regency buck Captain Gronow in the 1850s, wistful for his youth. When I was a boy they were all in Carmarthen, only they drank beer – gallon men, 2-gallon men, practitioners of a different style of boozing that lasted all day. You rarely saw them on the streets because when not at work they were in the pubs, getting bigger and bigger and bigger. They rarely left the town, and when they did they caused chaos wherever they went.

A friend of mine met one who had gone to London for a hair transplant. He had picked up a woman and in the exertions of the afternoon the transplant stitches had broken and were oozing blood, his new hairpiece having moved down to within an inch of his eye, where it hung like a cat. He was forcing drink on the woman. ''Ave a gin.' 'No thanks, dear, perhaps a fruit juice.' ''AVE A GIN. This is a pub, not a health farm.'

One of them became Carmarthen's only political prisoner (see *John X*, p. 53). Another, attempting to make love to his girlfriend on a riverbank, slid into the mud flats. In the dark, naked and covered with mud, he was beaten with paddles by coraclemen, nervous for their catch, who thought they had come upon a huge bull seal.

Then there was the town solicitor stopped by the police because he was drunk, who took off in his car and was chased to within a few miles of the English border. A restaurateur, taken by the police to the local hospital to have a blood test for alcohol content, vanished by hanging on to the springs beneath the bed, prompting a manhunt. His restaurant was later the scene of an incident remarkable even by Carmarthen standards. A neighbour, enraged by the noise during a function, came in with a chainsaw and, having demolished the banisters, started on the tables while the guests were still eating.

It was always like this. An awed local historian found that in the nineteenth century Carmarthen had more pubs and murders than Dodge City. But now a wonderful humour had come, with one species, avid for respectability, denying that any of it went on, a former headmistress castigating the press for reports that the town was a boozer's paradise. But then the two species never met. Late at night an efficient taxi service came into its own, when the drinkers needed ferrying home to their long-suffering wives. You saw their huge faces in the backs of the cabs, passing as impassively as the priest-kings of the East.

'When we came to Carmarthen, we went into a pub,' said the wife of a chief superintendent of police. 'There were two men there who knew my husband, and they'd been there *for two days*. They asked what I would like to drink. Port, I said. The next thing I knew I'd been given a pint of port. I was still staring at it when the barman, taking pity, took it away. I turned around to talk to someone, and the next thing I knew there was another pint of port on the bar.'

One day the anthropologists will come.

1986

THE SCHOOL

It certainly looked the same. Above the rugby pitch, which every winter proved as difficult to drain as the Western Front, there was the same straggle of grey buildings along a ridge. But one wing had gone, destroyed by fire, and the school lavatories, pans proudly trade-named 'The Flood', had been pulled down. For generations they were a place of sanctuary for smokers, against whom the previous headmaster waged a sort of holy war, until, suddenly wearying of his efforts, he had the whole lot razed to the ground. It is popularly believed that he considered this the greatest achievement of his career. There is grass now where the romantic little packets of five Woodbines were tremulously opened, long ago.

In place of the gutted wing another has been built, to house woodwork and metalwork rooms. That was the first shock. When I left the school, in 1959, woodwork and metalwork had as much place in the curriculum of the Queen Elizabeth Grammar School for Boys, Carmarthen, as the Black Arts.

I remember my first day there. After prayers the Head called five young men out of the wings of the stage. They were those members of the previous year's Sixth Form who had won State Scholarships, and they stood there stiffly as their names were called out. It was the first introduction of the little boys in the front rows to the cult into which they were about to be initiated. The masters, impassive in their black gowns, might be its high priests, but these were the heroes. Their glory was underwritten not only by the school, but, more significantly, by the society in which they had all grown up. Few things in life ever equal that. Anyone without experience of small Welsh towns will have little idea of the fame these boys enjoyed, their names chronicled in local papers, their parents congratulated in the streets. But it was such a brief glory. I remember my feeling of outrage when, fenced about with my own scholarships, I realised that next autumn others would set out to inherit the earth.

The grammar school was the one route that led out of the town to the professions, and to take it you had to pass exams. The school purveyed an education perfectly tailored for the scaling of the Ordinary and Advanced Levels of the Welsh Joint Education Board. Trained to argue lucidly as to whether Napoleon was Heir to the Revolution or Last of the Enlightened Despots, and come even more lucidly to no conclusion at all, it was possible for the more able boys to be quite unbeatable at A-level. And so it had always been – until now.

It was a strange time to choose to go back. In 1976 the Gram will be 400 years old. But it is possible that it will celebrate this from inside a comprehensive school five times its present size. The Ministry's instruction, evaded for so long, has abruptly become an ultimatum. There is a Cavafy poem about a small Roman town in the twilight of the Empire, in which the inhabitants listlessly await the coming of the Barbarians. Would it be like that?

The present Head, D.J. Evans, was an assistant master in my time. Even so, entering his study one felt like a successful revolutionary penetrating the secret police headquarters. How strange that this narrow little room, with its timetables and faded paintings, once prompted such terror. Only the quick, and the very quick, came out unscathed.

The most abrupt change since my time has been in the position of the Head. In my time he was an autocrat, answerable to no one (no Parent Teacher Association was ever established at the Gram). 'Where does the Head stand in modern society?' asked Mr Evans, and would not stay for an answer. 'If I insisted on a boy cutting his hair and he refused, could I deny him an education? I wouldn't have a leg to stand on. Smoking is forbidden and practised, just as in your time.' He smiled wearily. 'But when a boy comes to me and tells me he smokes at home and that he drinks with his father at the golf club, I feel pretty silly enforcing the rules.' Today the Head cannot even put a boy in detention after school; he would be held responsible if anything happened to a boy going home in the dark.

Change among the boys is not immediately apparent. They still jerk to their feet when a master enters the room. They still wear school blazers. Hair, apart from that of some boys in the Sixth Form, is short by English standards. But the wearing of caps, rigidly enforced in my time, has gone. 'They couldn't, not with that hair,' said the Head gently.

'The boys,' said Jack Thomas, the history master, 'are much more friendly than in your day. We treat the sixth formers as grown-ups, which you would find very strange, and they're quite frank with us. Of course, it's much less academic now.'

The school abolished 'streaming' this year. Something like half the Upper Sixth have announced their intention of going nowhere near a university. Eleven of their number have opted to leave and join the newly-constituted Dyfed local authority. As John Aubrey mourned, it was not so in Queen Elizabeth's day.

A boy in the Upper Sixth, hair falling lankly to his shoulders, shirt open to mid-chest, said, 'There's no point now. You can leave and make more money at Ford's.' There was a peculiar listlessness about the older boys. One said it must have been better in my time, with the discipline. Another said, without much interest, that it seemed a pity the School's academic results were falling off. Suddenly one felt it was not so much the masters who were awaiting the Barbarians.

It extends to the sports field. Dewi Lewis, the Deputy Head, said with some bewilderment, 'I was watching the boys when the whole school turned out for a rugby match. More than half of them didn't seem to be interested at all.'

A footnote to how much change has occurred in just fifteen years was my own incredulity at finding the Sixth Form, during a general arts period, experimenting with a light projector to make a visual interpretation of the *Planet Suite*. If we had listened to Holst, it would have been because the Welsh Joint Education Council had ordained we listened to Holst, and Holst would have been another rung on the ladder to the town clerkship or the lectureship or the general practice.

But now the school seems to have lingered on beyond its allotted span. The relaxed entrance requirements of the new polytechnics undermine its academic pride. The new little boys, products of different teaching methods, make a mockery of its discipline. A tradition, unchanged over 400 years, is coming to an end. This was a proud, competitive place where the few succeeded wildly but very many more failed.

'I met a bank manager in the National Eisteddfod this year,' said the Head. 'His daughter told me every time they drove past the Gram, he took his hat off.'

He shook his head with puzzlement. 'And he wasn't even one of the bright boys.'

1976

THE VALLEY

She opened the curtains a few feet more. 'It's almost time now,' she said. 'The sudden light comes out of the west at just after 4 o'clock. Look across the valley. There, at the mountain.' It stood against the sky some 20 miles away, an escarpment below which the land was in shadow. 'And here it is.' She could have been talking about an old friend fixed in his habits.

In what had been shadow there was suddenly a castle out of all the fairy tales I had read, a castle that was an exhalation out of sheer rock. It was there for just a few minutes, though these seemed to last forever, and was gone. But as it went, there was another castle, this time nearer, a castle on a green hill, more ruined, its towers like broken teeth. Then that went, and there was a folly tower above the trees, a rich man's plaything from 200 years ago, on which the spotlight rested. It was pure, blatant showmanship, as though some celestial Barnum was displaying his marvels one by one, then daring the watcher to say that he had ever seen anything like this.

'I've never seen anything like this,' I said.

'People say that. When they come to stay they sit at that window all day long, watching the light change.' A doctor's widow born in the valley, she had returned twenty years ago on her husband's retirement, as, she explained, she had always intended.

I nodded, for I knew that at that moment I was in the most beautiful place in the world. I was looking down at an eighteenth-century world where nothing jarred and all things were in perfect taste. The hills were rounded, the woods discreet, the castles, of which there were many, not big enough to dominate but just high enough to show above the trees, sufficiently ruined to be picturesque, no longer a threat to anyone. So no single feature took the breath away: there were no crags, no grandeur. This was a landscape so ordered that I felt I had strayed into an oil painting and might collide with some vast gilded frame out of sight beyond the hills.

It was not a place for dawns or sunsets but for summer evenings. Far below me, cows stood in the shallows of the river, the coils of which turned slowly like those of an old snake, and it was enough to nudge some parson into untroubled couplets, as once it did.

> Up Grongar Hill I labour now
> And reach at last his bushy brow.
> Oh, how fresh, how pure the air !
> Let me breathe a little here…

Of course you can, vicar. That was the Reverend Dyer, out for a walk, and his poem duly made all the anthologies of eighteenth-century poetry.

But it was not always like this. Say it was possible to drop a lens into a pair of binoculars, so with one eye I could see through space but with the other through time. What would I see in that second lens? Below me the water meadows fill with men, for this is a war front. Amongst them trundles the thirteenth-century equivalent of a V2, a trebuchet so big that sixty oxen pull it, as a war machine turns its full fury on the last descendant of a princely house in his castle above the river. This wooden machine hurls great stone balls, of which two or three survive in a shed at the county museum, up 80 feet and more to shatter its masonry.

More than a hundred years pass, and the valley fills with men again. This time there are over 8000 of them, a human swarm, more than anyone of that time has ever seen in one place, as a guerrilla army comes out into the sunlight of a July afternoon, and the castles and the towns begin to fall. The Tet Offensive has hit the Valley.

What follows is a journey to the sea down the valley, using just such binoculars, so the watcher again, closing one eye, then the other, moves in space and time. It starts out of time, at least out of recorded time, in the prehistory of the vast dry-stone fortress 400 feet above the river, amid bracken that stays red throughout the year.

This has walls 20 feet high and, at the main entrance, 30 feet thick, *with a perimeter of 6000 feet*, dimensions that would allow this fort to enclose all the castles of the Valley. But who built it, and why, on the eve of the Roman invasion will never be known. Even more mysterious is the large cairn at its centre, which may be from an even earlier time, possibly some sacred site it was built to protect in this place of forgotten faiths and forgotten wars.

Now turn the focusing forward to 1770, to the house beneath it called Glanareth but which for over two centuries has been called the Murder House. In a dip beside the road, this was derelict for years until in the 1990s a young family from Maidstone, unable to afford their mortgage any more, restored it – something local people would not have done.

For they had not forgotten a murder that required no detection to solve. On the night of 7 January 1770 it had snowed, then stopped, so all that the magistrates had to do was follow the lines of footprints leading away from the house, in the passageway of which a man had been hacked to death with swords. Ten sets of footprints, as the result of which nine men were brought to trial, the tenth, the ringleader, escaping to France. Their victim had been the local squire, William Powell, a man so hated that his own brother-in-law, when he heard, called out, 'Praise be to God! The villain is gone at last.' The trial had to be held in Hereford, for a local jury, it was thought, would have given the accused a standing ovation. But from Hereford six men did not come home.

The datestone is still visible, with Powell's name upon it and the date: 1765; he would have had five years to live when that was cut. The family, who spent much of the 1990s in a caravan while they worked on the house, has now moved in. The murder did not worry them; as far as they were concerned, said the wife, it was that which clinched the sale.

Behind the hills above it is the first castle I saw in that afternoon flare. You will remember it if you saw the Dimbleby film with the Prince of Wales, paintbrush in hand, in the meadows at its foot. There were storms behind him, storms in front, but, for a moment, tranquillity among the buttercups, as he sought to capture the old castle in watercolour. This, ironically, was the only way anyone could have captured it. It rises out of sheer rock, so you cannot see where rock ends and the castle starts, and has its own water supply, a spring at the end of a tunnel cut 150 feet down into the dripping dark. The castle is grim and terrifying, as it was meant to be, but the last act of its story is pure, wonderful farce.

There is a farm at its foot, which the tenant, like others in the valley, was encouraged to buy when an ancestral estate was being wound up. The only thing was that there were many farms and a great deal of paperwork. When the farmer came to read his deed of conveyance, he found he had not only become the owner of his farm, but somehow of the castle as well, which had not been for sale.

He has now converted a barn, acquired a drinks licence and serves meals. 'It's an old saying among farmers,' he said modestly, as he served ice cream, 'that the cow you find in your yard, you milk her.'

The great estates are all sold now, the sharp young men from Christie's coming and going with their inventories in houses so old they had no deeds, the late twentieth-century sale of one of them being the first in 800 years. The last of the families, wistful for bungalows, have gone, though one still lives in a small-holding, from which he can see the towers of his lost patrimony, around which the armies swarmed.

Downstream on a high hill is the second castle I saw, around the foot of which the ancient monuments people have built a dressed stone wall to keep the sheep out, the cost of this being well into five figures. But the sheep have somehow found their way in, and, having got in, cannot get out. The result is that the castle is now more impregnable than it was in its days of terror, its slopes so slippery a man cannot keep his footing should he climb them and so smelly he would not want to.

A Sunday afternoon below the steadily humming castle. I am watching from the river bridge a young couple in a boat, the girl in a bikini rowing, and in the sunlight I can see the sweat gleam in the blonde down on her back. She is beautiful, and there is no hurry anywhere in the world, until…

'Hoy, can't ew read? No Boatin'!'

The girl's voice is small and startled. 'I'm sorry, is there a sign?'

''Course there's a sign. No Swimmin'. No Boatin'. Now get out of there.' A thickset man in a waistcoat, he stands on the bridge like the angel set with a flaming sword over Eden, as the two scuttle up the bank with their boat. The cows watch. 'If they got away with it, this place would be like bloody Blackpool,' he tells me grimly.

'But why can't they row their boat?'

'Because the Electricity Board Pension Fund wouldn't like it, that's why not. They've got the fishing rights, that's why. Know what they charge per rod?'

The old order changes. Throughout recorded history things have disappeared in the Valley, nowhere more so than in what until five years ago were its lost gardens. With the gentry long gone, their houses sold or in some cases abandoned, the undergrowth had closed in to the point where you could pass the lichened walls around the parklands and not know there was anything beyond them except desolation. The past lay heavy. And then he came, conjuring vast sums out of the air.

Well, if not air, at least out of the committees administering the Lottery and the European Regional Funds, which may be the same thing in the end. First one garden, at a cost of a staggering £44 million, then, at a trifling £3.5 million, a second, that of the old house where the Reverend Dyer had puffed and written, which rose out of the 200-year-old paintings in which they had last been seen in all their glory. Beneath the folly tower on the hill, built by a Croesus returned from India, the waterfalls he conjured up flow again and the colonnades of flowers and trees are tilted to catch the sun. They have all come back.

And they are back because in the 1990s Johnny Appleseed, restored to life, came like a whirlwind to the Valley. Johnny Appleseed is a Mr Wilkins, a professional artist who can make accountants dance and the strangest figure in its history. The old magicians made women out of flowers; Mr Wilkins has made flowers out of money and in the process has dragged the Valley into the present.

But see that farm out in the flood plain? That's right, the small one where the river really writhes, which one day will be marooned. Put yourself in the place of the man farming that in 1933, when on the evening of 28 July 1933 a man comes running into your yard. The conversation goes something like this.

'Have you got a horse and cart?'

'Well, yes…'

'Thank God for that. Please, can I borrow it?'

'Why?'

'Why? I've caught a fish.'

There is a photograph. In the farmyard the angler, a short man with a fag in his mouth, is standing beside a trestle, but you notice all that much later on account of what is dangling from the trestle. It towers over the man by a good four feet and looks like the biggest herring in the history of the world. For he had needed a horse and cart, just as earlier he must have thought he needed the Book of Revelations to identify his catch.

A commercial traveller, out fishing for salmon, he had caught a sturgeon 9 feet 2 inches long, weighing 388 pounds, on a July evening 15 miles from the sea. It is always a July evening in the Valley. But it was a day of rain when his old friends, gathered on the bank, committed his ashes to the river, as he had instructed. A man who had taken its largest living thing was making amends.

The river is slow now. It slides by the town, which is there only because the river was there, though its inhabitants have forgotten this. Here the Imperial galleys came and the stubby little cogs of the Middle Ages. They brought wine and took away slaves and wool and, much later, convicts. But the river is silted up now, its coils twisting desperately in the mud.

Still there is one glory to come. At the estuary, as you cross the bar with the tide full, look above you at the last of the Valley's castles in the sunset. It stands on a hill with the water at its foot, just as it was when they sailed out, the old Peninsular general bound for Waterloo and death, and the medieval lord of this place bound for Agincourt and death, in his case on the French side. It would have been the last thing they saw when this was the gateway to the whole world.

2002

PART TWO
FOOTSTEPS

THE ROMAN

Just before the New Year, I met the man who had been the last Head of Classics at my old grammar school. When this went, he had gone on teaching Latin in the comprehensive, like one of those philosophers who, after the fall of Rome, were temporary curiosities in the courts of their new Barbarian masters. Trotted out to amuse friends and reassure envoys that there had been no real change, such men survived on whim. For, inevitably, Latin got dropped from the syllabus, at which point this remarkable man switched to French. He has no bitterness at the way things have turned out.

But I remembered his predecessors – one in particular – E.V. Williams, the jovial autocrat I knew, who spent his entire career not doubting that the brightest boys took Classics, for so it had always been in the four centuries of the school. He would no more have thought that there would be an end to this than a man around the year AD 400 would have thought that there would ever be an end to Rome. Yet it has happened in my time.

I have often wondered whether I would recognise a moment of history. Peering down from an embankment at men laying rails or standing in a confused crowd outside the first meeting of some enclosure commissioners, would I have appreciated the significance of what was happening? I doubt it. But sitting there, in a small country pub among the smell of chips and curry, I did feel this was such a moment. The last little light of the Roman world, which had burned for 2000 years, had finally gone out in the town of Maridunum, which men now call Carmarthen.

This, the oldest inhabited town in Wales, was a Roman civitas, or regional capital. When Gerald came through in the late twelfth century, some of its walls could still be seen, as can their outline from the air, now in a modern street grid.

The journalist Peter Simple, a demon lover of my shrinking race, maintains that the Welsh are the last Romans, which is not so barmy as you might think. This is Professor Gwyn Williams on the building of Offa's Dyke in the eighth century: 'The people to the west of that line knew where they were, they were in Rome.' In the Dark Ages they went on burying their dead in the Roman way, beside roads. You can still see one of these stones on the hills behind Neath, to 'Dervacus, son of Justus', and you know where the cobbles at its foot go: they lead to Rome. In the sixth century in north Wales, a man could describe himself on his grave as 'Venedotis cives', a citizen of Gwynedd, the last time in the Western world that a man would claim to be the cives of anywhere.

There were parts of Wales where, until the eighth century,

land changed hands in the terms and vocabulary of the Empire. Self-made kings claimed even more self-made Roman ancestry, one of them on his gravestone in Carmarthen Museum claiming to be a Protector a century and a half after Britain ceased to be a Roman province (the equivalent of someone a century and a half after a nuclear strike claiming to be a town clerk among the ruins of cities). Cut off from Europe, they dreamed their dreams. Poets reminded their princes that they would again ride through their ancestral town of London (which is why the severed head of the last prince was mockingly paraded along Cheapside in a crown of ivy).

A chronicler like Nennius, in the ninth century, could airily list twenty-eight cities ('These are the names of all the cities in the whole of Britain'), overlooking the fact that most were ruined shells and the others English trading posts. Reality was never a strong point with the Welsh.

Grass grew over the arenas, but another dark side of the classical world survived. Slavery lingered on in Wales long after it had become a thing of shame in the rest of Western Europe. But learning also survived, a ninth-century poet referring to the fact that he was the librarian in the fort at Tenby ('The writings of Britain were my chief care').

Then there were the monasteries and after them the grammar schools. And now it is all over and I am sitting in a pub with the last Roman. Does it matter? Oh yes, it matters. Up until the twelfth century the Welsh still called themselves the British. A.J.P. Taylor probably didn't know that when he waspishly castigated the modern use of the word Britain, 'The name of a Roman province which perished in the fifth century.'

But the last time I drove down the A40 some nationalist

clown, intent on dispossessing his race even further, had scrawled these words on the 'Welcome to Wales' sign outside Monmouth: 'BRITS OUT'. It may not matter much, but it matters.

THE DANCE OF THE THREE TOMBS

This is the story of three tombs, so near each other you can see all of them in the course of a winter's afternoon. The first, the oldest, is the most poignant. When its inscription was cut, the mason knew his world was falling apart.

CLUTORIGI / FILI PAULINI / MARINI LATIO. The language is still, just, Latin, and the lettering still in Roman capitals but also straggling, as the mason tried to commemorate in the grand old way Clutorix, son of Paulinus Marinus of Latium. When they buried him in the far west of Wales, the proudest thing they could find to say about this man was that his dad had come from Italy, and it is a fleeting moment of snobbery in the sunset of Roman Britain.

You will find the stone in the outside wall of the church at Llandissilio, on the A479 from Narberth to Cardigan, where it stood in the churchyard until a Victorian vicar decided to use it as building material. In the back lanes of west Wales the dance of the tombs had begun.

The second is the most mysterious. Three miles away, in a shadowy dingle near a farmyard, is the tiny church of Castelldwyran. Annual services used to be held here, but these stopped last year, and only ducks and a goat now walk through the dusty interior. Yet you feel anything could have happened here, and it did. In the nineteenth century another vicar stole a tombstone from his own churchyard.

Only this was no ordinary tombstone: it marked a king's grave, and not any king. Voteporix is mentioned in the only piece of writing to survive from sixth-century Britain (the writer, Gildas, thought him a gangster). But this did not deter the Reverend Richard Bowen-Jones. He put the tombstone in his own garden, perhaps to enhance a rockery, probably just to make way for his own grave, for when he died in 1887 Bowen-Jones had himself interred in the grandest tomb of all, surrounded by railings. The inscription on this is conventional enough, 'In Loving Memory…'.

But there is a second gravestone alongside this. 'Richard Bowen-Jones / Born 1811, Transferred 1887. / Here lie the remains of a "Classical Ass" / The accursed of his sons by the name of "Jabrass" / In the earth he is Ammonia and Triphosphate of Calcium / On earth a "Home Demon" and ferocious old ruffian'. Whatever your experience of monumental masonry, you will never have seen anything like this.

The words are cut on a slab beneath a very grand replica of a Celtic cross next to the vicar's own stone. The lettering on the cross is blurred and I had to rub earth into this to make out that it was to a Clara Gibbs Bowen-Jones (1817–1913), presumably the vicar's widow, whose death someone had chosen to record separately. That someone must also have been responsible for yet another small slab within the family railings, for the lettering on this is similar to that on the vicar's bizarre epitaph: 'C.G. B-J, 1913. V. B-J, 19…'. The last date is left empty.

He was, I found out from the farmer's wife, the vicar's son, Vaughan Bowen-Jones, who hated his father for the pressure he had put on him to succeed academically. This seems to have driven him out of his mind, although the local masons did well by it, chipping busily away far from the eyes of bishops and their consistory courts. A sister, embarrassed by having a king's grave in her garden, later gave the Voteporix Stone to Carmarthen Museum. But in the dingle the Bowen-Joneses, their boy and the old king await the Last Judgement, when they can really get their hands on each other.

Just as 15 miles away in the churchyard at Steynton, near Milford Haven, another sixth-century man, Gendilius, must be waiting to get his hands on one Thomas Harries of that village. All that is known of Gendilius is that he was given a Christian burial, as the ring cross shows on his tombstone. All that is known of Harries is that he was put in the same grave. And not only in the same grave.

When he died in 1870, aged 84, someone in Steynton thought not only was there a space going to waste in the graveyard, but also a perfectly good tombstone as well, one with no family to object after 1300 years, so another obliging mason cut Harries's name under that of Gendilius. They have taken this out of the churchyard now and hidden what has to be the most outrageous tombstone in Britain behind a pillar near the font.

This has been the dance of three tombs in the West.

1997

THE LOST PALACE

This turns on the purest elements of old romance, a lost palace, the last prince of a ruined dynasty, and they rise, like Schliemann's Troy, out of what should not have been, for the palace is where tradition and the old always said it was, except that in the libraries they did not listen. But chiefly it is the story of a woman who, two years ago, bought a chicken farm in north Wales.

In 1988 the 36-acre farm at Aber, on the coastal highway between Bangor and Conway, came on to the market. The A55 is straight at that point, and fast, so you may not have noticed the hamlet of Aber that the road sweeps by. You will certainly not have seen the house built of grey stone on the hill to the east of this.

Stop for a moment. It is a large house, quite grand, and as you stare you will find yourself wondering why you have not seen it up there before. For there are strange features: a porch with a room above it and a round tower tacked on to one wing. It is startling to see something so old after the bungalows and holiday caravans of the coast.

Many people were interested in buying the farm, including a Londoner who had already got planning permission to convert the barn in the farmyard into even more holiday homes. Remember that barn: it is now one of the most mysterious buildings in modern archaeology, which might so easily have become three cottages with plastic windows.

The farm was sold to Kathryn Gibson and her husband, an engineer, largely because the widowed owner wanted a quick sale and the Gibsons had not insisted on a professional survey. You do not need such things when you buy a view, and the Gibsons wanted Pen-y-Bryn because of the panorama of sea and island opening like a fan beneath them. Anglesey is on one side of the house and Snowdonia on the other.

They knew the house was old (in 1956 the Royal Commission on Ancient Monuments had decided that most of it was built around 1600, the tower a little later), but to the Gibsons it was more curious than anything, 'with its strange little tower'. That was two years ago. 'How long ago it seems,' says Kathryn Gibson. 'I was a housewife then, I had time to talk to my daughters.'

People come uninvited up her drive to stare at the walls now, and a few stand there in tears. A friend of mine working for CADW, the Welsh equivalent of English Heritage, described a colleague's reactions after such a visit. 'He came into the office in a sort of daze. Now this is a man who spends his life looking at old buildings, but all he would say was: "I've touched the arch through which Llywelyn walked."' Those of you with a weakness for such things will remember Schliemann's telegram to the King of Greece: 'Today I looked upon the face of Agamemnon.'

In three months alone, fifty experts of one kind or another have called at Pen-y-Bryn, so Kathryn Gibson's life, like that of royalty, is suddenly full of strangers. Many call, like I did, unannounced, but do not get turned away, for they know, and she knows, what her responsi-bilities are now. A woman in early middle age who thought she had bought a chicken farm with a view has moved into the lost palace of the last Welsh Prince of Wales.

After the Conquest a few stone keeps were allowed to stand, dwarfed by Edward's subsequent castles, but not the palaces or halls where the prince had held his courts; the timbers of these were taken down to be reassembled in Edward's castles, so that their location became a mystery. Like Carthage, the little state of Gwynedd had gone.

It is known that the two most important courts were Aber and Aberffraw on Anglesey, the oldest place, dating back to the origins of the dynasty in the late Roman Empire. These names mean a lot to the Welsh, but there has been a curious reluctance to excavate, for these are all they've got. Tread softly for you tread on my dreams.

It was left to Richard White, an English archaeologist, to dig at Aberffraw, and, as he put it, nobody had done so before because of the feeling that the grandeur of Gwynedd could have nothing to do with this sad village among 900 acres of sand dunes.

But a map turned up, in Bournemouth of all places, dated 1749. It showed the village and, in the middle of it, 'Here stood the ancient palace of the Welsh princes…'. There was another note saying that thirty years before this, the last stones had been removed. 'So that would have been the last time anyone saw the hall of the princes,' said Richard White, a remark that does not go easily from the memory.

Then in 1973 one of the villagers digging near the post office found something he kept quiet about for some time. It was a large two-foot head, a roof boss. Excavating at the spot, White found remains of a high-quality stone building, not the primitive timber hall it had been feared he would find. For the colonising power's policy of injecting a sense of inferiority into the conquered had taken effect. English writers had ridiculed Welsh law (formulated by the

Devil), the morals of the Welsh clergy, even Welsh costume (when Llywelyn came to London in 1277 it was said that crowds in Islington had followed his men, 'staring at them as if they had been monsters, and laughing at their uncouth garb and appearance'). And if everything had gone, the halls, the court archives, who was to argue with any of this?

In the English records there is the odd ghostly glimpse of what had been, as in a piece of accountancy prepared for the Black Prince who was trying to raise cash in a hurry. Seventy years after the Conquest, a baffled clerk wrote about the strange functions still being carried out at Aberffraw. 'These have to look after the wall, these the gate, these the garden plot...'

But the greatest mystery of the Welsh state was the court at Aber. Despite the surviving image of Llywelyn as a wandering prince with his war-band, moving like giant weevils from hall to hall to eat up the produce of the people, the most important personal events of the dynasty in its last century all took place at Aber. Princess Joan died here, King John's daughter and the wife of Llywelyn's grandfather; and David, prince before him; also Llywelyn's wife, Eleanor de Montfort, giving birth to their child Gwenllian, in that last year. And it was here for three days in November 1282 that the aged Archbishop of Canterbury came to negotiate in something which was about to pass out of history: the hall of a sovereign Welsh prince.

So Aber had a significance that the Welsh historian Jones Pearce was only just beginning to investigate before his death. He found, using the inventory prepared for Edward after the Conquest, that there was something unique about it: there were twenty-four families here, to which another eleven were added, whose only job was to look after the court. There was a 200-acre home-farm. There was also one building that the English did not raze, for twenty years later they charged the cost of its repair to the local community. So here, argued Jones Pearce, must have been the centre of the Welsh state.

But where? In the hamlet itself, to the west of a stream, there is a little green mound, the remains of a motte-and-bailey castle. This, it was said, was the court; and those who believed in the benefits of the Conquest seized on it as another pointer to the lunacy of a prince prepared to go to war with someone who had one room, Westminster Great Hall, into which this could have fitted.

It is 1988 now and, newly installed in Pen-y-Bryn, Kathryn Gibson has some local people call on her who ask, does she know where she is living? Mrs Gibson, as anyone might who has spent a week unpacking, feels she knows exactly where she is living, but it is now she is told that Pen-y-Bryn, not the motte, Pen-y-Bryn on its hill to the east of the hamlet, her Pen-y-Bryn, is the Aber of the princes.

Soon after this she finds a Victorian journal, *Three Weeks in Aber Village*, in which, to her astonishment, she comes on this paragraph: 'Mounting a steep rustic ascent you will find yourself before a Round Tower, the principal vestige of Llywelyn's castle at the present day. Attached to this Tower is an interesting looking structure built entirely, we are told, of the ruins of the ancient Palace. It is at present used as a farmhouse.' And then, in capital letters: 'THIS MOST PICTURESQUE HOUSE, FROM ITS PRIVATE ISOLATED CHARACTER, IS KNOWN TO FEW OUTSIDE OF ITS IMMEDIATE NEIGHBOURHOOD…'

In book after topographical book of the sort beloved of our ancestors, Mrs Gibson finds the tradition stretching back. Four centuries ago this was Leland. 'In a wood, in the parish of Aber, Llywelyn had a house on the hill, part of which now standeth…' And so began the quest that now occupies all of her life.

The more she read, the more it made sense to her: the old Roman coast road at the hill's foot, the bolt-hole into Snowdonia behind, Llanfaes (which was then a port across the Menai Straits to which the luxuries of Europe would have come to the princes and their Norman-French wives), with, in its priory, the men who would have formed a prince's secretariat. It had to be here.

She began visiting academic libraries. In Aberystwyth she came on a document clearly indicating that the palace and the home-farm had been to the east of the stream, the hamlet to the west. In the Public Records Office she found the 1303 repair bill, evidence that the English had departed from normal policy to preserve this place.

Then in Bangor she came on letters written by Jones Pearce to a former owner of Pen-y-Bryn, in which the historian said he believed a large stone in the cottage alongside the house was the altar of the court chapel. In the last two years Mrs Gibson has travelled Britain and on one occasion visited the Vatican. 'I suppose you could say I've been a bit carried away.'

But what was she to do next? She knew the tradition, she knew that Pen-y-Bryn had survived as a Royal Manor until the sixteenth century, when it was given to a local landowner for his bravery in the wars in the Low Countries. Yet none of this contradicted the Ancient Monuments dating of the house. So had anything of the palace survived?

It is one thing to live on a site where something happened, quite another to touch the stones those other hands may have touched. That is when the pulse starts racing. But how to go about this when what is before you is not an archaeological site but a house in which you live?

Praising God for dampness, Mrs Gibson persuaded her husband to hack away at a dark patch on the first floor of the tower. Here they found Victorian brickwork sealing off a Tudor fireplace, and then there it was: another fireplace under this, much wider and built of a large dressed stone, 2 feet under the level of the present floor. Now this becomes a detective story.

In the ground floor of the tower she found a trap door and beneath this a cellar. Again, the large stones. Tiny windows and the depth of wall you only get in castles. And in the wall a sealed archway. An old lady, formerly in service at Aber, had told her of a passageway under the house down which people had gone, following deep underground until they became frightened. 'You hear about these tunnels but you don't believe in them,' says Kathryn Gibson. 'Yet there's something there.'

At this point she called in Tony Parkinson from the Royal Commission on Ancient Monuments and Geoff St Paul from the Gwynedd County Council conservation department, who concluded that fireplace and tower were medieval. You might appreciate the stiff little comedy in an archaeological report: 'In 1956 the Royal Commission's description of the house... implies that the earliest phase dates from *c*.1600. In 1989 this description was revised in the light of further architectural details that were coming to light during renovation work...'

A computer scan of the field in front of the house picked out the remains of walls under the grass, and when this was cut away, the mortar that was found was thought to be thirteenth-century. Finds like this made Mrs Gibson think of a full-scale excavation, and she has formed the Aber Welsh Heritage Trust to raise funds for it.

Out of such an excavation might come a picture of the complete palace. The glimpses of it were tantalising, since no complete building dating back to the Middle Ages had been found. But such a venture would need a study centre, and it was then that Mrs Gibson remembered the barn, which was in a terrible mess, with cement blocks pushed in where the walls had crumbled. She began picking away at the broken render, and it was then that she saw, blocked up and shadowy, the outline of small mullions, groups of three and five in line, tiny apertures, windows of the Middle Ages.

Now it is possible to come on such things in Welsh farms under the centuries of bodging. The cowshed becomes a chapel again; the place where they kept the feed an exact replica of the hall in which King Harold sat in the Bayeux tapestry. I have seen such places, where it was all still there under the long agricultural centuries. So in Pen-y-

Bryn, Kathryn Gibson, once a housewife, pulled away at the walls of her barn until she saw the outline of a great arch and another matching one in the opposite wall, as though a road had once passed under them.

And Mrs Gibson had found the gatehouse of the princes.

1990

THE TET OFFENSIVE HITS
THE TOWY VALLEY

I t starts with a letter written in a castle – startling enough in itself, only there is something even more so. The letter is part of a series written over a fortnight in July, which together roll back the clouds so the Middle Ages uniquely become daily newspaper reports. You are in that Towy Valley between Carmarthen and Llandeilo now beloved of fly fishermen; but forget the water meadows and the picnic sites, for where you are, in 1403, is the equivalent of South Vietnam. People and animals have crowded into the little towns and the white-washed castles, for out of nowhere a great guerrilla army has come out into the open. The Tet Offensive has hit the Towy Valley.

It could be any US commander appealing for an air strike, for the letter has none of the elaborate phraseology of the Middle Ages, no 'may it keep you in worshipful prosperity'. The writer has pressed the panic button, and it is only the way in which he dates it, 'on the feast of St Thomas the Martyr', that reminds you of when the letter was written. His name was Jenkin Havard, a Welshman who, as constable of Dynevor Castle outside Llandeilo, was in the English Colonial Service, and a wind he had never thought to feel was blowing about his ears, a wind out of the remote past of his race.

'A siege has begun of my own castle and there is panic in those that are with me for they have vowed to kill all those who are in it. Because of which I pray you give us warning very quickly whether we can expect help so that if not we can slip away to Brecon… Written at Dynevor, in haste and dread…'

Stand on his hill, which rises as abruptly as modelling clay out of the Valley. Behind you his castle is again in a state of defence, this time by Welsh Heritage for behind their boarded doors workmen are pointing up the ruins before the tourists come. Now look down, close your eyes and listen to what he heard.

It would have puzzled him at first, this dull sound that would have come and gone but every time the wind brought it back was more insistent. And then, of course, he knew what it was: the ragged drumming of thousands upon thousands of bare feet in which he had begun to make out the shouts of men. From his castle, Havard looked down on the most terrifying sight on earth – a human swarm.

If you want to see what he saw, find one of those early photographs of a Zulu impi on the march, a confused mass of armed men moving without hurry, some chatting, some just looking round them, a few shouting and waving their weapons. What would have been so terrifying would be the mixture of the ambling with the underlying menace.

Havard, probably relying on his scouts, thought there were 8240 of them, an oddly exact figure for the Middle Ages when chroniclers referred airily to armies of 100,000. In addition there would have been dependants, carts for loot and animals being driven; he would have looked down on miles of moving humanity. A medieval army had little order but this would have had none; this was the world going by.

There would have been mounted men amongst them, landowners with a lot to lose, who had come late to this rising; also men with nothing at all to lose, who had come early to what for them was a peasants' rebellion. And the friars. And the undergraduates who had slipped quietly away from Oxford to join. And old mercenaries. They had come for different reasons but somewhere amongst them was the old man who was a dump for all their dreams. They called him Owen Glyndwr.

What sort of men were they? For a start they would be religious maniacs to us, which is why no historical novelist would dare attempt true medieval dialogue, for the hereafter leant on everything these men did or said. Heaven and Hell to them had the outline of geographical locations, and to us they would have been superstitious to the point of lunacy. Yet they were far better able to bear pain when the horrors of this world seemed so trifling, especially after two things that had shaken their world to its foundations.

The first was the Black Death. Half the population was dead, farms deserted, animals strayed; in a small country like Wales, with a population of perhaps 200,000, the desolation was everywhere. Still, the survivors knew some advantages: they had begun to move into the forbidden colonial towns from which English merchants had hitherto enjoyed trading monopolies. More amazingly, there were now Welsh constables in the castles that had previously skewered their countrymen to the thin acres. Men like Havard.

Then, the second thing. Four years earlier the King of England, Richard II, a holy anointed king of the Middle Ages, had been pulled down and replaced by his cousin and murderer, Henry IV. Men were now living in a world off all the known maps, where anything might happen. And it did.

He would have been rising fifty, a man old by the standards of his age, who had been at the English court, served in its wars and been considered sophisticated enough to be an expert witness in a heraldry case that then obsessed the English upper class. For him to emerge as the leader of a Welsh peasant rising would have been as unlikely as Roy Jenkins returning to Wales now and assuming leadership of the men who were burning the holiday cottages. These call themselves the Sons of Glyndwr.

Look at him as he rides by. Of his appearance we know only that he had a fashionable forked beard, for this is on the wax impression of the seal he sent to the French King and which survives in Paris. He would have been dressed in complete plate, with a dragon on his helmet (also on the seal), and on his shield the four lions of the last Welsh Prince of Wales, killed in 1282. His rebellion is just three years old and for much of that time he has been a fugitive. A few months back his ancestral estates were burned by columns under the teenager who was to become Henry V, and yet he is like a prince come out of exile.

It started in 1400 with a quarrel over land, a mere piece of commonland. The Middle Ages are full of such quarrels, and what is extraordinary is that a year on, in his one attempt to do a deal with the English, Glyndwr was still insisting only on his rights as a landowner. We know the scale of the beginning from the wanted posters, for Glyndwr had quarrelled with the English Lord Grey, and when he sacked Grey's town of Ruthin, he had 270 identified men with him. The only thing was, everyone else then joined in and within a month Henry IV, treating it from the start as a national rising, had invaded in what for him was to become an annual autumn event.

Henry never did understand the nature of warfare in Wales. He would assemble these huge armies and lurch in; next he would find himself unopposed at the sea and have to lurch out again. Rain and accountancy did for him. At fourteen his son did understand and used flying columns in what was a guerrilla war, yet even he pleaded desperately for funds ('if our men are withdrawn for us we must retire to England and be disgraced forever...').

What did Glyndwr want? Was he, like so many whom history calls great men, a sleepwalker who was swept along by events, or did these move to his choreography? We will never know, because at the centre of everything that took place, there is this void. Men rushed in to fill it, the peasants, the idealists from Oxford (their names bleakly record-ed in the Rolls of Parliament), the churchmen, the squires. They came in roughly that order, the last after his first set-piece victories when they smelled success. But of the man behind the whirlwind we know virtually nothing.

Yet everything was done in his name, and even behind the wildly escalating events there are glimpses of military purpose (the captured letters to the Scottish king request heavy cavalry), of foreign policy, followed by ecclesiastical and educational manifestos for an inde-pendent Welsh church and Welsh universities. And at some point in those three years a man who had at first merely sought redress in the courts (and today would have written to Esther Rantzen) had pro-claimed himself Prince of Wales.

Now he is in his glory. The hit and run raids are over and the guer-rilla bands are measured in hundreds; he is out of hiding and, with an army at his back, is moving in daylight on the old capital of South Wales at Carmarthen. For whatever his plans, or lack of them, there has been no mistaking his ruthlessness. He has unleashed civil war on Wales, split families, and in a time when the most fearsome piece of military technology is the longbow, he will lay waste a country so entirely that grass will grow in the marketplace at Llanrwst with deer in the churchyard and the ruin will persist for 200 years. It has been a war of atrocities.

Henry has had the bowels torn from living men, one of them, recorded a stunned chronicler, a man so rich he used 16 tons of wine a year in his household, which, at my reckoning, comes to 20,000 bot-tles a year. Owen has hanged the entire garrison of New Radnor castle from its battlements. You must remember this, for it is easy to forget such things, especially when the headiest element of romance is involved, which is failure. These wars last fifteen years, longer than any other rising in Europe, and there were men then who thought he could win. And he came close. He knew trouble was brewing in England with the Percy family; he also knew that war on the scale he was about to wage needed trouble in England for it to succeed.

So it was that on 3 July 1403 he appeared in the Towy Valley and the castles began to fall. Not through siege. His sieges rarely succeeded in military terms; castles surrendered after negotiation or just because their constables opened the doors, as on 5 July at Dryslwyn, four miles down the valley. 'Owen lay tonight at the castle of Dryslwyn, with Rhys ap Griffith, and I went there and spoke with him on a flag of truce. I prayed with him that he would give a safeguard under his seal for me to send home to my wife and her mother and their company, but he would not... I can write no more but pray that God help you. Written at the castle of Carreg Cennen, the Fifth Day of July, John Scudamore.'

This is one of the most mysterious letters ever written, as Scudamore was Glyndwr's own son-in-law, so he was either a bigamist or a man with a terrible secret he was trying to keep from his English paymasters. He certainly had a capacity for cheek, as when, twenty years after the end of the rising, he came a cropper when he tried to claim back as heir Glyndwr's forfeited land. But it also shows the divided loyalties of the Border upper class; Scudamore's own brother was to die fighting for Glyndwr.

Incredibly, the man who opened the gates of Dryslwyn was himself Scudamore's son-in-law, and had profited from the confiscated estates of him of 20,000 bottles a year. Intermarriage and changes of side are more complex than in any Australian soap opera, for the constable of Dryslwyn had his property forfeited, though he was subsequently pardoned.

'Dear Friend, I want you to know that Owen Glyndwr, Henry Don, Rhys the Black, have taken the town of Carmarthen, and

Wigmore, constable of the Castle has surrendered it to Owen and they have burned the town and killed more than 50 men.' Dated 6 July. Roger Wigmore was an Englishman and a career civil servant.

On 8 July, Richard Kyngeston, archdeacon of Hereford, wrote to the King, and you will gather from his first sentence that there were letters flying all over the place. 'Our most redoubtable and sovereign lord the King, please you to know that from day to day letters are arriving from Wales containing intelligence by which you may learn that the whole country is lost if you do not go there as quickly as is possible, with all the power you can muster, and march night and day… Written in haste, great haste, at Hereford…' In great haste. The terror was everywhere. The garrison of Kidwelly Castle, fearing an attack, sent two messengers to Bristol with a plea for help.

But then something very odd happened. While at Carmarthen, probably trying to decide what to do next, Owen, like the present Duchess of York after holidaying with her Texan, decided to consult a clairvoyant. A man living in the Gower was sent for and prophesied that Owen would be captured under a black banner somewhere between Carmarthen and Gower. This ensured that the man's home did not become a war zone and to us is an incident of complete farce. But it shows how difficult it is to get inside the skull of a medieval man, and also makes you wonder what Shakespeare was drawing on in his portrayal of the superstitious Glendower.

At any rate, there was no invasion of the South East. There was some probing of the defences of English Pembrokeshire to the west and then abruptly the great army had gone from the Towy Valley as mysteriously as it had come. For on 10 July, Hotspur and his father, the Earl of Northumberland, rose in rebellion against the King.

You must imagine the old man riding North. The years of a greater glory are to come, when the ambassadors of France, Castille and Scotland attend his coronation as Prince of Wales, and a French army lands in Wales. The years when he plans to partition England

and holds court in his castle at Harlech, where centuries later a small horse brass with the lions upon it will be found, all that remains of this glory. Then it all goes, his family in gaol or dead, and he is a fugitive again, disappearing like a fox into the landscape. There will be offers of a pardon to which he will not even reply.

No bard wrote his elegy and no one knows his grave, though a tradition persists that he ended his days on the Welsh Border with his daughter Alice and her husband, that John Scudamore who once wrote from a castle in Wales. The Scudamores are still there in their old home at Kentchurch where, at the end of a long passageway, beyond the pictures of hunting squires and magistrates, there is a painting 150 years older than all the others.

In this picture a man, tonsured like a monk, his face abstracted and grim, stares out at you. Somebody tried to clean it two centuries ago and this had a strange effect, for it revealed the lines of the drawing under the paint. You can see the tightness of the mouth and the cheekbones, and you know, whenever this was done, it was done from life. The cleaning has also brought out the eeriness of the painting, for the long hands have been made transparent and you can see through them the book they are holding. And behind are the white outlines of a house you recognise as the one you are standing in, when there was a tower and walls and this was defensible.

So who was he, this man for whom an early fifteenth-century Flemish master travelled all the way to the Welsh Border? Tradition has it that he was the household priest, a noted scholar and poet, but would Scudamore have gone to that expense to have his priest painted?

It is then that your imagination begins to move as you look at that frightening face, for there is a tradition that another man ended his days in this place, a man who left a country in ruins and even the village beyond the hill was a town until he passed through. When a man has caused such things, his face in old age would be the face in the picture.

1993

PART THREE
MEET THE WELSH

JOHN X, POLITICAL PRISONER

There was nothing contemporary about it. The men who stood round his grave might in other times have been his companions on cattle raids or have recalled with him their hangovers after Agincourt. As it was, each had some story to remember him by, which since 8 a.m. that day they had been exchanging in pubs opened especially for them. The drinkers of Carmarthen did it in the old heroic way when they mourned the passing of one of their number.

At the grave something odd happened. Someone must have leant too far forward, for there was suddenly a light clatter, which startled everyone. A comb had fallen on the coffin. He would have appreciated the irony, having spent years industriously sweeping forward the last few strands of his hair. And the comb was buried with him, as once it would have been, so X entered the hereafter with his grave goods like a Celtic warrior.

His name was John Davies, which surprised many there, as he had always been known as John X. Nobody is sure how he came by this sobriquet, some saying it was something to do with his father, others that this was how he had signed himself on betting slips in the illegal days. He will be missed by the bookies of Carmarthen, for there was a wreath of a green field, a little horse upon it, and the instruction, 'Enjoy your last ride'.

It may have been his experience of the turf's vagaries, but nothing in life seemed to surprise him – least of all his own misfortunes. He spoke in a low, quick monotone, his voice not rising a note, even when describing the extraordinary two months when he was the town's one political prisoner.

He had gone to Southampton to see off a friend who was emigrating, got drunk and awoke to find himself on the high seas. The captain was sympathetic and said he would be put ashore in the Canaries, where the next ship would take him back.

But these were the Franco years and the Spanish police, faced with a man who did not have a passport, behaved in their usual enlightened way. They put him in gaol and forgot about him, except that at 10 a.m. each day they would beat him up. It was the regularity of their habits that intrigued X.

His family, now frantic over a man who had vanished off the face of the earth, contacted the Foreign Office, which as usual did nothing, and in the end it was the *Daily Mirror* that got him out. X travelled back as a guest of the shipping line, which meant that he could eat and, more importantly, drink anything he wanted. He sometimes referred to this return voyage as a Golden Age.

He did not have regular work in the time I knew him. There were hobble jobs, the odd bit of labouring on building sites or gardening (someone told me he had trained as a landscape gardener, but then there were many tales about X). His life was spent in pubs in a town that had elevated boozing to an art form.

X once had a council house with two lodgers, men after his own heart. Coming home one night, the two collided on the path, fell down and went to sleep. X told me that when he looked out of his curtains in the moonlight, a sparkling frost had crept over them. 'I thought, that's funny, someone's dug two graves in my garden.' Nothing else. There were two graves in his garden, and that was that.

A larger society might have viewed such men differently, but here they no more questioned what they were doing than the men of the Dark Ages would have questioned what the cattle raids were about. They were myth-makers and what they were about, batty as it might seem, was style. Anything outside this, and the stage of the town, was remote and faded, like a colour photograph left too long in the sun.

X went to London once, got off a train at Paddington and went into a pub in Praed Street. Some hours later he came out, had a haircut and caught the train home. 'London? I've been to London,' he would say airily. 'I had a haircut there.' There was also Basingstoke, where I think he had a sister and where, he often told me, everything would come right if he could only get there. There were many send-offs for him but somehow he never managed it. On the M3 I often think about X as I drive past the bleak, bleak brick precincts – for Basingstoke was his Avalon, his Isle of Apples. 'I am like a seagull, Byron,' he said once. 'I happen to have landed in Carmarthen, and when the weather clears I shall be gone.'

Only he never did. Aged fifty-five and unmarried, he was hit by a lorry on the A40 near Nantgaredig, walking at night away from the town after a day in the beer tent of the local agricultural show. His body was brought back to the town, as Carmarthen claimed its own. He was a nice man.

A YOUNG MAN SKIPPING

I n 1980 Johnnie Owen, boxer, died without regaining consciousness after his attempt on the world bantamweight title in Los Angeles.

When I saw him he was skipping. There was just the sound of the rope hitting the floor and an alarm-clock ticking. He did an hour a night to start his training, expressionlessly, increasing the tempo, switching hands. In the morning he had run 14 miles. In the afternoon he had chopped trees. And in the nights he skipped. It had been like this ever since he had turned professional three years earlier, every day, every week, every month; neither illness nor holiday disrupted the routine.

The gymnasium, if you could call it that, was an old miners' institute in New Tredegar, high up in the valleys of South Wales, where they become deep and very narrow. There are no road signs here, for no strangers come. There are no banks either, and the advertisements in the shop windows are faded. Prosperity and industry have gone and just the people are left.

The gym was dirty and very cold: peeling posters on the walls, old punch bags hanging from the ceiling like eighteenth-century gibbets. In the night someone had thrown a brick through the window and, as the rope quickened, there was a scraping noise as glass was swept from the ring. The irony was that there seemed to be more hope here than in the terraces outside. Older men watched approvingly as the champ exercised. Neither he nor they had any doubts that this was just a beginning, that the crowds and the purses lay ahead: a young man skipping, a young man in the wings.

I met Johnnie Owen in the springtime. A shy, very thin boy of twenty-four, he had high shoulders which he pushed even higher so that his body streamed away from them like a suit on a coat-rack. He had that strange, waxy pallor that you get in the Valleys, which has people talking about the Welsh being Italians in the rain. He was so thin that after every public appearance middle-aged women wrote to his manager accusing him of starving the boy.

He hardly spoke at all. When I rang him first he said 'Yes' six times, very politely, very quietly, a small, small voice on the telephone. Not that it mattered, for his father Dick Owen did not stop talking. They could have been a ventriloquist and his life-size doll sitting there in the cluttered parlour of a council house in Merthyr, with the cups and plaques and photographs of a young man with his arms raised everywhere.

Dick Owen talked of the Merthyr boxers, all of whom he had known. 'Must be about twelve pros around here, not counting the old ones. Where are they now? Still around. Nine times out of ten they're broke, chasing the rainbow. They finish boxing and there's nothing in the bank. I got eight children, all boxers. Well, the three girls don't box, but I think they'd like to. It goes back in our family. My grandfather boxed, put the gloves on with anyone, he would. And my father was very athletic. There was a gym in every pub round here then. Steeped in boxing, this place.' He lit another cigarette. His son, a non-smoker, watched him with a look of amusement tempered with some awe: for him smoking, like talking and the world outside boxing, was something very strange.

'I had the four boys on one bill once. They all won. 'Course, the problem was weight. Couldn't get a weight on any of them, they was so light and small. Had to give them a pie each before the weigh-in.'

'I was 6 stones 6 pounds at fifteen,' said a voice so tiny it did not seem human. 'I was 4 foot 8 inches.'

'I used to be like him,' said Dick Owen, patting his belly affectionately. 'Good livin',' he said to nobody in particular. His son has never smoked a cigarette, never tasted alcohol and never, said his father proudly, ever run after women. 'Curiosity will get him in the end. He'll want to go out with his friends and I'll be terribly annoyed.'

Johnnie Owen had the same job for eight years after leaving school, as a machine setter in a nut and bolt factory. That meant he could only run for 4 miles each morning. Every night he was down the gym. Had he sometimes wondered where his teenage years had gone? Dick Owen said nothing. After a pause the small voice said, 'Yes.'

And there was the chopping, said his father. The chopping? Every afternoon. It built the arms up. They had never wanted for firewood since Johnnie took up chopping. 'That's the difference between him and his brothers, they'd always ask why. And then,' he nodded sombrely, 'then a woman would come along and they'd start drinking. Finish.' It was also probably a respite for the deforestation of Merthyr.

Owen rose at 6.30 every morning. Sometimes he did a 14-mile hill run, sometimes an 8-mile run up the hills with a one-in-five gradient. It was beautiful country, said Dick Owen.

'When the sun's out,' whispered his son. 'You can't see too much when it's raining.' He ran every day, whatever the weather and whatever his state of health (he remembered having flu once). He had run in six inches of snow, socks wrapped around his shoes and then only his tracks were up there, disturbing the whiteness. Once he saw a fox, and once a squirrel, three days on the trot. 'And once there was a goose,' said Dick Owen. 'Bloody big thing, black it was. Came out of this stream like Concorde.' Did he run as well? He winked conspiratorially. 'We got a car.'

And then there were the breakfasts and the lunches and the dinners. Dick Owen cooked all these for him, in between work shifts as a moulder in a local rubber factory. He dared not leave meals to his wife ('I know all the little touches and the calories'). His son slept until lunch, and in the afternoons there was the chopping. In the evenings there was the gym. He did not go out at night. Too dangerous, said his father, too many dreamers in the nightspots of Merthyr, all fancying their chances. Not that there was much chance of anyone falling out with the boy. He beamed. 'How can you quarrel with 'im when 'e don't talk to you?'

'I've always been quiet,' said the champ.

So the days passed. The only break came just before a fight, when sparring partners (at £150 a week, with expenses) arrived. Then the runs became shorter and the chopping restricted.

Johnnie Owen thought he had about three years left. The smaller weights retired early, having used up more energy, said his father. And there was much less money in being a bantamweight, for the crowds like to see the big punches land. How sad it is to write all this now.

The most he had ever earned for a fight was £7000 (even for his world title bid he earned only £10,000; at present his hospital bill is running at £250 a day). He had bought a small general store on a nearby council estate – his first and only investment. His mother ran that for him. He thought he might like to keep a pub one day. It seemed to be his most worldly ambition. But would that not mean talking to people? Barmen, said the champ innocently, would do that.

I asked him about the hurt in boxing. 'It has crossed my mind what it would be like to really hurt somebody. I hit someone very hard once and my mother said after, "What did you want to do that for?" But all I've ever had is a cut eye.' A grin streaked across the pale face. 'Man from the estate here, went out for a walk. Fell over and broke his nose.'

The next step then was the world title. No, he wouldn't recognise the champion even if he saw him in the street. He was a Mexican. A good body puncher by repute.

He leant back, bewildered by all this talk. Dick Owen, who cleans the trophies and keeps the ten scrapbooks up to date, pointed out mementoes of old fights, the British championship, the European in 1980, the twenty-five professional wins. Last year he won the Lonsdale Belt outright. I asked if I could see it. Father and son exchanged puzzled glances and then the champ went to look. There was a long pause and then a door slammed. Through the window Johnnie Owen was stealthily opening the boot of his car. He had forgotten that the belt was there. He had once, muttered Dick Owen, seen him carrying it about in a Tesco bag.

In the gym his manager Dai Gardiner was talking of his plans. Next year, he said, with any luck there would be the world title. But he was not going to rush it. Dai Gardiner has announced that he is quitting boxing.

Every day now for weeks I have remembered that pale face and the sound of the rope. I have forgotten the televised pictures of the thin body fluttering to the canvas. The real tragedy was a long time before, that of a young man in the wings, a young man skipping.

1980

THE CORACLEMAN

David Rees of Carmarthen meets Red Indians in the hills of Montana. 'Standoffish lot, the Sioux,' said Rees. 'Which is not that surprising when you think what's been done to them. But then I introduced myself. I said I knew what they had been through, that I too was living archaeology, part of a way of life which went back before written history, but that there was a great difference between us. Their rights had been given back to them, ours were still being taken away. The next night I went in and they all stood up as if I had been at the Little Big Horn. "Howya doin', Dave?"'

David Rees is a builder, at least he is by day. At night, when seven stars stand in the sky, like Dracula he is something else. On land, against the moon with his boat on his back, he looks like a huge beetle out of Kafka, but in the quiet of the River Towy, drifting with the tide, a net spread out between him and his partner in the darkness, he is a coracleman.

A medieval traveller in Wales 800 years ago saw such men and marvelled at boats 'made of twigs, not oblong nor pointed but almost round, or rather triangular, covered both within and without with raw hides'. The point is, he was startled enough to record this, for a tradition, already fabulously old, had dwindled to the rivers of the west. But when Caesar saw them in Kent before the birth of Christ, these boats were a common feature of British rivers, and he was so impressed by the fact they could virtually float on a rain puddle that he used them in his Spanish campaign. And the traditions of the men who made these boats were old then.

Now there are just two rivers, the Teify and the Towy, both in the extreme west of Wales. Two hundred years ago there were 400 coracles on the Towy, a whole fleet into which one dark night there blundered a startled Press Gang, moving upstream with muffled oars, who must have felt they had come on something out of pre-history. The Press Gang was sent packing.

But that was before river boards and fly-fishermen and licences. Some 22,000 licences are now granted on the rivers of west Wales to fly-fishermen, a vocal pressure group in a time of dwindling fish stocks. There are just twelve coracle licences on the Towy, of which, at £389 each for a season cut back to five months, only five were taken up this year. When David Rees met the Indians in Montana, it was a meeting of throwbacks.

'They make treaty after treaty with us, then they break them,' says Rees. 'Ten years ago the licence was just £100. When they tried to get that up to £500 we appealed to the Secretary of State for Wales, the way the Indians used to appeal to the President of the United States. "You're going to be given Heritage Status," said the man from the National Rivers Authority. Never saw him again. Never saw the Heritage Status either.

'Easy to pick on, we are. The river's dying. When I was a boy forty years ago there were thousands of elvers. There are none now. But they daren't pick on the companies with permission to pump the effluent in. They daren't pick on the trawlers which intercept the salmon on the high seas. But it's cheap to pick on us and give the impression they're doing something. They want us off the river, just as they wanted the Indians off the Frontier.'

When I started writing this I wanted to tell the story of a river and a town. The town is Carmarthen, where I was brought up, the river the Towy. The town is where it is because of the river, for even though the sea was 7 miles away, the river was navigable and, as such, one of the highways of the Old World, up which trade came and went. All trade. Until 1852, when the railway came, the town was a port from which a third of the population made its living. Then, in my lifetime, a four-lane carriageway was torn through the alleys and streets between the river and the town. Like an old whore who had married money, Carmarthen had turned its back on its origins.

This has happened in other towns, but nowhere with such brutality. There are no bridges or crossings of any kind across this road. In one of the most beautiful valleys on earth, no child and no family will ever walk the banks of the Towy at Carmarthen again, where I walked with my parents. To compound the lunacy, the local council has built picnic tables there, which would be the equivalent of opening a chip shop on the summit of Mount Everest. The result is that people have forgotten what their town was or why. It was when I met someone who had not forgotten that an article intended to be the story of a river became the story of one man.

Like Water Rat in *The Wind in the Willows*, Rees lives on the river in a house he built himself three miles from Carmarthen, below the road where the marshes start. Quite how he managed to get planning permission for this is one of the mysteries of the late twentieth century and one of the few victories over its bureaucracy. Down there he is among reeds and mud and cormorants, in a secret place you cannot see from the road. But the irony is that when he built here, it was a return. Rees is the first man in centuries to live above the Black Pool, the lost and forgotten deep-water harbour of Carmarthen.

The Romans, who built Carmarthen, called it Maridunum, the fort by the sea. Their merchantmen would have moved through the reeds, bringing luxury supplies or exotic wild beasts to an amphitheatre capable of seating 5000. Perhaps even the odd galley came, beating oars upstream. But 1000 years later, by the 1430s, the river had become so silted that a harbour had to be built three miles down from the town. This was where they anchored, the vessels bringing wine from Bordeaux, and where, from boats, these were loaded with wool for the return journey. All traces of this had disappeared in mudbanks and in deep woods so thick they could almost be a rainforest. From time to time cars unable to take the corner at Green Castle plunged into this, one woman, badly injured, waving her petticoat to summon help. But the Woodland Trust has now magically built paths through the woods to the water's edge, and when you walk them you come on mysterious things, stubby lichened walls and a stone surface underfoot. Up these, from the three-masters anchored below, the packhorses would have come, bringing quiet contraband from forgotten quays.

The people of Carmarthen know nothing of this. But men have survived whose predecessors were on the river before the Romans came, and are still there, though triremes and three-masters have long gone. They use terms so old that only medieval Welsh scholars might recognise their origin. Words like *astell orlais* for bulkhead and *clyfwchwr* for that moment of twilight when the tide comes, a time for fishing. Fluent Welsh speakers, which not one of these is now, would not understand these terms, but the coraclemen do, for they have been passed down from father to son. It is as though in Greece you met men who in their craft use words Achilles knew, using them because, in a shrinking world, they are the last secrets of what was once a secret society.

'Who were we? The poorest of the poor, the lowest of the low. We were the Carmarthen Mob,' said David Rees. Catch you a salmon for tuppence, lay on a full-scale riot for less. They lived in their own quarter, those slums by the river that were razed to make way for the four-lane carriageway. We heard stories about them, about fights and babies bitten by rats, but most people in Carmarthen did not meet a single member of what was a hereditary caste based on a handful of families. We just saw them once a year, when they entered a full-sized boat on wheels for the town carnival. They pulled this through the streets, twenty of them singing 'The Volga Boat Song', all stripped to the waist and being lashed, really lashed, with a rope's end, a crone in the boat smoking a pipe. All the other entries were what you would expect in a small-town carnival; this was different. This was barbaric and terrifying, and fifty years on I have not forgotten it.

But the first time I talked to a coracleman was when a national newspaper instructed me to do so, he, then in his nineties, having been made an MBE 'for services to coracle fishing', which made it sound as though the salmon had nominated him.

He told me stories of the river, of the night a huge sturgeon had plunged into the net. They hadn't a clue what it was because of the darkness; all they knew was that they were being pulled upstream like speedboats. He told me of the poverty and the fighting, and I realised his was a town I knew nothing about. My town was based on change, on the grammar school and getting on. His had never changed. It had its own traditions and a folk history passed on which no historian had written down. The lowest of the low…

'My great-grandfather, he loaded the cannon on Carmarthen Quay on Mafeking Night,' said Rees, watching the tide come in. 'It was a Russian cannon from the Crimea. Used to stand in front of the Fusiliers Monument. He put too much powder in. That was the last anyone saw of him or the Russian cannon.

'They were like something off the Frontier, these men. This bloke, he used to come out of the Jolly Tar, a pub on the town quay, every Saturday night at stop tap, his Jack Russell on a lead behind him, the dog dragging back because he knew what was coming. His owner would cross the road and stand there above the river. "If Jesus Christ could walk on water, then so can I." The next moment, whoosh, him and the dog. Every Saturday night. And of course every Saturday night they had to rescue him. Not the Jack Russell though. That could swim.

'They had this siege mentality, it was them against the world, not that they had much idea about the world. Theirs was one mile of the River Towy, from just beyond the town bridge to the railway bridge downstream, and they were known as the Red Light Boys on account of the red lights on the railway bridge. There was no need to go further, there was that much fish, and they had names for every bend in the river in that mile, every pool, every inlet, every island. Gwely Tomos, Thomas's Bed, after a man who fell asleep in his coracle and was drowned. Cook's Bank. Banc yr Alma, after the Crimean battle. Beyond the Red Light they were not too sure where anything was. I heard one old boy claim that the dwindling fish stock was due "to them catching the salmon in the sea beyond the Bar". Beyond the Bar? "Yes, in Greenland." He thought Greenland was the other side of Carmarthen Bay.

'But they were as hard as nails. After the booze and fags and fog, nothing could carry them off except old age. I remember my grandfather, well into his seventies, borrowing a motorboat for the day so he, my father and I could go cockling in Ferryside on the estuary. I was a small boy. Anyway, we filled three sacks – we used to pickle the cockles then – and we were about to load them when this man came down the beach.

'He was in uniform, peaked cap and all. He said he was a Fisheries officer and it was against the law to fish on a Sunday. "We're not fishin', we are cockling," said my grandfather calmly. The man put his hand on my grandfather's shoulder, and grandfather hit him. I can see him now, lying on the ground as we put the cockles in the boat. My father was terrified. "They'll be waiting for us when we get back," he said. "Don't be silly," said my grandfather. "He was an escaped lunatic, that one." "But he was in uniform." "Stolen," said my grandfather. I lay in the bottom of the boat, convinced something awful would happen to us. But there was no one waiting at the quay. We just went home. For years I thought I'd dreamed the whole thing. But I hadn't.

'Some of them were on the river at eight years old. This little boy, he caught a salmon. "When you go home," said his father, "you'll have a whole boiled egg to yourself." They never ate the fish, they couldn't afford to.

'I suppose I should have stuck more to school, but once you get on the river there's no going back. It gets into your blood. You drift on beyond the town lights, and there are no traffic sounds, just the sounds of the river in the moonlight. I've never been frightened of the river, except when that bloody film *Jaws* came out. We were seeing fins everywhere after that. And once I was fishing in fog when this body went by. "Bugger that," I said, but my partner said, "It could be your mother." So we paddled after it, I could see the white face, but then the moon came out from behind the clouds. It was a pig.

'But it's amazing what you find. See this.' It was a silver jug with a hinged lid. 'From the markings it's by R. Wallace of Connecticut. See here, these thirteen stars? They were the thirteen original states, so God knows when that was lost or from what trader. One chap, he was fishing under the bridge when there was a screech of tyres, then running footsteps and a splash as something landed right in his net. A bloody shotgun. He took it to the police just as this chap was being brought in for a shooting. Apparently the man's jaw fell to the point where he couldn't speak, as he stared at something he thought was at the bottom of the river. He confessed to everything, he thought he was among the greatest detectives in the world.

'I am forty-seven now and I've been on the river since I was a teenager. Dusk to dawn. The stars coming out and the stars going in. A coffee and a fag, and all that beauty. I saw Halley's Comet from the river. All that history, those nicknames, the Yankees, a family one of whom did a bunk to the States after a shooting, the Shippoes, a family which unloaded cargo. "Ship ho!" Good God, where else in Britain can you see a living tradition a Roman centurion saw? And they've turned their backs on us, except when some TV company wants to make a film, just as with the Sioux. They make headdresses for tourists. I make coracles for Heritage Centres now.'

There is one in the Heritage Centre built by Carmarthenshire County Council. They have, of course, built it on the other side of the four-lane carriageway, where it stands in solitary and mocking grandeur on the riverbank. One day someone will get across.

2000

A DARK HORSE IN EBBW VALE

Mr Dai Burchell was shoeing a horse. 'Can't run if ew don' have no foot,' muttered Mr Burchell as the gleaming neck turned. He does the farriery himself, as there have been no farriers in living memory in Ebbw Vale. Or trees.

'What would it have been like round here?' He took the nail out of his mouth. 'Go down Blaenavon way, bloody marvellous it is round there. They do have trees by the road and all. Up here they've seen them off long ago.'

The high hills look as though a giant hand has thrown an old blanket over them to hide their shame. Far below them in the one main street, shops have closed in a debris of bleached advertisements and broken glass. There are derelict houses, derelict chapels, and though a hand has written 'Free Wales' on a wall, it has done so in discreet small letters in case someone might. This is a place of the dead.

Only they have forgotten to inform the living. It is midday, and the

Ebbw Vale Leisure Centre, the S of which is dangling, is full of squash and soccer players. There is no shortage of leisure, with 24 per cent unemployment. They have forgotten to tell Dai Burchell, too.

David Burchell, aged forty-seven, was born in a hunting lodge near the Severn Bridge ('Why? We was living in it, that's why'), son of a farm worker who moved to Ebbw Vale in boom time. A steel-worker himself, he took voluntary redundancy two years ago and used his £13,500 pay-off to set up as a trainer of steeple-chasers – in Ebbw Vale. Today he is one of the most successful of Britain's 800 registered trainers, and this is where the film spins off the reel.

Take Two: A Day in the Life of One of Britain's Most Successful Trainers. Some 400 acres in a pleat of the Berkshire Downs, a string of racehorses against the dawn sky, a line of trees a windbreak around an eighteenth-century farmhouse, and Captain Burchell, a lean leathery face above the sheepskin. So it would be in films or in the novels of Mr Dick Francis. But it is not like that here.

In Ebbw Vale the terraces on the hills are as steep as the upper circle in a theatre, and you get good views of the steel works, the rain and your neighbours. At the very top, where the roads end, there are what seem to be inhabited garden sheds but no sign of racehorses. Hearing pop music, I knocked on one door. There was a pause and then a large and amiable young man, stark naked, stood in a bedroom window, a flap of curtain held about his middle. 'Come too far you have,' he said chattily. 'That's his place down there, by that house.' Mr Dai Burchell must be the only trainer in British racing to be based in a street.

Horse and Hound could not disguise its awe. 'The tiny yard directly overlooks the Ebbw Vale steel works and it amazed me to see the inmates contentedly watching the hustle and bustle of the indus-trial area in the valley below.' Yet earlier this season it was from here that Mr Burchell, with seven winners, six seconds and a third out of just twenty runners, was the second most successful trainer in racing.

There is a break between the houses and a short muddy track leading to a farmhouse that was here before men mined coal in the valley. 'Nothing here before this,' said Dai Burchell, '1400, this was built.' It was a sheep farm. Somehow it survived the houses pushing up and round it, cutting off its fields, but 19 acres of these – and the sheep – are still here. And now the horses are back, but horses the like of which the valley has probably never seen in all its history: horses that go like the wind.

Ruth Price, aged twenty, was exercising a horse in the circular indoor school that Dai Burchell has built on the hillside, by levelling it and using old railway sleepers in its construction. She went round and round. What was it like to ride a horse that could go that fast? 'It's all right,' said Miss Price in that maddening way with which young people respond to a direct question. Miss Price came round again. 'I'll tell you what it's like,' she relented. 'We take them down to Aberavon Beach, and the first time I thought wings were coming out of my head.'

In summer they turn the horses out in the fields above the town. This is a constant source of worry to Dai Burchell. 'The kids can't leave them alone. Racehorses, see. They want to see how fast they can go. But get one of these worked up and they *go*.'

Living where he does, Dai is aware that he is a man out of place and time. He is separated from his wife, who finally, he says, could not take any more of the horses. His son David, aged sixteen, stayed to work with him as one of his three young helpers, but his two teenage daughters left with their mother. He said sadly of the younger, 'She was one of us, but she had to go with her mother.'

He uses the phrase 'one of us' to describe an older species who somehow clung on here, the horse people. His neighbours, he said, were interested only in cars and pubs and clubs. Once he went to see his local MP, Michael Foot, with his problems, but Mr Foot told him that it was his job to represent the majority.

Mr Burchell is an amiable, open man, living in the sort of domestic chaos in which ten-year-olds would be content to live for the rest of their lives. Curry and chips for lunch, and great heaps of biscuits, copies of *Sporting Life* in a pile that reaches almost to the ceiling, bottles of whisky and opened boxes of chocolates. House-proud Welshwomen would probably commit suicide on the doorstep, but the horseboxes are immaculate, and you are left with the impression that the human quarters are the servants' wing. Athletes at rest, long faces peering mildly over the half doors, the horses seem to share this impression.

His father, said Dai Burchell, never understood what he saw in horses. He bought his first, a pony, at the age of eleven, and kept it on a patch of waste ground, riding it over the hills. 'I've no idea what fascinates me about horses, but I'd have them even if there were no races. I just like to see them and get them fit. Also the jumping, that's the excitement and it do prove a point, like you do it better than anyone else.'

He was quite a successful jockey, always over the jumps, always on days off from the steel works. But though for the last twenty years he has trained horses under a Jockey Club permit, which allows you to ride horses you have trained yourself, his ambition was always the public licence, which allows you to train other people's horses. Redundancy gave him the chance. He and his brother built the indoor school, new boxes with stones from old cottages, installed their own central heating and rented an extra 80 yards of hill-top, which gave them gallops of over a mile and a half. So to Ebbw Vale came a Jockey Club man and two years ago Dai Burchell got his licence. After all, everything was there in its own odd way. The heating system in the tack room, made entirely out of scrap-iron, as *Horse and Hound* recorded, gave out more heat than many costly commercial systems.

Dai Burchell was dreaming aloud. If he won the football, he said, he would buy a real farm, somewhere around Chepstow, where he could grow oats and hay and be a self-contained unit. He has seen such places. Once he went to Harry Wragg's place at Newmarket, and he talks about it the way returned Crusaders must have talked about Byzantium. 'The stables and the lawns all laid out in front of you. With us it's all make-do and mend. But there's nothing too expensive and it's all geared to horses. It's great, man.'

He has no illusions about his place in the scheme of things. 'We're right down the bottom of the ladder. We're the bread-and-butter boys.' His are the National Hunt races at places like Taunton, Hereford, Chepstow, Ludlow. Once he dreamed of winning the Derby; now he dreams of winning a race on every track. It was a matter of building up, he said. He had eight horses, while someone like Henry Cecil had 130.

But almost from the beginning he began winning races. Just hard work, he said. He starts at 6.00 in the morning, taking a bowl of oats round each of his lodgers, oats with usually a bit of stout in them. At 8.00 he takes four out on a gallop across the hills, walking them for 20 minutes up through the streets. In the afternoons he drives another four down to Aberavon Beach. It is usually 9.00 at night before he finishes.

Hard work and – he looked very innocent suddenly – picking the right race. 'You get the best rider and you enter him in the worst race.' He is a punter himself and, so rumour has it, was £30,000 up at the end of last season. He backs his own horses, and after one race it is said that he and his friends were £15,000 up. The bookies began to hear about Dai Burchell last year.

There has been much publicity. 'This reporter rang up, asking if he could come down. He'd been totting the winners up or something. But I said to him, "We don' have time for that." Then I had something to hide, he said. 'Course he came then, and it hasn't stopped now for eighteen months.' It has meant that the horses now come to Ebbw

Vale from places like Bath and Shropshire. It costs their owners £55 a
week. ('And that's half what most trainers do charge. Some do want
£200 a week'). The longest stay has been seven months. "'E kept on
winnin'. But the good 'uns don' stay long enough.'

There was a knock at the door. It was an old colleague of his from
the steel works. 'Take a horse out for you tomorrow, Dai?' It was not a
request one would imagine a caller making of Henry Cecil. But the
horses, said Dai Burchell after he had gone, did need exercise. 'You
know someone, you'd lend him your car, wouldn' ew? Specially if you
know he do look after it.' The one great problem, apart from the
curiosity of small boys, was the weather. 'It affects us here. We had
two inches of snow some days ago. And there's the rain. We can't
guarantee any horses in January and February up here, not with the
hills.'

I told him about someone I had met, a Jockey Club handicapper.
Dai Burchell grinned. He would like to have met him, he said. But
then he liked everyone he had met in racing. Tidy people, tidy
people.

He himself was always doing now what he had always wanted to
do, he said. He ran the horses as though they were his own. Down the
hill the horse-box trundles to the races, driven by Dai, and at night it
returns, sometimes with Dai in a new suit. For the winning streak has
gone on. Brown Rifle winning at Stratford and Taunton; Kilsight at
Bangor; Beaming Lass at Uttoxeter and Bangor. It is the stuff of which
dreams are made. Was he a happy man? For a moment he looked puzzled by the silliness of this. 'Oh, aye,' said Dai Burchell. 'I am paid to
go racin'. That's what it do boil down to.'

In the main street far below there was a Chinese restaurant, the
Sun Do Take-Away. Infectious thing, grammar. Dai do get his lunches
from there.

CLINT EASTWOOD OF THE CLEDDAU

H
e does not think of himself as a quarrelsome man. 'I have belonged to a male voice choir for twenty years,' said Watcyn Richards, slowly so the logic could sink in. 'No man can be a member of a male voice choir for that length of time and be quarrelsome.' Yet in that time he has collided, to use his word, with the District Council, the Ministry of Agriculture, the National Rivers Authority, the Milk Marketing Board, Barclays Bank, the National Westminster Bank, a High Court judge whom he informed in his own courtroom that he was 'as bent as a piece of old wire', and the local hunt, thirty-six members of which he kidnapped one afternoon.

'I've not set out to do this, but I seem to have fallen foul of everyone in authority,' he says. 'Yet in all that animosity I have never lost an ounce of sleep. I put that down to regular choir practice.'

You may have noted something familiar about all this, with the exception of the Haverfordwest Male Voice Choir. Think of high blue skies and of men who stand tall against them, men who also did not think themselves quarrelsome but collided, in their case, with cattle barons, carpetbag politicians and town bosses. It could be Clint Eastwood speaking in the quiet moments before Hell came to breakfast.

Watcyn Richards, in his fifties and a farmer at Camrose, Pembrokeshire, looks like a Western hero, 'a big strong-looking type, an inch or so over six feet, with dark Celtic features,' writes his Boswell, Roscoe Howells, in *The Farmer And The Bureaucrats*. 'To me he is the man who saw it through.'

We all daydream about the Western hero, but even had we the guts to do so, we would not behave like such a man, fearful that his terrifying simplicity has no place in real life. 'You and I, we'd say "Bugger it", and walk by,' says Derek Rees, a local reporter who has known him for twenty-five years. 'Only Watcyn doesn't say, "Bugger it", nor does he walk by. He's a one-off job, he is.' What follows is a record of the Western hero in action, not on the plains of the Midwest, but in west Wales. It is the story of one man's collisions.

HE COLLIDES WITH THE HUNT

Watcyn did not object to the South Pembrokeshire Hunt crossing his land. What he objected to was their galloping over seeded pastures and over new fences, so he had sent word to tell them. But the man on the horse is the old symbol of authority and Mr Richards was just a tenant farmer, so the hunt galloped on.

'I was waiting for them in the lane beside my farm. There were thirty-six of them on horseback and I had my shotgun. They wouldn't turn back when I told them, so I fired in the air to get their full attention, after which I drove them in front of me back into my yard. I had locked the far gate, so as soon as I got them into the yard I locked the other one as well. I told them they'd had due warning, but they were shouting so much I left them and went off to phone my solicitor.

'I asked his advice. There was a pause and he said quietly, "Who exactly have you got in the yard?" I said I thought I had the chairman of the bench and most of the local gentry. He said he'd phone me back in 10 minutes, which he did, saying that perhaps a better approach would have been to write to the Master of Foxhounds, saying it was my intention to close off the land and enclosing a map. "Right," I said. But when I got outside they started shouting at me all over again, saying how they were going to have me, which I found puzzling. "Gentlemen," I said, "it seems to me I've had you, and I was just about to let you out, but now I won't." I kept them there until the evening, by which time the hounds were all over the county. I've not had any trouble with the hunt since then, and they've agreed to pay for all the damage they caused.'

HE COLLIDES WITH THE MIN OF AG

In 1985 Watcyn Richards wrote a letter to the then Prime Minister. 'Dear Mrs Thatcher, I am delighted you are taking an active interest in trying to stamp out the abuse of drugs in our society. Whilst you are at it, could you also take an interest in the abuse of drugs in the farming industry, which is being carried out for the benefit of drug manufacturers with the connivance of the Milk Marketing Board and your own Ministry of Agriculture.' No reply.

He was concerned about two things. The first was the massive dosages of antibiotics being administered to animals. The second was the instructions issued by the Ministry of Agriculture on the withdrawal period after such treatment, before their milk could be sold or cattle sold for beef.

'If you want to know what he was on about, just listen to this,' says Anton Lowe, a Haverfordwest vet who had earlier said 'Goodbye' when he heard Mr Richards' name. 'There was a cortisone drug we could prescribe for beef cattle without any withdrawal period. We could inject this and put the animal into the slaughterhouse that same day. Then the manufacturers announced there should be a thirty-six-day withdrawal period. The rules change overnight, from three days in one case to sixty-three. And it's only because of the EC that proper clinical trials are being done now. In the past people accepted it, it was the System. Only Watcyn didn't accept it.'

It started when traces of antibiotics turned up in his milk. When this happens the farmer is penalised by having to withhold the milk. But, he argued, almost every form of medical treatment involved antibiotics, and the matter came to a head when a ten-day-old calf was taken ill with white scour on his farm. Normally treatment with antibiotics would have had the animal on its feet after 24 hours. This time it died, the vet reporting that it appeared to have an immunity to antibiotics. Next day Watcyn Richards, carrying his dead calf in his arms, appeared at the Ministry of Agriculture offices in Haverfordwest and dropped the animal on to the desk of a startled assistant District Veterinary Officer.

'He does seem to enjoy a good fight,' says Mr Lowe. But, with the weekly injections of choir practice, this has only once turned to fisticuffs.

HE COLLIDES WITH THE HSE

Watcyn Richards is a great admirer of the Steyr tractor, made in Austria, and bought one at a local agricultural show. There was one snag. The Health and Safety Executive had condemned its cab because the noise level inside was two decibels too high (this, despite the fact that many farmers work in a daze of pop music). No problem, said the British suppliers; they would fit a new cab blessed by the HSE. The tractor came but Watcyn Richards found it was now almost impossible to change gear and completely impossible to close the doors.

He called in an engineer who listed twenty faults. He then called in an HSE inspector who reported it was impossible to distinguish design faults in a tractor that was no longer new. The tractor was by then just three weeks old. In response to his desperate appeals, the inspector returned and this time identified two safety faults in a Fordson tractor that happened to be in the yard at the time. He did not mention the Steyr.

Mr Richards sent it back to the suppliers, went along himself and, after being called a Welsh bastard and threatened with a spanner, hit someone. Later he was served tea and sandwiches, but the tractor came back unchanged. He has found a way of changing gear, though no one else can. Still, the tractor has its uses.

When a grove of elms died on his land, he pulled them out, which left him with a small ravine. This he began to use as an in-fill site, only an Environmental Health official heard and said he needed authority to operate a refuse tip. Mr Richards replied that it was just an in-fill area where building site material got dumped, not a refuse tip.

The official called, and as it was a wet day, Mr Richards offered to drive him across the fields in his Steyr tractor with the new cab. He went up and down a steep bank, the doors frantically semaphoring, and no more was heard about the refuse tip. But on occasion even a Western hero can come unstuck.

HE COLLIDES WITH THE BANKS

Like many farmers in the late twentieth century, he got into trouble with a bank that had enthusiastically lent him money. Barclays had advanced him a sum that enabled him to buy Bunkers Hill, one of the two farms he was then running; the other, Whitethorn, he already owned. He fell behind with the interest, interest was charged on interest, and Barclays foreclosed on him. The final straw came when the Revenue tried to charge him capital gains tax on this.

He was out walking across his land one night when near the in-fill he saw papers blowing about. Shining his torch on one he saw it was the trading account of a local businessman. The next morning he was back and saw that some black plastic bags had split open revealing the personal financial details of customers at the local NatWest Bank, which was then having some building work done. One man, he noted with interest, had an annual turnover of £9 million.

He phoned the manager who came with an assistant and, as Mr Richards afterwards informed the *Sunday Express*, 'went white', for Mr Richards did not hand them over. Instead, he buried them, being, as the paper reported, 'not kindly disposed to banks'.

A Western hero sees the world in simple terms, and he had the wacky idea that one bank might put right the depredations of another. It took a High Court writ and a court in London sitting *in camera* (during which Mr Richards, reflecting on the moral character of the judge, was threatened with contempt) before he dug them up.

So what, as Edmund Gosse once asked with awe, had prompted Mr Thomas Hardy to stand up in the arable land of Wessex and shake his fist at his Creator? What has prompted Mr Watcyn Richards to stand up in the meadows of west Wales and shake his fist at authority?

It started with an illness. As a young tenant farmer he had joined the Ministry of Agriculture's Brucellosis Accredited Scheme. The disease in cattle produces contagious abortion, and the Ministry had the laudable ambition of making Britain brucellosis-free. But then the disease came to Watcyn's farm, and from 120 gallons of milk a day he was down to 40 within a year; eight animals were dead. So he appealed to the Ministry who confirmed that the cause was pollution in the River Cleddau, which crosses his land. They further identified this as coming from slurry – cow shit – seeping into the river from his neighbour's land, from a lagoon the Ministry itself had approved. The result of this discovery was that an official placed an order on Watcyn Richards forbidding him to use his best grazing land, 23 acres of water meadow.

Anything else, he was told, was the responsibility of the Public Health. He appealed to them and was told it was the responsibility of the Rivers Authority, and when he appealed to this, nobody came. Then one night he saw a pipe leading from his neighbour's slurry lagoon to the river. It took many phone calls before the river inspector turned out, and then all he did was remove the pipe from the river; he would not confront the culprit.

Eventually there was a case, the neighbour pleaded guilty and was given a conditional discharge. By then Mr Richard's losses were estimated at £7000 and he could not afford a civil case to recover them. It occurred to him that in the vast shadow of late twentieth-century bureaucracy, where civil servants now outnumber farmers, a man was completely on his own. It's you and me, Jesse.

HE COLLIDES WITH THE COUNCIL

Watcyn Richards already had planning permission to build a bungalow but did not start work until five years later when eviction from Bunkers Hill made this a matter of urgency. He wrote to inform the District Council that work was progressing, at which point an official phoned to tell him the planning permission was out of date. He was invited to reapply.

This he did, though the council's own building inspector who had called told him it was a formality, and to carry on. What followed was a council demolition order on the almost completed bungalow. The reason given was breathtaking. Mr Richards had been farming Bunkers Hill when he applied for his first planning permission, and the bungalow was designated a dwelling for use in agriculture. When he reapplied the council's legal department asked to see the deeds of

Bunkers Hill. It didn't matter that Mr Richards still had a 20-acre farm and was also renting land; they had to see the deeds of a farm he no longer owned.

The matter went to a public inquiry, in the course of which the inspector asked for a map of Camrose village and was told this was not available. A messenger was sent to the council offices and returned with the news that either such a plan did not exist or it could not be found. A bemused inspector found for Watcyn Richards and awarded him costs of £6733.77.

HE COLLIDES WITH EVERYBODY

In 1989 he decided to build a fishing lake and submitted a plan to the Ministry of Agriculture as a farm diversification project; the Ministry promised him the mysteriously exact figure of £1,193.75 on completion.

In 1990, having dug his hole in the ground, he contacted the Ministry, which informed him that he needed to get a certificate from a qualified engineer 'for any raised reservoir'. He replied that there was no raised reservoir, just a hole in the ground now full of water. There was a site inspection, after which he was told he still had to do two things. The first was that he had to remove the gratings from the overflow, as these could easily become obstructed. He replied gleefully that the gratings had only been put in at the insistence of the National Rivers Authority. He heard no more on this.

But the Ministry was strong on its second demand. He had to fit 'an inlet throttle pipe' six inches in diameter. Now by that stage the lake was full, being fed along an open ditch from a nearby stream; a ditch was easy to clear when the leaves fell, but a pipe, he knew, would be a different matter. Still, he wanted his £1,193.75, and if the Ministry wanted its pipe, the Ministry would get its pipe. He got them to agree to a larger one, nine inches in diameter, and this was fitted. That first night it rained, by morning the pipe was clogged and water had flooded the road. The road was the responsibility of the Highway Authority.

The cars came again, this time containing a man from the Ministry, one from the NRA, two from Welsh Water and a man from the Highway Authority. There was a lot of talk and the man from the Highway Authority said he would personally see to the removal of the throttle pipe; Mr Richards got his £1193.75.

The bungalow is finished now. Watcyn Richards is still there, drowning quietly in paper, for when he took up farming all a farmer was required to keep was a Movement of Animals book, recording the animals he bought and sold; now the forms, and the advice, arrive in every post. The bungalow is an archive now. Fearful of further collisions, he has constructed a safe in its foundations; a Western hero might have kept a Winchester 73 here but Mr Richards uses it to store his files.

In the evenings he walks by the lake and watches the carp under the lilies. This summer he found a Viper's Bugloss on the banks, a plant rare in Pembrokeshire, but has not told anyone about it in case a man in some office puts a protection order on it. Such men, he believes, are capable of anything.

1994

THE PRINCESS AND THE CAPTAIN

An old captain has died in Caernarfon, the son, grandson and great-grandson of seafarers. Richard Turner was 72, and I mourn the one human being who, because of something I wrote, was moved to action. It was an unnerving experience.

Some years ago I wrote an article about Gwenllian, daughter and only child of Llywelyn, the last Welsh Prince of Wales, stolen as a baby by English troopers to live out her life as a nun at Sempringham Priory. It was a sad little story and at most I hoped it would make people pause over the cornflakes to remember a life forced into the footnotes. I had not met the Captain then.

The Bishop of Grantham, Bill Ind, was at Sempringham to dedicate a plaque in memory of St Gilbert, its founder, when up the path to the little church, which is all that remains of the Priory, he saw a seventy-year-old man come, staggering under the weight of something on his back. The Bishop, in full canonicals and presiding over an ecumenical assembly of several hundred dignitaries, was a bit pre-occupied that day, for dozens of pre-ordered Portaloos had been delivered, not to Sempringham, but to Sandringham. He did not expect things to get any worse. But things did. Up the path came a man with a tombstone for a Welsh princess six centuries dead. The Captain had brought a memorial for Gwenllian.

As the Bishop recalls, he had not asked permission of the Crown, which owns the land; he had not even approached the diocese. The Captain had just ordered the stone ('chap called Jones did it for me'), put it in the boot of his car and driven 300 miles to erect it. There was some consternation in the Church over his epitaph ('Died at Sempringham, 7.6.1337, having been held prisoner for 54 years'). Some might think she had had a vocation, said the Bishop mildly. But in the end they allowed him to have his stone on the old road leading to the Priory. A local mason put it in place and it has become a little shrine, with flowers put there each month by the Captain's cousin, a commercial traveller from Halifax, his beat mysteriously extended.

The Captain was not a Welsh Nationalist, being bitterly opposed to a Welsh Assembly, which he thought would be dominated by the southern Welsh. It was just that on his long night watches at sea he had begun to brood on what he saw as the lost inventory of his race. Scotland had the Stone of Scone, its crown jewels and royal tombs. Wales, its tombs plundered, its regalia stolen, had nothing. To the Captain, Edward I was a contemporary politician, whom he hated.

I wrote about that lost regalia, in particular the piece of the True Cross that had belonged to the last Prince. The final reference to this was in 1548, when the gold backing was sold, but there is a tradition that the relic was built into the roof of the new St George's Chapel at Windsor. After Sempringham, I suppose, I should have known better, for the inevitable phone call came. The Captain had been to Windsor. 'Why? To nick it, of course.'

He had an odd telephone manner. He never introduced himself, but would launch into a conversation he assumed had already started but had been interrupted. It did not help that he sounded like Bluto, Popeye's enemy, at his most gravel-voiced. But that day he was rueful. 'Couldn't get near it. That roof is a hundred feet high. I hadn't read that in the guide. It was too high and I am too old.'

Bishop Ind, who must have thought little would surprise him again, was rung up and asked abruptly if he had any influence over the Dean of Windsor. The Bishop thought he had once sat next to him at dinner, and the Captain did not pursue the matter.

He phoned many people. He harangued bishops when Welsh Water turned a medieval friary into a sewage farm. He instructed startled historians to pursue new areas of study. And it wasn't just history. His great love was opera, and he wrote to Norma Major, among others, suggesting that pressure be put on the BBC to broadcast an evening of Gigli. He had, he explained, forty-four lost years at sea to make up. Mrs Major replied with a polite, baffled letter.

A Roman Catholic, although he had been married three times, he lived alone at the end, cooked for by local nuns, whom in return he allowed to watch Association Football on his television. 'He was like a character out of one of G.K. Chesterton's novels,' said Bishop Ind. 'In one sense, dotty. In another, quite wonderful.' He, too, will find it hard to forget the Captain.

1997

THE MALE VOICE CHOIR

There are sixty-five of them on stage. Sometimes there are more, but time and wives, those old enemies of promise and especially of male voice choirs, exact a toll, and tonight there are sixty-five rising as one man to the signal of their conductor. They are not young, there are many grey and white heads among them, and certainly not one would meet the minimum height requirements of any British police force – these men being bred, like Jack Russells, to go underground. Only there is no underground now, as the Treorchy Male Voice Choir, with not a working miner among them, celebrates its fiftieth anniversary. The tenors, their faces lifted to the spotlights, begin, and then, like the surging of the sea and as expressionless, the bass section joins in. They can move you to tears or want to make you march to a drum, though there are no drums, just the single piano (Mrs Marion Williams B.Mus), the conductor (Mr John Jenkins BA) and the voices. But what voices... with the choke full out, they can shake a concert hall like a jet awaiting take-off. So look at them for a moment, these little men standing to attention in tuxedos renewed every eight years. What you are seeing is the end of a way of life.

Outside religious sects there has never been a closer community than that of the Welsh Valleys. Geography sealed them in, the terraces of identical houses inched their way up the hills, and three things cemented their sense of community: the pit, the chapel and the male voice choir. These men worked (and sometimes died) together, they worshipped and sang together. But the pits have closed, the chapels are closing at the rate of one a week and the young are streaming out of the valleys to find work.

Nobody knows for sure whether some male voice choirs even exist now. One, it is said, has an average age of eighty and has not sung in public for as long as anyone can remember, but it is thought the members still meet like the last Jacobites, six proud and elderly gentlemen ('nine, if it's a fine day').

Yet among the rusted winding gears, among chapels that have become squash clubs and mosques, there is still the Treorchy Male Voice Choir, with its annual EMI recording contract, its three American tours in four years, and with devoted English fans who have been fans for so long that they are on first-name terms with the choir. The two coaches sweep out of the Rhondda thirty times a year, and at each concert there is a packed house. Over the years the choir has grown into something of a myth. Cartoonists caricature it, comedians make jokes about it, for it is said they had their own version of the wedding ceremony: 'Do you, Gladys/Glenys/Gwyneth, take this man, also the Treorchy Male Voice Choir?'

But there was no need to invent jokes: life supplied these. 'Perhaps you could keep me some cake,' said Bryn Howells, chorister, being told the date of his son's wedding. 'I shall, of course, be on tour with the boys.' And in the end it was the wedding date that got changed. Every year on the first page of the choir's magazine, *Excelsior*, grown men have their attendance records at rehearsal paraded, and see noth-ing odd in this.

They have sung (and drunk) with Tom Jones ('That boy might have made a light tenor, if he'd practised'). They have sung with Ella Fitzgerald. ('And all of a sudden our old conductor, John Cynan Jones, said, "Stop." Now this was in a recording studio with an orchestra. "I'm sorry, Miss Fitzgerald, but you're singing it wrong." You have to admire a man from the Valleys doing that.') But it was a confrontation between gods: in the fifty years of the choir there have been just three conductors.

Three years ago they recorded an album of hits by the rock group Queen. So they have gone from 'Amazing Grace' to 'Were You There When They Crucified My Lord', 'The Battle Hymn of the Republic' to, now, Freddie Mercury's 'Good Old-fashioned Lover Boy'. 'To sur-vive, a choir has to change its repertoire,' the former chairman told me. 'We can't go on singing "Crossing the Plain". Good God, we'd sung that so often, we'd started seeing Red Indians.'

Not only has its repertoire changed, the choir survives in a changed world. 'Big thing, the emancipation of women,' pronounced Norman Martin, choir archivist. 'When I was young, three choir prac-tices a week plus a Saturday concert was no problem. Now if they let the men out at all, the women want to come as well.' Family commit-ments, sniffed Mr Martin, who last year had a 90 per cent attendance record at rehearsals. 'We just put up with it in the old days,' said Mrs Pat Howells, wife of Bryn, he of the wedding cake. 'Some weekends I didn't see him until Sunday morning in bed, and then he usually had a terrible headache.'

It is a choir tradition that there are two concerts and two coaches, just as in the old moralist prints there were two Ways, the Broad and the Narrow. The public hears the first concert and when that is over the first coach leaves for the Rhondda; this contains the teetotal and the respectable members of the choir, and is known as the Deacons'

Bus. The other coach contains the Rodneys, valleys slang for good-time boys. This does not leave.

It is now midnight, three hours after the concert ended at the Spa Centre in Leamington, and in a rugby clubhouse on the outskirts, the Rodneys are well into their second concert of the night. Entrance is by invitation only, for the Rodneys, some still in their tuxedos, some in blazers, are singing for themselves. The stewards have been squared and the blinds drawn, though some of the singers are due to report for the dawn shift at the Royal Mint in Llantrisant, a hundred miles away. The Mint is now the major local employer. 'I'd check my change for the next few weeks if I were you,' said a man at the bar. 'God knows what sorts of coins these buggers will be making in the morning.'

A lot of thought goes into the location of these second concerts. In Treorchy men pore over maps and make many phone calls to rugby club secretaries, sergeants' messes, even the odd tolerant hotel, and when such negotiations break down, they take pot luck. They once held a concert in a gents' urinal in a service station on the M5 ('perfect acoustics'). And it is fascinating to spot who is here from among the gentlemen I watched on stage earlier. A man, I am told, is born either a Deacon or a Rodney, and remains one until time, or wives, intervene.

There are no hymns now. One by one they rise and each man does a turn tradition has assigned to him, so one tells jokes bluer than any in Bernard Manning's repertoire, and then one sings in a perfect high tenor an old Welsh song about lost love and the corn ripening. When he finishes there's a sudden silence and I notice that my friend, a 17-stone lecturer in political economy, is crying quietly into his double vodka.

Roger Morse, twenty-two years a top tenor, reflects on married life. 'When I got married, I was already in the choir. My wife always said, "The choir comes first." She's a good girl.' And where was Mrs

Morse now? 'At home.' Wives do not travel with the Treorchy Male Voice Choir. It has been known for wives to travel with other choirs, but not with the Treorchy. The only one who does is Mrs Wendy Jenkins, wife of the conductor, and she is tolerated because on stage she turns the pages for the pianist. At Leamington Mrs Jenkins, like the Deacons, is long gone.

'Yes, we have been known to leave people behind. One old boy, we'd gone 40 miles down the motorway before we realised he wasn't with us. So that was 80 miles we had to go to get him, and then he was cross because we woke him up.'

Adrian and Valerie Dicks, a couple in their sixties, have stayed for the second concert, being the choir's number one fans. They first heard them sing near their home in Cheltenham, and since then, primed by a list of venues from the Wales Tourist Board, they have missed just one concert in Britain. They break their holidays to do so, they follow them to Blackpool and Skegness and send birthday cards to all the choristers. 'Once we'd started, it became a bug,' said Mr Dicks, who sells plumbing equipment. 'They sound so different from English choirs. It's a much higher note that sends a shiver up my spine.'

This note was deliberately encouraged from the start. In 1946 the men who had answered the scratched appeal among the ads in the local cinema were told by their first conductor and the choir's creator, the great John Haydn Davies, 'When you reach a certain note and you drop out, you're a second tenor. Beyond that, and you're a top tenor.' Thus, in the town's senior school, where they have rehearsed ever since, Haydn Davies developed what has become known as the 'Treorchy Sound'. There are thirty top tenors alone in the choir, such a luxury that the conductor was once heard to address his twenty-two second tenors, 'Second tenors, turn to the wall. I do not want to see you, let alone hear you.' Haydn Davies was a legend in his lifetime and afterwards.

'In 1964 we had the battle of the giants at the National Eisteddfod in Swansea,' said Dean Powell, top tenor and at twenty-four one of Treorchy's youngest members. He was, of course, not born at the time, but a choir is like a regiment: the first things a recruit learns about are its past glories. 'All the Big Five choirs were there, ourselves, the Morriston Orpheus, Rhos from North Wales, Manselton [which became the Swansea Male Voice] and Pendyrus, also from the Rhondda. It was the first time we had all met in competition, and our conductor, John Haydn Davies, was ill with fever. But he insisted on appearing, and he was swaying about all over the place, bringing the boys in at the wrong moment. In the end he fell over and they carried him off on a stretcher… But we won.'

Rivalry between the great choirs was intense. But there are no competitions now. After it had clocked up seven consecutive wins at the National Eisteddfod, Treorchy, like the Harlem Globetrotters before them, withdrew into a world of exhibition matches (concerts in their case). Partly this was a recognition of social change, the choir's second conductor, John Cynan Jones, informing them in 1967, 'Boys, the National is held in summer, and it was all very well when you went to Barry and Porthcawl for your holidays. But in the '70s and '80s you may start going abroad and you won't want to come back from there.'

It was Cynan Jones, when he took over, who extended their repertoire into light music ('Stephen Sondheim, Paul Anka, Andrew Lloyds Bank, you name them, we've sung them…'). A carapace of showbiz began to form over the choir, as it had over the Globetrotters; the difference is that 90 per cent of the concerts are for charity, the rest being used to meet choir expenses. Only the conductor and the pianist are paid, and even then it is a small honorarium.

John Jenkins is the choir's third conductor. He took over in 1991, when Cynan Jones retired because of ill health and the position was advertised in the Welsh press, with the choir six weeks from an American tour. Jenkins, shock-haired and with a wild gap in his front teeth, did not apply, for this is Wales, where little is done in the open. He just let it be known that, like Barkis, he was willing.

It has become a commonly held fear that one day the supply of what they call their officer class, the graduate conductors and accompanists, will dry up, for the music departments at the Universities of Aberystwyth and Swansea have both closed. But that day is not yet, and the respectful delegation of three presented itself at the door of John Jenkins, school inspector and well-known conductor of brassbands. Only this was a door in Swansea, and it was another sign of the times. Both his predecessors had been Valleys men, and Treorchy remains unique among choirs, in that 80 per cent of its members still come from within a three-mile radius. Now every Tuesday and Thursday night Mr Jenkins drives over the pass from Swansea for rehearsals.

'How would I dare change a listed building?' he asked, and did not stay for an answer. In fact, he did so by extending the choir's repertoire even further. An awestruck John Redwood MP records in his anniversary greetings that Treorchy had sung Sibelius's Kullervo symphony – in Finnish. 'A lady from Penarth taught us,' said John Jenkins. They have also sung in Latin, Japanese and Russian ('We may not understand them, but we have sung in them'). Curiously enough, Welsh presents almost as much of a problem, only four being Welsh speakers.

Dean Powell BA is one, having taken his degree in Welsh. He was sixteen when he applied to join, even though he comes from Llantrisant, 10 miles away, and went through the whole rite of passage. The first step is the audition before the conductor, after which the applicant is assigned a senior member of the choir as a sort of musical minder. It is on this man's say-so that he finally sings in public, and then only after thirty practices. This rule is absolute. 'I was hoping to make my debut in front of the Queen at Powys Castle,' said Powell. 'Sorry boy,' they said. 'You've only done twenty-nine practices, it'll have to be next time.' And that was how it turned out, only next time, on a boiling hot night, was in a windowless little gym in the local leisure centre.'

After that a man gets his spurs of knighthood, which in the case of the Treorchy Male Voice Choir consists of the club tie, in navy blue with a red dragon and a harp. A man is given only one tie in his lifetime.

'You've got to be understanding,' said Mrs Pat Howells, after thirty-eight years of marriage, thirty of them to the Treorchy Male Voice Choir. 'Tuesday and Thursday nights go out of your life, also any idea of a Saturday night out. I've done a lot of knitting in my time.'

'You mustn't think of it as a hobby, like darts,' said Roger Morse. 'It's a commitment, a way of life. You ask if I can see life without the choir, I have to answer: "With difficulty." We have a six-week break in the summer, and then it's like having an arm cut off.'

So it is 2.00 a.m. in the Leamington Rugby Club, and the choir, whose rendition of 'Were You There' had an entire gospel congregation in the Deep South on their feet shouting hallelujah, has just finished the 'Lunatic's Song': 'Come inside, you silly buggers, come inside,' sang Dean Powell and Roger Morse and Roy Stevens, forty-five years a miner. And then they are gone into the night, these last footnotes to an industrial South Wales.

1996

GOD'S OWN NUISANCE

In 1903, in one tremulous little 12-second hop, just 10 feet off the ground, Orville Wright made the first powered flight by a man. True or false? As one the human race bellows, 'True', a vast monosyllable streaming up to the stars. And then, breaking a silence as absolute as that which fell in heaven after the opening of the Seventh Seal, a single small voice speaks. 'False,' says Mr Roscoe Howells of the seaside village of Amroth in west Wales.

It does not matter that outside the village no one has heard of this flight. His father, a builder, told him that the local carpenter Bill Frost, whom both knew, flew in 1895, eight years before the Wrights, which would make flight a nineteenth-century, and a Welsh, invention. Only the undercarriage caught in the top branches of an ash tree, his plane crashed and the old carpenter was too poor to build another. Frost, a generous man, offered the patent he had taken out to the War Office. 'A FLYING MACHINE. William Frost, Carpenter and Builder,

Saundersfoot, do hereby declare the nature of this invention to be as follows…' Roscoe Howells has the patent. He has the War Office's reply as well. 'This Nation does not intend to adopt aerial navigation as a means of warfare,' wrote a Mr William St John Broderick, then Under Secretary of State. The reply does not surprise Roscoe Howells. In the course of a long career as farmer, novelist, historian and polemicist, he has come to the conclusion that everyone in authority, with the possible exception of his cousin Lord MacLaurin, formerly of Tesco, now of English cricket, is part of a rising curve of lunacy. Nor is he concerned at finding himself in disagreement with the rest of the human race. Disagreement is his private gymnasium.

To the Managing Director, Bowater Scott. 'Dear Sir, For longer and stronger than I care to remember we have used nothing but Andrex. Yes, we have tried the odd roll of something else, but, wipe for wipe, Andrex beats them all. At least it did until recently. Whatever is this new rubbish you have substituted? Don't tell me you are now catering exclusively for the yobboes hurling your wares from the football terraces…'

By appointment to HM The Queen. 'Dear Mr Howells, I was very concerned to read of your dissatisfaction with the New Feel Andrex. This product has been produced in response to wider demand for a softer and more absorbent toilet tissue. In general, this new specification has been well received but it appears that you have been unfortunate enough to purchase a faulty pack. I therefore enclose a replacement which I hope you will find more satisfactory.' *Y (Mrs), Consumer Relations Officer.*

'Dear Mrs Y, What a noble gesture, and what splendid public relations…'

Mr Howells, now eighty-one, lives near Saundersfoot, not far from where he was born, where Bill Frost flew into a tree and where for 200 years his family has lived. His novels are set here, and his history books, the latest of which, *From Amroth to Utah* (Gomer, 2001), records the mass emigration of locals prompted by Mormon missionaries, though in one case by a man who, anxious to get his hands on a cottage occupied by two old people, called down their chimney, 'Joseph and Elizabeth, The Lord commandeth thee to go to Salt Lake City.'

Mr Howells has never felt the need to travel, for, whatever it gets up to elsewhere, in Amroth authority goes its fascinating way. In the spring of 1996 the local council closed the one public lavatory in the village. But the Pembrokeshire National Path ends in Amroth, and walkers come in from the cliffs like cowboys hitting town after a cattle drive. By June the local pub was getting through 300 rolls of toilet paper a week.

'People were knocking as early as 8 o'clock in the morning, and we couldn't very well tell them the next loo was only half a mile away. It might have been too late,' said Roger Harries of the Amroth Arms, a man now in awe of the human digestive system. In reply to an appeal for a Portaloo, the council announced it was applying to itself for planning permission for one. Two-thirds of the way through a crowded summer, the Portaloo came, but the next day it was locked. The Environmental Health had inspected it and closed it down.

In the meantime work had started on a new public lavatory, but changes to the original plan meant a door opened the wrong way; progress was slow. Ten days later a new Portaloo was delivered, but this came locked and the council had lost the key. In response to now frantic appeals, a workman broke in. He then fitted new locks.

In late summer the old village hall was demolished, the council feeling this would be an eyesore beside their new loo. In its place, at a cost of £10,000, an ornamental wall was built, in a garden with plants. Roscoe Howells, formerly clerk to the parish council and chairman of the late village hall, watched in wonder, knowing that the autumn gales would come, with waves breaking over the sea wall to send sheets of salt water into the garden. By October 1996 the gales had killed every plant and overturned the ornamental wall as casually as a child overturning his toy bricks. They had also killed the new plants about the loo now nearing completion. Just before Christmas this was opened at a cost of £100,000, though local estimates put it at twice that. 'I had never seen such opulence, oh the tiling,' said Roscoe Howells. The council then, to his great joy, locked it for the winter.

Disagreement came early to him. In 1937 the prefects of Christ's College, Brecon, like many other young men at the time, loudly announced their pacificism. But when it came to it, only two refused to join the school cadet force, Howells and a boy with a disabled arm. The headmaster sent for Howells. 'You are adamant about this, are you? And you know what it means? I shall have to withdraw all your privileges as a prefect. You still won't change your mind? Then good day to you.' He was at the door when he heard a groan. 'No, I won't make a martyr of you, which is what you want. Just go.'

Then there was the war, which, because of his work on the family farm at Amroth Castle, he would have been excused. Instead, being Roscoe, he registered as a Conscientious Objector. 'I didn't want anyone to say I'd used farming to get out of the Army.' Nothing must be sidestepped: the long career as God's Own Nuisance was beginning.

The Army requisitioned Amroth Castle, forcing the family to move out, and within a week the banisters had been cut up for firewood and the silver cupboard broken into. An appeal by his father to Lloyd George had the place derequisitioned, but within six months the Army was back. A full colonel turned up to say it was being taken over again. Mrs Howells, Roscoe's mother, asked him if they had considered requisitioning the two other big houses, one belonging to Lord Merthyr, the other to a senior Army officer. The Colonel said they had, but these two houses were too near the sea. *Too near the sea?* A man can throw stones into the sea from Amroth Castle, which is why today it is a caravan park. 'And you ask me why I don't like authority,' said Roscoe Howells mildly.

Disaster called in the early 1960s when, now married, he and his wife were farming near Pendine. Encouraged by the Ministry of Agriculture, they had built up their milking herd to thirty-five pedigree Guernsey cows, for the future, they were assured, was rosy, a new wonder vaccine having eradicated brucellosis, that terror of dairy farmers, which causes a cow to abort so there are no calves and no milk. Roscoe Howells duly had his entire herd vaccinated and was ruined by brucellosis. That was the end of his farming career, and he still feels betrayed. There was no compensation and, worse, he himself had been infected.

It was a nightmare condition that baffled doctors, for its effects changed shape. One man could be stricken with diarrhoea, another with constipation, a third with insomnia, a fourth with a form of sleeping sickness, and this could be permanent. Roscoe Howells suffered so badly from arthritis he had to have two hip replacements and was prescribed so much streptomycin he has to wear two hearing aids. As a result, any form of background music is a torment.

To the Managing Director, National Express. 'Dear Sir, I am contemplating for the first time travelling by coach. I should be obliged therefore if you would tell me whether the sound with the video is all-embracing or on headphones only…'

'Dear Sir, While our original coaches were fitted with individual headsets we found the equipment unsatisfactory and difficult to maintain in constant use. Please accept my apologies for your journey…

Y, Consumer Relations Officer.'

'Dear Mr Y, There is no need to apologise, for I shall not be taking the journey. Whatever the cost in money and torments various, I shall go by train.'

For the past twenty years he has been a full-time writer, ever since an attempt to convert the farm into holiday flats ended when his first wife died. An agricultural columnist before the brucellosis, he has since become a novelist and historian, the novels and histories being set on the coastline of West Wales. 'You should only write about things you know.'

From Amroth to Utah, a history of emigration from the area, is his twentieth book. Like just about everything else he has written, it is a narrative with targets: the Pembrokeshire National Park ('the Ayatollahs of that mighty quango'). Television ('that social destroyer'). The indifference of fine Victorian gentlemen to conditions in the old coalmines of Saundersfoot ('It was a time when Christian-motivated people were much concerned about the Slave Trade'). This is history written by a man with a catapult, but it is none the worse for that.

It was in *Old Saundersfoot* that he first mentioned the story of Bill Frost. 'When he was in his eighties my cousin told me that his mother, then a girl in service in Tenby, was walking home when another girl told her, "Let's go up Stammers Hill and see that man's flying machine. Poor chap, they say he's gone off his head...". Still, people had said similar things about the Wright Brothers, and there was a grandeur about Frost's one recorded comment, "I could ask no one for advice, I had no books to refer to... I walked alone."'

But it was what happened after the publication of *Old Saundersfoot* that surprised some. Until then the story had been folklore, but from America an engineer wrote, enclosing a Patent Office certificate. Folklore had become a technical drawing, though it was hard to make out what the flying machine looked like. From the patent it was made of wood and consisted of an upper winged assembly incorporating gas cylinders to give it lift and a lower streamlined chamber in which the pilot sat, operating a helicopter-style motor fan by foot pedals, thus turning it into a sort of powered hang-glider. There was some sound thinking involved.

Roscoe Howells was surprisingly unmoved by these developments. After all, he had known it all along. 'Look at that face,' he said. He has a photograph of Frost sitting in his garden, an elderly gent with a long white moustache. 'That couldn't tell lies. Bill Frost flew.

Everybody round here knows that.' And for a bizarre afternoon in his company I wandered round Saundersfoot, meeting elderly gentlemen, all equally off-hand. Ah yes, Bill Frost. Carpenter. Had two goats when he was old. Of course that was after he flew…

And for Roscoe Howells there were other matters on which the world had to be put right. There are men in boardrooms and county halls today for whom the invention of the computer must count as the darkest day in history; once one was acquired by a man in Amroth. For most of us, rage and a sense of wrong are stillborn. We draft letters to the offending agency, we polish them in traffic jams or in bed, but at dawn they fade into the light of common day. In a flat overlooking the sea they never fade.

Mr Howells finds himself in a long queue at his bank. *To the Head Boss, Barclays Bank*, 'The whole world being in a state of flux, there would seem to be some confusion as to the identity of whoever it is to whom I am writing.' He writes on behalf of elderly neighbours alarmed at the closure of their post office. He writes to a regional head; there is no reply. He writes to the Postmaster General. The post office reopens.

His method is simple. The first complaint coaxes a head out of the corporate defences. If that head is surly ('We have contacted our legal department for advice'), the fun starts. 'I have a copy of *Salmond on the Law of Torts*, if that is of any help,' and then the row rises through the hierarchy, a manager's bluster giving way to the strained politeness of his superiors ('Any involvement of our legal department would be a waste of everyone's time').

Usually there is a reply. *The Managing Director, R. and J. Hopkins*. 'Dear Sirs, Some time ago I bought a pen at St Clears Post Office. I was so pleased with the pen I bought three more. I thought you might be interested to know that. Would you also be interested to know that they are now of no use to me? Of course, you will know why they are of no use to me, won't you? I cannot buy refills for them.

Every time I ask at St Clears Post Office I receive the same answer. They are waiting for the man to call…'

'Dear Mr Howells, Please find refills for your pen. This company did NOT supply your friendly post office, and we have no control over HIS purchases from HIS wholesaler. PS, perhaps you could sell your spare refills at 25p each to the post office…'

'Dear Sirs, What a lovely surprise. I really feel I should offer to pay for these refills, but I read somewhere the other day that we must learn to accept graciously as well as to give. So thank you. It was my birthday yesterday (Sunday).'

Four months later, scribbled across a compliments slip. 'Please find a few blue refills and some black. We have discontinued the pen…'

2001

PART FOUR
THOSE I DIDN'T
GET TO MEET

AMONG THE SUMMER STARS

Pub conversations fascinate me. I love the outrageous claims and the disconnected way they rush and veer all over the place like a wildly-deflating child's balloon; I love the romantic fantasies that always surface.

It happened in a pub in Carmarthen, one of those bleak establishments with strip lighting, of which my wife, persuaded to go out one night, said: 'I just don't know why you mess about, why not just go straight to Wormwood Scrubs?' She had been a little unhinged by sitting in such a pub next to three women who, for a whole half-hour, had discussed their vacuum cleaners.

Anyway, this night there were present a Builder, a Policeman and myself. The Policeman and I had known each other since we were children. But although I knew the Builder's

mother, I had not talked to him before, and was pleasantly surprised as he began to talk about the history of the town, which,
it became obvious, meant a lot to him. He told me about the
listed building the local training college had finally managed to
demolish, and of an even grander building that a milk factory
had razed to the ground, demolition being the town's one civic
passion.

The Builder grieved over wrecked porticoes and plaster-
work, and bought me a port and brandy. The Policeman listened
with the impassiveness of his kind, the talk turning to a house on
which the Builder had worked, Fern Hill in Llangain, where a
hangman had once lived. The Builder mentioned that he had
read that hanging produced an erection, at which the Policeman
spoke for the first time. 'Not in the ones I've cut down,' he said
quietly. There was a little pause after this, at the end of which I
bought the Policeman a double gin and murmured that I didn't
know what all the fuss was about, that impotence was something
all sensible men should look forward to.

'Exactly,' said the Builder. 'Be a chance to talk to the wife.'

Inevitably there were many jokes, which we, in turn, pre-
tended not to have heard before, at the end of which, just as
inevitably, we started talking about old town characters. There
was the deceased businessman whose bankruptcy had been
spectacular. 'When I went down the tubes,' he had boasted, his
one tooth scraping the air, 'men read about me in the Reading
papers.'

Then there was the local graduate who went off his head and
in the small hours wrote cryptic messages in felt-tip pen in the
town's phone boxes, things like, 'Nixon, Madonna of Napalm'.
It was the discovery of these that prompted a visiting reporter

from the London *Times* to write that Carmarthen was a town remarkable for its political sophistication.

I mentioned the man who, as an innocent of seventeen, went into the Army in the last war, to find that a single cigarette bought him a woman in the jungles of the Far East. On his return he descended eagerly on market day Carmarthen with 400 Players and was cuffed the length of Lammas Street by large and indignant matrons.

And then the Builder told us this story.

'Did either of you know Y?' He gave the name of a scrap-metal dealer. 'Beautiful-looking man, physique the colour of bronze, looked a bit like Geronimo in the photographs of the Old West, but odd, very odd. Couldn't stand cats. He said that once, with his own cat beside him, he had been sawing wood in a barn when he became aware of this huge tom watching the two of them from a window. "And this tom, boys, he leapt down and devoured my cat." Not attacked his cat, but *devoured* it. I've not forgotten that. Afterwards he couldn't bear to be in the same room as a cat, not after the… devouring.

'He died young and in a lot of pain. He had this ingrowing hair in his bottom, a sinus they call it, and he would not go to the doctor on account of his gypsy blood. Gypsies are like that,' he assured us. 'They're terrified doctors will find they're growing tails.'

'Come on…'

'Well,' he spread his hands, 'I'm just saying what I've been told. After that, all kinds of complications set in, so he took to his bed. "Boys," he said, "I want you to do something for me. I want you to come round and take the slates off my roof so I can lie here and watch the stars." And this was done. The slates were taken away, it was August, and he just lay there watching the summer stars.'

The Builder, it was clear, was a man of romantic tendency. 'The trouble was, everyone went on their holidays and forgot about him, so the next time they went round they found he'd been dead for three weeks. Melted into his bed, he was.'

'Under the stars?' I asked, moved by this narrative.

'Under the summer stars.'

There was another little pause, broken this time by the Policeman. 'How much did you get for his slates, Ralph?'

GOVERNOR STEPHENS'S
PICTURE BOOK

The Book has not been anywhere. It is today where it was first compiled 150 years ago, though the man who compiled it would not recognise any of the buildings. The book is in a basement below the County Offices at Carmarthen, themselves built on the site of the County Gaol, built on the site of the Castle. The basement houses the County Archive.

It is the size of a family Bible, the Book. It has never been published, so what you see, inside those peeling leather covers, is what a long-dead man wrote. No print, no typesetters, no editors stand between you and him.

Richard Ireland, lecturer in law at Aberystwyth University, has been reading the Book and writing about it for five years, but feels about it now as he did when he first opened its pages. 'This is a marvellous document, the faces are incredible.' The Book is an office record, the Register of Felons at Carmarthen Gaol covering the years 1844 to 1871.

It was something all Victorian prison governors were required to keep, entering in it the names of their prisoners, their crimes and sentences, on page after copperplate handwritten page. But in 1858 something strange happened in Carmarthen Gaol, the result of which is that you turn a page and abruptly it is not an office record. The long-dead, some sunk in misery, some grim, are staring back at you, for in 1858 Governor Stephens, an old policeman from the Met, began taking photographs of his inmates. A very early photographer, he used a summerhouse as his studio.

Presumably this was to be a means of identification, for amongst the handwritten columns there are entered details of height and complexion ('pale' or 'sallow' are not that much to go on). But it is the effect, all these years on, which is so extraordinary. He may not have realised it, but when Governor Stephens started pasting in his photographs, the Book became one of the most moving records of human life.

His name is John Evans. He is fourteen years old, and in the summer of 1864 he attempted to steal some strawberries. Attempted, you will note; he did not even get to eat them before the full righteous weight of the State descended. Hot on the rights of property (of which they had a great deal), Victorian magistrates, the colonels and the captains and the squires, sentenced John Evans to two years in a reformatory. But before this he had to serve two weeks in Carmarthen Gaol with hard labour. Do you know what hard labour is? You walk inside a treadmill like a mouse, on and on and on, three hours at a time, grinding a little corn in the process, for the Victorians were a utilitarian lot when it came to punishment. But worse are the old ships' ropes, hard as hawsers, which you must unpick with your fingernails to make caulking for the seams of boats. And you are fourteen years old.

Like a little cornered animal, a boy stares out of the Register. Yet there is curiosity in his face, the curiosity of someone wanting to know whether there is any end to the lunacy of this world. For having done all that to him, the world now wants to take his photograph. It is probably the first time John Evans has had his photograph taken and it intrigues him. His cravat is rakishly tied, and they have not totally crushed him.

Others they have. George Adams, aged forty-five, sits with his eyes downcast. A servant from Narberth, he is in custody awaiting trial on the charge of stealing a donkey. George Adams will soon die in custody, still awaiting trial on the charge of stealing a donkey.

The photographs are tiny, just half an inch by three quarters, but the detail is extraordinary. The expressions are also indelible, as Richard Ireland said, for these are not the mug-shots of modern police records. These people, not used to being photographed, could not hide their feelings. You are among the broken here.

There may be a slight difference in dress, the men going in for cravats and side whiskers, the women for severely drawn-back hair and shawls, but these are people like you and me, except they are out of another time when things were done differently.

Jane Davies, twenty-five, a servant girl from Tenby. A pale, scrubbed face, quite expressionless, very young. Fourteen days for concealing the death of her baby, a strange charge, which makes the sentence monstrous. But then, as Richard Ireland says, it hides a lot, that charge. Really Jane Davies is being charged with infanticide, but Welsh juries are notoriously reluctant to bring in a verdict of 'guilty' in such cases, for they know what that would mean in Victorian Britain.

A nineteen-year-old woman, charged with murdering her four-month-old child, is acquitted, and the extraordinary thing is that in almost thirty years nobody, not a single person, gets hanged in Carmarthen Gaol, even when found guilty of murder.

The first photograph of all is of James Jones, twenty-eight, sentenced to death on 18 March 1858 for murdering his sister-in-law. It is not a good photograph (the Governor must have been nervous), but even in its blurred state the features are tough, even brutal. There was some suggestion of mental illness at the trial but the judge brushed that aside. Yet in spite of that, James Jones was reprieved, his sentence commuted to penal servitude for life.

The result is that the ultimate horrors of the penal system do not stalk these pages, especially its bungled executions. In 1829, in the living memory of some in the Register, the rope broke here and the condemned man, David Evans, had to be hanged again, shouting that this was illegal. The hangmen would call again, alighting from the down train, being followed everywhere by the crowds that had been waiting, for in the late nineteenth century hangmen were like pop stars. The *Carmarthen Journal* even carried accounts of their wardrobes: 'Mr Berry then entered the cell, unostentatiously dressed in a plain suit of dark clothing *and wearing a red Turkish fez*.' The italics are mine.

But for the period of the Register none called, though murders there were, the most extraordinary being in 1844 before the photography began. A Mr Evan Lloyd is charged, not with one, but with 'Murders'. Described as 'a labourer', he is said to be 'single, with no children', which is more or less as you would expect him to be, for Mr Lloyd is just nine years old. He is acquitted and nothing more is heard of him or of his murders.

But in the magistrates' courts there are few acquittals. Theft of tea worth two shillings, a first offence: three months with the inevitable hard labour. Theft of two shillings in money, again a first offence: two months with hard labour. A young Irish girl, first offence, guilty of stealing six shillings in money: one month with hard labour as a 'rogue and a vagabond'. David Miles, aged thirteen. A small face in the photograph, and a puzzled one. But he has just been given seventeen stripes with the birch and is serving six days with hard labour – *for stealing a pair of boots*.

These were poor and desperate people, prepared to steal shawls and risk two months with hard labour (the actual sentence handed down), or a leg of mutton (six weeks, also with hard labour). The irony is that the men who handed down these sentences and were so keen on hard labour had probably not done a day's work in their lives.

How small the prisoners were. In Carmarthenshire in the nineteenth century you were a man of above average height if you were 5 feet 5 inches, and few women, at least amongst the poor, were over 5 feet. It is no wonder they were prepared to add legs of mutton to their diet. But one of them, it was said, ate nothing at all. Among the photographs is one of Evan and Hannah Jacob, she looking down, he staring grimly at the camera. They were the parents of a Victorian Nine Days' Wonder, Sarah Jacob, aged twelve, the Fasting Girl.

The story starts when the vicar of Llanfihangel-ar-Arth writes to *The Times* to say that he has seen a miracle child, able to live without food or drink. The devout come on pilgrimage to see her and leave gifts of money at her bedside. But the medical profession becomes interested, and four nurses are sent from Guy's Hospital to watch her in relays. After eight days, on 17 December, Sarah Jacob dies. It is a terrible story, out of which only one person comes out well, the little girl prepared to endure agonies of hunger and thirst and not betray her parents. The doctors who tested their claims should have stood in the dock beside them, but in March 1870 it is Evan Jacob who is sentenced to twelve months with hard labour for manslaughter and his wife Hannah to six.

'There is no humour in the Register,' said Richard Ireland. 'But what you must remember is that these were felons, found guilty of what the authorities considered serious crimes. Alongside them in the gaol there would have been others convicted of mere misdemeanours, like Ann Awberry, town prostitute and drunk, and a favourite of mine. She was a permanent resident there, throwing her chamber pot at the Governor and singing so loudly all night long in her cell, people who lived nearby would queue in the morning with their complaints.'

In 1874 Margaret Davies, aged thirteen, pleading guilty to breaking into a grocery shop and stealing eight shillings, a pound of sugar and three ounces of tea. She did this, she said, to help provide for her sick mother and five younger brothers and sisters. Six months, with hard labour.

John Nash, a local man, built the gaol, then went on to build Buckingham Palace. Some of his bleak grey limestone walls survive and are the first things you see when you come up from the basement where the Register is kept. They were also the last things George Adams saw, awaiting trial, charged with stealing a donkey.

1999

IRA JONES, FLYING ACE

The hamlet is called Pass-by, and the world did as it was told. This used to be on a main road and was somewhere on the way to somewhere else, but it is not even that now, for the main road got moved. Pass-by had a bakery, but that closed. So only funerals stop, for the chapel called Cana is still there on its ridge above a hamlet where the dead, my own grandparents among them, far outnumber the living. Some forty years ago it was found necessary to open an overspill graveyard, and this, bounded by a small brick wall, is already one-sixth full. In this bleak place Achilles lies.

Take the A40 west of Carmarthen, and three miles along its dual carriageway you will see a right turn to a village called Meidrim. The hamlet, and the chapel, are just beyond the turn in one of those lost eddies of tarmac that road improvement brings. It will not be difficult to find the grave. All the others, row by regimented row, are polished black slabs, but in the far corner is a Celtic cross in rough-cut granite on which there is an eagle soaring. The only thing is, you will not be able to make out the inscription, for in less than thirty years the wind and rain have done for its gold lettering and the grave is as mysterious as any megalith to a forgotten hero of the old world.

Some seven centuries ago in the *Black Book of Carmarthen* a monk wrote down the poems recording the last resting places of such heroes on moors and headlands. Apart from Arthur, their names mean nothing to us now, their scuffles with swords at some ford even less. They are men out of the dawn, when war was glory and single combat, which perhaps even the man transcribing the Stanzas of the Graves thought would never come again. But it did briefly. In the dawn of a new form of war, in the skies over the Western Front, men, whose successors were to fight above counties and their successors over whole countries, these men fought above parishes, often alone. Which is why we are here, in this little graveyard we did not pass by, at the tomb in the west of a hero in the old style. In the shadows of the setting sun we can make out a name, Ira Jones, and, with some difficulty, a line of initials. DSO. MC. DFC and bar. MM. We are at the grave of a man whose strange destiny it was to be a throwback. Here the last paladin lies.

My uncle had been at school with him, so I grew up with the legend. I was told about a man who, in middle age recalled to the colours, took off in a training aircraft against a German bomber over Swansea, armed only with a Very pistol. I was also told about the boozing, which was on almost as heroic a scale, when, a senior RAF officer, Ira Jones one night stole a steam train from Cardiff station and set off up the line. I saw him once in the street, a dapper little gentleman with a moustache; he was popping into a pub, just as Achilles might have done or Shakespeare's Fluellen or any hero who has run out of wars and for whom only the littleness of life remains, in his case a job in the Ministry of Pensions. That such a man should be in living memory is extraordinary.

He died in 1960 after falling off a ladder, according to the reference books, though his family maintains it was after tripping over a doorstep. Either way, it sounds like the twentieth century's little revenge on a man who could write, 'I have been in 28 aeroplane crashes, the machine somersaulting on the ground on each occasion, and only once have I been hurt; this was when I was a passenger and broke an arm…'.

I knew all this, but what nothing had prepared me for was the three volumes of autobiography, *Tiger Squadron*, *King of Air Fighters* and *An Airfighter's Scrap-book*. All are out of print but not impossible to find. If you can, do so – for you will never have read anything like this.

No stiff upper lip narrative, it is the honesty that is so incredible. First there is the hair-raising bloodlust of a killer setting down in practical terms the best way to bring down Germans and recording his own delight as he does so. But at the same time there is his description, often step by step, as in the novels of Conrad, of what it would be like to fall, or to burn alive, the British authorities, unlike their German counterparts, having refused to issue their pilots with parachutes. This never happened to him, but it did every day in his imagination. The terror is there every waking and sleeping moment, and is endured. Forget the silk scarves and the champagne in the mess: if you want to know what it was REALLY like to be a flying ace in World War I, these are your books. No Englishman, certainly no public school Englishman, could have written them. Only an outsider could have done so.

Ira Jones had just about every disadvantage life could have given him. He was tiny, less than 9 stone and only 5 feet 4 inches tall at the age of seventeen, after which, as he ruefully recorded, he grew very little. He stammered. He had, or acquired, a considerable drink problem. Other disadvantages were there from birth. He was born near the village of St Clears in 1896 into the Welsh-speaking rural working class, 'of parents', he wrote, 'whose ancestors tilled the soil', which meant they were monoglot Welsh small-holders and farm labourers tethered as effectively to the land as in feudal times. And there was more. Though he was never to mention this in print, he was born illegitimate, at a time when this mattered and mattered intensely. None of this is on the memorial to him in St Clears, 'raised by public subscription to perpetuate the memory of a man of whom Wales was justly proud'. Above the lettering, in mosaic, the eagle is flying again.

'For about 15 minutes we circled the aerodrome. Leaning over the side of the observer's cockpit, I watched, fascinated, as the patchwork pattern of the fields unrolled beneath us. I saw men like ants walking on the ground. I looked up into the limitless blue kingdom of the sky, and I prayed, "Oh God, please let me do this forever…".'

He was nineteen and training to be a telegraphist in London, when, having failed to get into the Army, he got himself accepted as a mechanic by the Royal Flying Corps. At Hendon he had his first flight, and it was the beginning of the rest of his life. He became an observer in France, flying with a Captain Bell, a monocled joker who, when he crashed his plane, reported, 'Sir, I got into the backwash of a sparrow.' The observer's life depended on such men. He later tried to imagine what would have happened had Bell been killed in the air. He did not have to try hard, for he had seen it happen to others, but it is imaginative writing of a high order. At twenty this is what he lived with.

'The weight of the dead body leaning across the control column causes the machine to dive eventually. The observer has no parachute; he must resign himself to his doom. The wires of the helpless plane scream as it dives faster and faster to the ground with the observer huddled at the bottom of the cockpit waiting for the end.

'There is a tearing, ripping sound as pieces of the covering are torn by the winds, and is slowly bereft of its fabric. Now it is a mere skeleton, but still the observer holds on. What thoughts must flash through his mind. Then a heavy thud, a splintering noise, a huddled heap…'

Observers, he wrote grimly, were rarely decorated for bravery. One man who managed to climb out of his open cockpit and over the fuselage into the pilot's place was turned down by the authorities on the grounds that he had only acted on self-preservation. The authorities were much exercised about self-preservation, and on these grounds did not issue their pilots with parachutes, arguing that they would abandon their planes at the least excuse. So Ira Jones saw his friends fall or stay in their burning planes, and in the mess it prompted an obsessive black humour. 'Are you ready to die for your country, Taffy?' asked Mick Mannock VC. 'Will you have it in flames or in pieces?' Mannock, whom Jones thought the greatest ace of all, was to have it in flames.

It was against this background that he began to shoot Germans who had successfully baled out. The authorities may have frowned on this, but Ira Jones did not believe in the chivalry of war. He felt he owed it to his dead friends at a time when the average life expectancy of a pilot was six weeks, and prayed for the moment he first took to the skies as a pilot, 'Oh God, please let me kill at least one German before I die.' And when he did, and saw the plane crash in flames, 'I gloated over the roasting of the departing Hun.' When they recovered one body, they placed it in a hangar, dressed in pyjamas and a dinner jacket, and toasted it in champagne. These are not things Errol Flynn or David Niven did in films.

They watched as a German observer baled out and a freak shot separated him from his parachute. He dropped like a stone ('He must have been very surprised'), while the parachute gaily floated around, and Mannock tried to work out how many times the man had bounced. They were very young, they lived with death, and this terrible humour was their one release.

Like craftsmen, they passed on tips to each other. It was best not to attack a plane from behind, for that way you just filled the observer with bullets and his collapsed body shielded the pilot. It was also advisable not to get too close in an attack, as there was the risk of blood obscuring your own windshield. But it would be a mistake to think of these youngsters as just angels of death.

There were four types of air fighters, wrote Ira Jones. First there was the man who loved flying and fighting, who, when he shot down an enemy, saw him as so much charred wood and steel. Then there was the man who liked flying and fighting, but as a duty. When he shot down a plane, he thought of the man. But there was also the pilot who just couldn't take it (or 'funked it,' as he wrote, for he was not long out of school). Somewhere amongst these was a man who had to steel himself to endure the flying and fighting, for at night he was tortured by dreams, seeing the face of his victim and hearing the screams for his mother. This might have been closer to himself than he would have admitted in public.

There was one August night in 1918, he confided to his diary, when nightmares made him jump out of bed twenty-two times and he was obliged to tie his pyjama strings to the post. It is in the diary that you get the sense, undiluted by memory, of what it was like. He had been told, reflected Ira Jones, that it was a big mistake to keep a diary.

That same August, early in the morning when he liked to fly alone, he came on a German formation flying at height and, unseen by them, managed to join it ('a tremendous nervous strain'), attacking only when two planes peeled off to dive on a British spotter plane far below. He fired and one crashed into the other (he saw the pilot in the flames), at which point the other seven dived on him. He just got away, crashed his plane on landing, and when he was extracted from the debris was told to get dressed properly, as he was about to meet the King. The meeting passed into folklore.

George V asked how many German planes he had shot down. 'I started, "Th..th..th." The King tried to help. "Thirty?" I shook my head. "Th..th..th." "Thirty-five?" "Th..th..th." The King looked away to put me at my ease. "Thirty-three," I said.' That is his official version, but the one I heard had him telling the King, 'Shouldn't worry, sir, they were all bloody Germans.' He was awarded four medals at once and, given leave, looked so young and small wearing these between trains in the streets of Cardiff, he was actually arrested by a policeman.

He knew the end of the war was in sight when the sky began to empty ('sometimes we had to go as far as 20 miles behind their lines to get a scrap'). He wanted to attack the Germans in their aerodromes, but the authorities thought that too risky. And then it was all over.

He had hoped for one last fight, when, suddenly in a break in the cloud, he saw the German armies beneath him beginning to walk home. The moment should be filmed.

'As the clock neared 11 a.m., we flew closer to the retreating mass, and as soon as the hour had passed we flew over them. *They took no notice of us…*' And then? He and his squadron returned to base, above which they performed aerobatics, like schoolboys when their rivals refuse to play any more. Everything was unreal.

'It will surprise, maybe startle, a great number of people to learn that a certain percentage of the members of HM Forces were disappointed when the Armistice was signed…' It may have been bravado, but it may also have been a recognition that whatever he had become was the result of war, so much so that he could not think of life without it.

He tried to find another, volunteering for the ill-fated British intervention in the Russian civil war between Reds and Whites. This was a mistake. The Reds (or Bolsheviks) had no planes, so there was nobody to fight, just troops to strafe or the unending forests of North Russia to bomb. Was it their objective, he asked his commanding general hopefully, to bomb Moscow? No, he was told, it was to train loyal White Russians, then withdraw with honour. It was a confusing war.

He watched a mass execution of mutineers, one of whom, a sergeant, survived the machine guns, so an officer had to walk over and shoot him, the sergeant spitting at him. Another time, having run out of bombs, he dropped beer and whisky bottles on the Bolsheviks. He liked the whistling sound these made, and often dropped them afterwards; it helped to break the monotony ('and of course if a bottle dropped on their nuts it would no doubt give them a headache'). And then that war, too, was over. 'So 'tis back to old Blighty for yours truly / A sadder but wiser young chap / For the Lord played a joke on Creation / When North Russia was dumped on the map.'

And after that? There were bombs to be dropped on Iraqi tribesmen, the British cut-price way of administering the country. There was rugby football to be played (as a scrum-half he turned out for first class sides like London Welsh and Richmond). He was at one point the rugby correspondent of the *Sunday Dispatch*, in which capacity, it was said, he would guarantee your name got a mention provided you bought him enough whisky.

He also acted as personal pilot to an industrialist, who in the 1930s in Berlin introduced him to Goering, another ex-ace. Had the two, the industrialist enquired, met in the air? '"He wouldn't be here now, sir, if we had met." My employer laughed out loud, but Goering did not.'

Then there was World War II when, as a 'retread', he joined up again, this time to train young pilots, and took off alone to attack a Junkers 88 over Swansea, armed with the Very pistol. He fired this at the bomber, which made off. 'You're too old, Taffy,' said King George VI when he heard about this episode. 'It's a young man's game.' But there was too much boozing by now, and he was to leave the Service under a cloud. 'Socially, I avoided him as much as I could,' said Wing Commander Sammy Sampson, one of the pilots he trained. 'I knew his alcoholic habits, and I was there to learn how to fly a plane.'

After that there was the Ministry of Pensions, where he helped many an ex-Serviceman. And the pubs. He would stand by the bar, and after a few stiff ones would fill the tap-room for you with the scream of engines and the rattle of machine guns, just as his predecessors filled it with the thunder of horses' hooves and the whoosh of arrows. Then that, too, was over, and the throwback was among his own kind.

> A grave for March, a grave for Gwythur,
> A grave for Gwgawn of the red sword...

And a grave for Ira Jones, at Pass-by.

1999

THE LEONARDO OF LLANDEILO

It is December 1858, and in west Wales the small town of Llandeilo is preparing to celebrate the return of Lord Dynevor, its greatest landowner. Thomas Jenkins, the town carpenter, has been put in charge of the entertainment, in particular of the fireworks. In his diary he records a busy week.

December 1 To Carmarthen to procure Militia Band, also fireworks worth £6.12.0.

December 3 Made 30 torches. Labour and materials, 15/9.

December 6 Lord Dynevor and family arrived at 6pm. Town illuminated. Made 20 fireballs…

December 7 Dynevor Castle caught fire at 8pm…

There are no comments, no expression of surprise. It could be Oliver Hardy writing, for nothing is beyond the poise of a great comic figure. But, unlike Ollie, Mr Jenkins kept a diary.

The three tombs are at the north-west corner of the churchyard in Llandeilo, a town so dominated by death that its main road had to be cut through the graves. The three are not hard to find, for they stand in line. Here Thomas Jenkins is buried, also his two wives, his children and their children. But it is a single job description that stops you in your tracks. 'Sacred to the memory of Thomas Jenkins of this town, Carpenter and Diarist, 1813–1871.' What follows is a quest for a remarkable man.

For in addition to being a carpenter and a diarist, Jenkins was an architect, astronomer, antiquary, musician, inventor of a cast-iron passenger-carrying tricycle, scientist, caver and undertaker. This man could make boats, violins, artificial legs, wax figures for the Great Exhibition of 1851, also coffins. There were many coffins, so many that in the graveyard on the hill Thomas Jenkins must be surrounded by his craft. In the middle of the nineteenth century Renaissance Man was alive and well and living in Llandeilo, only Renaissance Man was a member of the working class. Where do you look for him 150 years on?

It is a wild morning, and I am standing on Llandeilo Bridge with Lynn Hughes. This bridge is a work of art, completed in 1848, the largest and finest single-span bridge in the country. 'Jenkins built the pumps to divert the river,' says Hughes. 'He bought the timber, the iron and the stone. For a guinea a week he built the centre form-work for the arch and he invented an engine to test its strength. Yet you won't find his name on any commemorative plaque – he was just a working man from the town.

'But I am old enough to have met men for whom his exploits were a living memory, who had been told about them by their fathers. You could say I grew up with Thomas Jenkins.'

Old men would point out his work: the elegant inn signs and bas-reliefs on the walls, like those outside the Castle Hotel; the Doric columns that support the porches, for Jenkins loved columns. Many of these have gone, but even now, walking through the town, you come on puzzling features, such as the extraordinary grandeur of the frontage to a takeaway Indian restaurant. 'That's probably him,' says Hughes. 'And see that sign over the alley opposite, on that wooden arch? That speaks of Jenkins to me.' The sign reads 'Public Hall & Literary Institute', the lettering still visible with its elaborate twirls and scrolls. Up that alley there met the Llandeilo Mechanics' Mutual Instructing Institution, which Jenkins founded in 1843. This is the man who passed into local folklore.

The private man only emerged in 1976 with the publication of his diary, later republished by the National Library of Wales. That took some nerve on the part of his family, for the diary records a fascination for life so complete that Jenkins even noted the occasions when he had sexual intercourse, usually with his maids, two of whom he was obliged to marry as a result. Like Pepys, he resorted to code, and was laconic when he recorded being ordered to pay one shilling and six-pence a week towards another illegitimate child. Yet suddenly in the midst of these one-line entries there occurs one of the great deathbed scenes in Victorian writing, as Jenkins records, hour by hour, the death of his great love, Sarah Davies. She was twenty-one years old.

But the main impression is of one man walking. We forget just how much our ancestors walked before the railways came; they had to, on account of the stagecoach fares. In 1838 Jenkins earned 12 shillings a week but it would have cost him 2 shillings to make a 30-mile return journey by coach. And not only did our ancestors walk, they were prepared to turn night into day to do so. 'May 3, 1836. Left Carmarthen for Haverford West at 15 minutes past 1 a.m. Got to Nar-berth at 8 a.m. and Haverford West at 12 noon...' There followed a day of sightseeing with his uncle, this after walking 29 miles in less than eleven hours. The following day he returned, 'feet sore, the weather being warm'. It was not just the men who walked. At one point Jenkins records that his wife left Llandeilo to walk to Car-marthen at 4 a.m., though she was pregnant at the time.

And even at the slow pace of the old world there were traffic accidents, such as a horse taking fright in Bridge Street, Llandeilo, and plunging over the parapet, killing two passengers in a carriage. So you can share Jenkins's wonder at the arrival of the railway. He walked to Swansea, took a ship to Bristol and there got on a train for the first time. His comment is to the point: '20 minutes – 12 miles.'

On 21 December 1849 he is almost as brief. 'Made a homomotive carriage with three wheels.' No plan survives and Jenkins does not describe how it works, this man-powered carriage, but on the following day there is this: 'Left for Carmarthen in the carriage at 5 p.m. Arrived 7.30.'

'For him to average 6mph means that on the flat or downhill he must have been touching 15 to 20 mph,' said Lynn Hughes. 'All this in a thing made of cast iron. He must have had some kind of belt drive and pedals. But what I find so amazing is that when he set out to make something, it rarely took him longer than a day. "Made a blast fan." "Made a turnip cutter to my own plan." "Made two hand pumps, also horse pump." "Made an air furnace." "Made a circular saw."'

Then there were the local caves, into which he ventured prepared for anything. 'I took a pistol and Peter brought his clarinet.' But at Llygad Llwchwr, near Carreg Cennen Castle, he was alarmed enough to bring a ball of twine, which he attached to a stalactite in case they got lost among the side passages, when they went 567 feet underground. The fascinating thing is that he and his friends chose to enter at 8 p.m., and then emerged at 1 a.m. Our ancestors had a strange sense of time. On another occasion he hit a stalactite with a hammer. It made, he recorded, as fine and loud a noise as any bell in Llandeilo steeple.

The old world intrudes from time to time. He takes the 6 a.m. coach and records: 'A tremendous storm of hail and sleet blowing in my face' – so he must have been on the roof, where the fares were cheaper. He meets the famous wizard, Henry Harris, but records only: 'He is in a decline, can't live many weeks.'

'1835. Went to Carmarthen Fair. Saw a giantess, a Hottentot woman, a flaxen-haired negro, two serpents, a crocodile, alligator, porcupine, American sea serpent, boa constrictor etc. Saw a woman raise 300lbs by her hair.' It is the old poise that did not desert him, even when castles were burning.

He was in love once: a widower with four small children when he met Sarah Davies. He was in his late thirties, she was twenty, and theirs was a formal courtship. They wrote each other many letters, each one of which he notes, for they must have meant a great deal, as did their encounters. 'Took tea with Miss Davies.'

Sarah Davies came from Aberdauddwr on the B4337 north of Llandeilo, not far past Edwinsford, where the little bridge he built still stands. It was here that he came to her deathbed. She died a few weeks after her twenty-first birthday, in such a state of religious ecstasy that she saw Heaven opening. Jenkins made notes. 'She said: "The sun is setting, but it will soon be light again," offering up a short prayer and singing several scraps of hymns. She desired that she should be buried at Bethel, near the brook in which she had been baptised at 12. She requested that I should make her coffin and design her headstone…' And all this was done.

The chapel is two miles from the village of Farmers. You see the brook first, then the stone groove into which a wooden dam was inserted to make the water deep enough for baptism. Above this, on a hill, is the chapel. Her grave is not hard to find, being one of a matching pair made of slate set into an elaborate limestone frame, both cut by Jenkins, who did make her coffin, and then placed an account of her death in a stone jar.

It is quiet there, as it must have been when he returned to spread flowers on her grave. All you will hear is the sound of water, just as he heard it, this remarkable man of whom just one crumpled portrait survives. A long, abstracted face stares out of the past.

1998

ARTHUR'S KINGDOM

His own society … him? Who at the end of his life worked out that forty years of writing had brought him exactly £635. Who often had to wait ten years for a book to be published, and then, when one was, the *Guardian* said of it that it was 'the most acutely and intentionally disagreeable work yet seen in English'. Not a man who will ever figure in any of the *Sunday Times* magazine's helpful little guides to twentieth-century success, even had he been aware he was living in the twentieth century, which is doubtful. He looked like an old rugby forward and believed in fairies; he believed in the Holy Grail, too, which he sought in places like Stoke Newington. He has been out of print for years.

Yet the members of his society will be meeting again tonight, as they do every year on the Saturday nearest his birthday in Caerleon, the town of his birth in 1863. They meet in the town of his death, too, Amersham in Buckinghamshire, in the King's Arms he enthusiastically patronised, for he loved gin, and after gin, sauternes (and mixing the two called it punch). After lunch they walk through Amersham churchyard, past the strange stone catafalques with the headstones turned away, as though some order of knighthood had been interred there. He would have appreciated that, also the fact that in the same graveyard Ruth Ellis is buried, the last woman to be executed in Britain. The macabre was his playpen.

So who are they who every year stand at this grave? It can never have happened before in the history of any literary society that its members are more famous than the man they honour. The president is Barry Humphries, the patron Julian Lloyd Webber; you will have heard of them but not of the man himself. His name was Arthur Machen.

Some writers attract followers as jam attracts flies. There will always be a Byron Society, for there will always be wistful upper middle-class women with time on their hands. Large men with moustaches will make up the Kipling Society and passionate chaps in specs will talk airily of the £2000 a time they command for lectures as representatives of the Brontë Society in Japan. But who is Machen?

'I shall always esteem it as the greatest piece of fortune that has fallen to me, that I was born in that noble, fallen Caerleon-on-Usk, in the heart of Gwent.' Only one record survives, a fragment of a talk he once gave on the BBC, but you do not forget the huge ruminating voice, tobacco-stained and ripe. He was an actor once, with the Frank Benson company, but was not a success: given three lines as a door-keeper, he would dominate the stage. Having heard his voice for a minute or two, you hear it in everything he wrote.

'For the older I grow the more firmly am I convinced that anything which I may have accomplished in literature is due to the fact that when my eyes were first opened in earliest childhood they had before them the vision of an enchanted land. As soon as I saw anything I saw Twyn Barlwm, that mystic tumulus, the memorial of peoples that dwelt in that region before the Celts left the land of summer. This guarded the southern limit of the great mountain wall in the west; a little northward was Mynydd Maen – the Mountain of the Stone – a giant, rounded billow; and still to the north mountains, and on fair, clear days, one could see the pointed summit of the Holy Mountain by Abergavenny. It would shine, I remember, a pure blue in the far sunshine; it was a mountain peak in a fairy-tale…'

Where are we? Six miles from the M4 actually. Estate agents might not recognise any of it, or even the people who live there, but a lot of us do. We are in the land of wonder, which is why Dylan Thomas stole some of that paragraph for his *Under Milk Wood*. Though he lived on until well into his eighties, Machen never lost that sense of wonder, even though the lonely young man living off green tea and stale bread in London lodgings became Micawber in the public bar, 'an old man sunk in poverty and obscurity, but he talked as though the world were his oyster,' recalled the writer Anthony Lejeune. He moved in wonder, insulated against the world, and the streets of south London rose shimmering out of place and time, so his readers look on them like explorers who have come to a white city in the jungle.

There are terrible things, too. In his short novel *The Great God Pan*, published in 1894, to which the *Guardian* took such exception, a doctor operates on a young woman's brain; she has a vision of Pan, becoming insane and also pregnant (Machen was always a bit airy on physical detail), and gives birth to a daughter with the power to provoke suicide in the men she meets. The book ends with the daughter's own suicide, 'changing and melting before your eyes from woman to man, from man to beast, and from beast to worse than beast…', a progression that will be of interest to feminists. Machen later remarked that the kindest critical comment he got was that the book, if nothing else, made you believe in the Devil.

I can think of no other literary career like it. He went from obscurity to being a cult figure (especially after an American admirer helpfully titled the first book written about him in 1918 *Arthur Machen, novelist of ecstasy and sin*), but never experienced fame and what fame brings, namely cash. Yet in his own lifetime men were prepared to spend more on one of his first editions than he had ever earned himself, and what made this even more bizarre was that his most famous book went into folklore at such a rate that most readers will be unaware that he, or anyone else come to that, had written it. Cruelly, he did not make a penny by it.

This was when, in his fifties and newly married, Machen had become a reporter on the London *Evening News*. This was an extraordinary experience, especially for his readers, for he wrote in the old way (his sentences, said someone, seemed to reach out for the horizon), but he duly appeared in the paper, and in 1914 there was a story by him called 'The Bowmen'. It concerned the victory at Mons.

But in Machen's story the British line is breaking and the grey German hordes are about to rush through when there is a cry of 'Harry and St George' and out of the sky the great arrows come. The ghosts of the archers at Agincourt have returned. Now this was written just after the actual victory at Mons, but suddenly amazing things began to happen. Men at the front claimed to have seen German corpses with arrows in them, and there was even a staff colonel called Shepheard who, travelling behind the lines in fog, said he had seen 'hooded, cloaked figures of silent gazing men rank beyond rank… They rose slowly and stared fixedly at me. Their cloaks were grey, almost luminous… I touched at one and it came off in my fingers like a soft dust. Then slowly they sank into the ground…' This will tell you more about the lunatics then loose in the General Staff than about Machen, who was stunned at the popular reaction to what he called his 'indifferent piping in the Evening News'. The paper, which owned the copyright on the tale, rushed it into book-form and sold 100,000 copies.

Machen, who had a vein of commonsense in him somewhere, was always wary of his admirers. The composer John Ireland, who said his life had been transformed by Machen, introduced himself after reading *The White People* by saying he, too, had seen some children dressed in antique clothes. Machen replied with a single sentence on a postcard, 'So you've seen them too.' In penury he had to contend with men who published books on every house he had occupied in London; he refused to write a preface to this ('I should look a terrible ass') but cheerfully supplied photographs ('One of the best is my cloaked figure in the wet street; I think that both the street and I are most picturesque').

Comedy, like the Holy Grail, was always hanging around somewhere. Pilgrims who turned up expecting to meet a pale-eyed seer who had looked beyond the veil of this world met a sturdy man in an Inverness cape who 'downed an amazing succession of neat gins, one after the other, which didn't affect him in the least'. A letter came from Winchester College and, recognising a kindred spirit (for it was about the old Celtic church) and assuming the writer was a master, Machen invited him to the Café Royal, where a stunned schoolboy found himself drinking absinthe with the great man. The same schoolboy, subsequently a lifelong friend, recorded Machen's opinion that 'Ta ra ra boom de-ay' was the supreme masterpiece of English music.

Machen the mystic translated Casanova, all six swelling volumes. His old friend Waite, the greatest living expert on the Cabbala, ended up a manager for Horlicks, and there was an irony even about the few honours. When his native Monmouthshire decided to honour him with a seventy-fifth birthday lunch, they got their sums wrong and a seventy-four-year-old Machen turned up, taking it in his stride, as he took everything else, even his sacking from the *Evening News*. He had published an obituary of Lord Alfred Douglas in which he used the word 'degenerate'. But Bosie wasn't dead, and sued. Machen, who had always said that journalism was no occupation for a gentleman, retired to Amersham and the King's Arms, where he was unaware, never carrying money himself, that the barman subsidised his gins.

He would have accepted the society formed in his honour just as he accepted everything else.

It was founded in 1986 by Rita Tait, who had moved to Caerleon with her husband, a head of department at Newport Art College, and by Godfrey Brangham, a pharmacist in Usk. Rita, formerly chairman of the management committee for Transcendental Meditation in all Wales, had found her way to Machen as naturally as the great man found his way to gin. 'Our Rita was always a bit odd,' her mother said.

Godfrey found his way to him because of a dip in the road between Usk and Caerleon. 'It's just a little dip, but when you come out of it, normality is far away. You're entirely surrounded by green hills, the sky is a line of blue as at the seaside, and there's a feeling of something around you which you can't quite grasp. I thought I was the only one who ever felt it, that wonder, until I read Machen and found he'd based everything on it. Nothing at all matters when you find a guy speaking to you.'

That was twenty years ago, and he found himself up against the problem that Machen's books were all out of print in Britain (though not in Japan, Germany, Argentina, Holland, Spain and the USA), and there was the odd inclusion in an anthology but nothing else. Godfrey went to W.H. Smith ('We'll let you know,' said a woman who never did), and then one day he called on a small second-hand bookshop in Chepstow.

'"Now that's a name I've not heard in a long time," said an old gentleman, and he looked me up and down like someone with a pedigree puppy for sale who needs to decide whether it is going to a good home. He took me into his office and opened a locked cupboard. And there they all were, his books.' Godfrey Brangham, who had never been in a second-hand bookshop in his life, realised that from then on his life was going to be full of them. Collecting Machen at that time, he said, must have been like being a homosexual in the 1950s in a small country town. It was just that as the years passed, he noticed prices were rising and knew there had to be others out there somewhere.

'The other day I saw someone advertising *The Green Round*, his last long book, and he wanted £4200. It's about a chap having a vision in a seaside resort in west Wales, and the only thing that stops me buying that is the knowledge that I don't have the money and that if I did, my wife would leave me. That's the joy of book-collecting. Rarer still is the first thing Machen ever wrote, a poem called "Eleusinia", which is terrible, about Greek mystery rites. Only one copy is known to exist and that's in Texas. That really is the Holy Grail, and at the moment I'm in the process of tracing the Hereford printers who brought it out, just in the hope that when they handed the business on, they might have handed on other things as well. I was in a book-shop with a friend once and I asked him, "What happens if we find 'Eleusinia'?" He looked at me and said, "Well, I'm bigger than you, Godfrey."'

'If you should find one, ring me,' said Rita Tait. 'Don't bother Godfrey.'

The story of how they met is as strange as anything in Machen. Godfrey Brangham had heard that a former headmaster of Newport Grammar School had done a PhD on Machen and wrote to him. When they met, the old gentleman seemed puzzled and said that only the week before someone else had written, a Mrs Tait from Caerleon. Going on the premise that people interested in Machen were a bit on the odd side, he said that he would not give her address but that he would give Brangham's to her.

'I answered the door when Rita called and she looked stunned and asked if my father was in,' said Godfrey. 'Every Machen reader expects every other Machen reader to be around 110.'

Out of this meeting in 1986 came the society. 'I'm not sure why,' said Rita Tait. 'I often find myself cursing the fact we started the bloody thing, but I've got to be organising something.' They have 200 members now, some of whom, like the man who wrote the music for

The Silence Of The Lambs, are fascinated by the horrors, others by the wonder, some by the prose, one or two by the quest of collecting a man so safely out of print. There are friars, doctors, psychiatrists, also the Australian bibliophile Barry Humphries, 'a serious, refined, warm, down to earth person' whom the world wouldn't recognise.

Members receive a beautifully produced magazine twice a year in which more and more of Machen's writing is unearthed, while they themselves trail steadily across his locations, in the hope, as one member wrote, 'that some cape-fluttering, pipe-smoking character of bibulous aspect might materialise for a second or two, clutching a glass of Corton 1910, then disappear with a hearty belch towards Wentwood like a self-propelled balloon…'.

And I am standing near that small church where his father ministered and where he himself sensed Celtic mysteries and dreamed of the Grail 'like a rose on fire'. The Church authorities have been trying to sell it for years, with the bonus that the graveyard will remain in use, the dead laying siege to the property should you buy it; no one has.

The land falls away in tiers and above you, among the trees, you can see the rectory where the young Machen mooned away his adolescence. Little has changed, though priest, church and mystery have gone. If you close your eyes, you can hear that voice again, remembering the nights when he came down to deliver the day's manuscripts to the postman. Listen…

> And I, with time to spare, walk slowly, meditatively, down the hill, holding my manuscript, hoping the day's portion has been well done. As I come to the stile there sounds faint through the rising of the melancholy night wind the note of the postman's horn. He has climbed the steep road that leads from Llandegveth village and is now two or three fields away.
>
> It grows very dark, the waiting figure by the stile vanishes into the gloom. I can see it no more.

1992

PART FIVE
A GAZETTEER

LLANSTEFFAN

What would they make of you,
Henry Gwynn, this St David's Day,
the stalls a blur
of middle-aged applause
for the English Royal Box?
What would they make of you,
who died at Agincourt?
No great death, nothing to
nudge the chroniclers and leave
you rampant in eternity.

The Towy estuary was far
from that wet field, and your
high castle of Llansteffan.
Only a lawyer's hand,

a spikey brown, commends you
to our notice, confiscating
your estate because you died,
trampled with the thousands in the mud
at Agincourt, on the French side.

ANGLESEY

The churches of Anglesey are very old. In a wall at St Cadwaladr's near Aberffraw is the first memorial to a king in western Europe, an early seventh-century Cadfan, 'the wisest and most renowned of all kings'. But the churches of Anglesey are also very locked, for the most part with no indication of where the key can be found. 'Mrs Hugh had it because she cleaned the brass, only she's moved. Old Mr Beynon was the churchwarden and he definitely had one, but he died. The vicar must have one, but we don't know where he lives.' If you like churches and meeting people, come to Anglesey.

At Llangefni, the county town, are the tombs of the Tudors, whose descendants got on, that old Welsh obsession, in their case with a vengeance, becoming kings of England. Only the church at Llangefni was locked. I saw a gate marked 'Rectory' and climbed the hill, but the rectory was also locked. No answer. I tried a surgery, but they did not know, and it was then I had a flash of genius. I called on the local undertaker.

He was a nice man, and we sat among the cold pastels of his funeral parlour, but even he did not know. 'I dealt with the vicar, but he retired.' As he phoned around, I asked about the Tudor tombs. 'Haven't noticed those. In my business it's straight in, straight out.' A half-hour of chat and phone calls yielded the information that someone called Olwen might help, of whom all that was known was that she had been burgled recently and lived in a brick house. If you have a talent for detection, you could do worse than exercise it on the lost church keys of Anglesey.

An air of fallen grandeur hangs over the island. For a thousand years a royal dynasty ruled north Wales from here, from the village of Aberffraw, now lost in 900 acres of sand dunes. Their palace is under the council houses and only one thing, one solitary footnote to their state, survives. In the village church – for here with the help of a Mr Hughes I did find the key (although we had terrible trouble with the lock) – turn to the west wall. Bricked up is the ghostly outline of a single, grand, decorated arch from the twelfth century, which is out of scale with everything else in the little church. Princes walked through that, but Mr Hughes, a churchgoer, looked at it in bewilderment, noticing it, as he confessed, for the first time.

It is a strange place, this Anglesey, not like Wales at all, being flat with few trees but a lot of stone breaking through the light soil. From the mainland the mountains of Snowdonia look down on an island that could have been towed here from the Mediterranean. Once called the Mother of Wales, it was its Ukraine, the bread basket of the country, but the agriculture is pastoral now and there are many deserted farmhouses.

There is only one good road, the A5, which tears through the centre of the island to Holyhead and the ferry to Ireland. The traffic using it never stops. But the new security at the port means this is now sealed off from a town where Swift lingered, cursing the contrary winds, and Holyhead is a dwindling little place, no longer even somewhere on the way to somewhere else. Tesco is opening a supermarket there later this year, distractedly, like an empire that has just been reminded of a remote possession. In the windows of village shops, the photographs are so faded that it is difficult to see what is being promoted.

In Aberffraw the butcher's shop has closed ('due to illness') and earlier this year the fish and chip shop closed, which, in Wales, means the end of the world cannot be far off. And yet, 'There's a chip shop 4 miles to the east, and another one 5 miles to the west,' said the barmaid. 'Myself, I think the chips in the west are sweeter.'

So life goes on and a more bizarre life you will never encounter. 'Fancy a lobster?' said a man with a wild moustache as I came out of the village phone booth. There had been no attempt at introduction, no comments on the weather, just 'Fancy a lobster?' My daughter, I told him, would kill me if I bought one.

'I'll boil it,' he volunteered. I explained that whoever did the boiling, there would still be guilt by association. 'Fair enough,' he said, disappearing up an alley. His trousers, I noticed, were sawn off just below the knee. 'That would be Will Wacko,' they told me at the pub. 'He likes fishing.'

Attempts to buy fresh fish occupied much of my week, for every day I saw boats out in the bay and every day I saw them disappear round the headland. I met the poet R.S. Thomas, an old friend, who assured me I would never get any fish on Anglesey. I met him again two days later and told him I was still looking. 'You've got a closed mind,' he said. But finally I met a man who knew a man and was told to be at the pub in the village square at 7.00 sharp.

At 7.03 a car stopped with a screech of brakes and a man I had not met jumped out. 'Fish?' he said. I nodded, and from the boot he produced in plastic bags four large pollack and nine mackerel, before driving away at high speed, having refused all offers of payment. The Aberffraw Connection had been made.

'H'm,' said Thomas, interrupted in a catalogue of his hates, which that week, in addition to such perennials as the English, included the South Wales Welsh, red sandstone and Jack Russells. Thomas lives in the north of the island, where from his window he has an unrivalled view of his lifelong hate, a nuclear power station. He once published a book of poems entitled *H'm*.

We walked together up the hill from a cove in which we had been watching what he thought might be a peregrine. At eighty-four he walked as easily as a young man, stopping only when I picked up a feather and asked what it had come from. 'Red Indians,' said Thomas.

And why not? Everybody else seems to turn up in Anglesey. In the tiny square at Aberffraw there is a post office, a pub and an off-licence. The pub is kept by a Scotsman who moved here thirty years ago, but when he and his son talk, it is either in broad Scots or in north Wales Welsh; recognisable English does not figure. The off-licence is kept by a former Ethiopian diplomat. This remarkable man met his English wife when he was in the Ethiopian embassy in Turkey and, with the fall of the old regime ruling out a return to his native country, the two of them read through *Dalton's Weekly* and came to the edge of the world to keep an offie in Aberffraw, the Casablanca of the west.

If you are a connoisseur of the bizarre, this is your island. At Llanfaes on the Menai Strait, on the site of the priory where two Princesses of Wales are buried, Welsh Water, run by Welsh-speaking Welshmen, built a sewage farm. No English company would have dared. In Beaumaris the council has reopened, this time to tourists, the most terrifying place I have ever been in: the Victorian town goal. For years forgotten in the back streets, it has everything in place: the treadmill, the whipping block, even the walk from the condemned cell to the gibbet. The whole building screams claustrophobia and human misery. But the day I was there a dance troupe was practising its routines in the dark passageways – '1–2–3–4–5, now turn.' The dancers strutted their stuff, the cheerful young women at the cash desk sold tickets and I found my sense of reality dwindling to a pinhead.

At the end of Holyhead seafront are the white, crumbling towers of a Disneyland castle, which looks as though it had been built by giant children but was in fact built for the engineer who came 150 years ago to construct the port's breakwater. I walked up a lane and passed a sign that warned me not to go farther on account of explosives, not to smoke or wear hobnailed shoes. I found one of the stables occupied by a cheerful man who told me that summers were all right there but in winter the rain fell in parallel lines.

'And the engineer?'

'He killed himself here. He looked down one day, saw the channel he had designed had a kink in it and he couldn't bear the shame.'

The island's other stately home, Plas Newydd, was built for the first Marquis of Anglesey, that tough old bird who, with surgeons sawing away at his leg after Waterloo, asked the onlookers whether they did not admire his vanity. His sperm count was equally legendary, and he was followed to his grave by more living relatives than any man in England. In the dining room is a masterpiece, Rex Whistler's mysterious mural of a Mediterranean sea, with ports and castles and a line of wet footprints leading out of the picture. Louche young men drape themselves on the boats. The extraordinary thing is that all this seems to have been painted long ago and to be older than even the Neolithic tombs of Anglesey.

I walked into the interior of the tomb at Bryn Celli Ddu, the Hill of the Black Grove, put up by a people of whom we know nothing except that they buried their dead. Smooth green turf covers it, there are great stones lining the interior, but whether this was a place of terror or majesty, or just one of quiet religious observance, we shall never know. It was already 3000 years old when princes walked in Anglesey. The title the greatest of these chose was Prince of Aberffraw and Lord of Snowdon. The photographer Antony Armstrong-Jones is Lord of Snowdon now.

On my first morning, staring out of the bedroom window, I saw a clump of mushrooms in the field that was all there was between me and the sea. In a few minutes, I said to myself, I shall put my trousers on and go down to pick those for my breakfast. But down the lane came an Englishwoman in white shorts and her son, both walking slowly. At the gate they paused, looked and, without hurry, walked across the field to pick every mushroom.

'The English have always got their trousers on,' said an octogenarian poet, whose name for the moment escapes me.

1997

MANORBIER

Some nights out of pity I pop up to see the Duke of Edinburgh. All day long, dressed in chain mail, he has sat in his cell with an expression of such fury that they have turned his face to one side so as not to frighten the public. That done, I cross the courtyard to the tower where, underneath a cell occupied by a murderer, the Duke appears to have found peace. Dressed this time in a shawl and a long black hat, and labelled 'A Welsh Lady', he sits intent over a spinning wheel. There is no room for ghosts, even in a castle, when the owners have taken delivery of a job lot of old waxworks from Madame Tussauds. Amongst these was a plenitude of Prince Philips.

Every afternoon, just before 5.30, they ring a bell and a few minutes later the great doors close, leaving my wife and me alone, apart from the Duke, the assorted murderers and a terrible cat called Miss Beamish, which stalks pigeons, seagulls and the odd small dog. Night comes over the sea to Manorbier Castle in the far west of Wales where

I have always wanted to stay.

One reason is the comedy. In the 1920s Charlie Chaplin touched Douglas Fairbanks Snr for a loan of Nottingham Castle, which the latter had built for *Robin Hood,* the biggest film set ever. As Chaplin explained, all he wanted was to film a short sequence in which, after the drawbridge had been lowered, he would emerge to put the cat out and pick up a pint of milk. But Fairbanks would never let him.

Manorbier had already been the setting for the TV series *The Lion, the Witch and the Wardrobe* when it first opened for holiday lets two years ago. Since then the castle visitors' book has been filled with the baffled comments of small children who have rummaged in the wardrobes, trying to find their way into Narnia. Others have sought their own Narnia here, having received, 800 years late, the one holiday postcard sent from the Middle Ages. 'The house stands visible from afar on top of a high hill which is quite near the sea... Hazelnuts grow very tall... Between the castle and the church a never-failing stream winds along a valley floor which is strewn with sand by the sea-winds...' The writer was Gerald the Welshman, and we can even date the postcard. It was March 1188, and he was recruiting men for the Crusades when homesickness overcame him. He remembered Manorbier Castle where he was born, he remembered the church where, as a boy, he had run, when news came of a night attack on Tenby, four miles away, and the beach where in happier days his brothers built sandcastles but he built churches.

So little has changed. The hazels he wrote about still grow tall, the stream runs, and church and castle face each other from their respective hills, for the extraordinary thing about Manorbier is that it did not sink into the usual cycles of decay. The reason is Joseph Cobb, a Victorian solicitor, who had one known weakness – castles – and the means of indulging this weakness. A railway speculator in boom time, he owned or held leases on just about every castle in west Wales, but at Manorbier, Cobb moved in.

That the castle survives in such a complete state is due to him, for he re-roofed and re-floored it, even glazing the arrow-slits, but then he went further. Inside the castle he built himself a house, constructing this against the curtain walls so that it has a medieval undercroft for a cellar and a tower as one bedroom. Today all hell would have been loosed, but Cobb did make one cheerful concession to history: his chimneys cannot be seen from the outside, though a TV aerial now can, showing above the battlements.

Throughout the twentieth century some bizarre lodgers came and went. Professor Joad of *The Brains Trust* lived here, as did two ladies, gardening by the Steiner method and planting at appropriate phases of the moon, who filled the courtyard with flowers. Virginia Woolf decided to become a writer ('That vision came to me more clearly at Manorbier, walking down the edge of the sea'), but the last tenant was the most bizarre. Texaco rented Manorbier for an executive then over-seeing the construction of a local oil refinery, so every night Corporate Man came home across a drawbridge. Then, ten years ago Beatrice Plunkett, whose mother had inherited the castle, moved in, to her family's bewilderment.

'I came in a sea mist. I had taken a taxi from Tenby and we couldn't see anything. When I told the driver to stop he said, "No, no, there's nothing but old ruins here." We went round again and again and on the third time I had to tell him this really was it. He stared at me, threw all my luggage out, then shot off into the mist. It was like the start of a Hammer film.'

This is a place that seems to be off-shore from the rest of the world. Roses, valerian and honeysuckle grow on the walls (with lime from the old mortar and the salt in the seawinds, the plants have had to sort themselves out here). Jackdaws nest on the other side of Cobb's glazed arrow-slits, peering out incuriously as you climb the spiral stairs.

Beatrice Plunkett moved out two years ago, but it was not until this summer that I realised it was possible to rent Manorbier. What is it like to rent a castle? I'll tell you what it is like. The moment that huge door, too thick for any letterbox, closes, it closes on the world. You who are bullied or faint of heart, this is your holiday home. If you have ever known fear in an inner-city street, if you live with insecurity, come to Manorbier Castle, a place that should be made available on the National Health Service to all freelance writers. No bugger can get you here.

1998

WHAT THE SOLDIERS
BROUGHT HOME

The maddest exhibit I have ever seen sits behind glass in the regimental museum of the South Wales Borderers in Brecon. It is a small jar with the accompanying inscription, 'Bottle of sweets taken from the E-Boat Admiral's cabin when they surrendered at Felixstowe, May 20, 1945.' There are some left in it. But fair play on the Admiral: had you or I had a similar date with Götterdämmerung, we too would have hit the humbugs as we made our last slow voyage across the North Sea. The South Wales Borderers with due solemnity added, 'Presented by Mr Sweet'.

Until then the maddest exhibit I had ever seen sat behind glass in Carmarthen Museum, next to the tombstone of a sixth-century king. It was a pair of cufflinks, and the inscription read: 'Dylan Thomas's cuff links. It is thought this was the only pair ever owned by the poet.' The present curator has now hidden them.

All museums were collections of oddities in their beginnings, until curators got it into their heads that they should be places of historical record. The British Museum still occasionally puts on show Dr Dee's Magic Mirror in which the Elizabethan alchemist saw demons, but no one else ever has, and I have stared hopefully for hours into its polished surface. They also have the idol which prompted the poet William Empson to write, 'A supreme god sits in the Ethnographical Section.' But such exhibits are rare now. For the bizarre, the poignant and the ludicrous left on the prim beach of the present, you have to go to one of Britain's sixty-nine regimental museums. Here, arranged in neat rows, catalogued with great care, are the things the soldiers brought home.

And in Brecon, with the barrack square of the Royal Regiment of Wales outside, I am staring at a small, bedraggled teddy bear. This was found in the trenches at Gallipoli by a Sergeant Bean DCM, who never did find out who the someone was, someone very young, who took an old friend with him into the Hell that was the Dardanelles, from which only the bear came home. If the jar of sweets is the maddest, then the teddy bear in Brecon is probably the most moving of all museum exhibits on earth. The old friend is threadbare now.

I have been fascinated by regimental museums ever since, many years ago, I visited that of the Yorks and Lancs in Sheffield. The chap who was showing me round was a red-faced major who had clearly enjoyed a very good lunch. We had stopped in front of the regiment's Boer War display, included in which was one of the bars of chocolate Queen Alexandra had had sent out to the troops, when I wondered aloud whether it might not still be edible.

'Good point,' said my guide. He fumbled with a bunch of keys, managed with some difficulty to unlock the case and reached in. He broke the bar in two, and gave me half. 'Mine's bloody bitter, what's yours like?' All that, as I say, was a long time ago, and since then I have never met a museum curator who was prepared to eat his own exhibits.

I noticed that when Major Martin Everett, to whom I told that story at Brecon, produced a Boer War biscuit, he carefully kept this in its case. This was that Major Everett, the curator of the Borderers Museum, of whom, when I rang earlier to fix an appointment, I was told, 'He's a bit tied up I'm afraid, he's entertaining some Zulus.' As the late Eric Morecambe used to say, there's no answer to that.

But the Regiment and the Zulus go back a long way, as anyone who has seen the film *Zulu* will know. On 21 January 1879 six companies of the Borderers were annihilated at the battle of Isandhlwana. A day later B company held Rorke's Drift, the most celebrated single action in which the British Army was ever involved, when twenty-two VCs were won. And this is where you come on the peculiar drama of the regimental museum.

The captains and the kings have departed long ago, and to the visiting Zulus, Isandhlwana and Rorke's Drift are part of their oral culture, events they have heard songs sung about and tales told. There is no sense of time in oral culture, so these could be yesterday or as long ago as Hastings. Then, as has happened, they come here, to a museum in Wales and see the actual flimsy shields that would not have deflected a water pistol and which their ancestors held up against repeating rifles. It is as if the Picts had turned up on a package tour to walk round a Legion museum in the sunset of the Roman Empire. 'They did find it a bit strange,' said Major Everett. 'Luckily nobody asked for anything back.'

There is a sadness about the Zulu exhibits, these pieces of wood and beads, which were all this people had when their Iron Age culture clashed with the industrial technology of a distant empire and for a little while held its own. The photographs of their dead royalty are here, and to these visitors it must have been like seeing pictures of Kings Harold and William. King Cetshwayo is here and his headdress, also a photograph of his brother before he was exiled to the end of the world, which in his case was the island of St Helena.

This remarkable individual is shown naked apart from a very small loincloth.

'Hang about, haven't you made a mistake?' I said. 'This chap's… er… not a chap.'

'No, we've made enquiries into that,' said the Major. 'Once you became a Zulu chief, you didn't actually do very much. You tended to put on weight.'

And the soldiers brought them all home… You come on things from places you did not even know the British Army had been to, like swords the Crusaders might have used, which they brought home from Eritrea in 1950.

'What were we doing in Eritrea?'

'I don't know, possibly it was some kind of police action,' said Major Everett.

In the three centuries of its existence the Regiment has been *everywhere*. Wars with the French in Belgium. Wars with the French in the West Indies. Wars with the Americans in the War of Independence. The Sikh War. The Indian Mutiny. The Regiment was seventy-six years in India alone. The Andaman Islands.

'What the Hell were we doing in the Andaman Islands?'

'Just a place we happened to be,' said the Major. 'The Regiment won five VCs there, when they saved some of their comrades in the surf. It was 1867, and they had gone to find out what had happened to nine British soldiers who, it turned out, had been eaten by cannibals.'

With twenty-three VCs, the Borderers, now part of the Royal Regiment of Wales, was the most decorated regiment of the line. The museum has sixteen of the medals, including all but one of those awarded at Rorke's Drift. The last of these, awarded to Private Robert Jones, came up for sale some years ago, but the asking price, £94,000, was beyond the means of the Regimental Museum. Ireland, Egypt, Ireland, Nepal, Ireland, St Helena, Malta, Ireland. We have forgotten, though they have not, how century after century there was always a heavy military presence in Ireland. And then suddenly in the midst of all this, '*March 22 to July 27, 1861, at sea.*' Four months at sea, and the Regiment was coming home from India. The tours of duty of the Empire were not the brief postings of the late twentieth century.

'I have been writing to someone whose ancestor, just back from Spain, joined the Regiment in 1814,' said Major Everett. 'Only the Regiment was in Nepal. And it wasn't just a matter of getting on a boat. He got caught up as a guard on a convict ship, went to Sydney then back to Bombay, after which he walked to Nepal. It took him eighteen months to get to the Regiment.'

Until 1873, when it acquired a permanent barracks in Brecon, its existence had been nomadic, on its home postings moving from one garrison town to another. But then, though the world travels continued, the Regiment had a home of its own and finally it was time to unpack the cases. There was so much stuff that in 1934 the curator of the Brecon County Museum, a lieutenant colonel, offered them a room to show off a portion of it to the public. It must have been an odd mixture of exhibits, for, while the County Museum travelled in time, it did so only in Breconshire, but in one room it travelled the world, at least those parts of it coloured the pink of the Empire.

But time was running out for the Empire, and, ironically, place for the Brecon County Museum, which in 1947 decided it wanted its room back. So that year the Regiment moved its stuff down the road and into its own barracks. In 1969 it amalgamated with the Welsh Regiment to form the Royal Regiment of Wales, but it held on to its museum. This is now housed in the Militia's old Armoury, where a new entrance on the street opened in 1967 to solve the problem facing most regimental museums. These are deep behind the secure wire of an MOD complex, and few members of the public, apart from the odd kinky individual, take kindly to the prospect of being frisked by a sentry on a family day out.

'At the moment we have 20,000 visitors a year,' said Major Everett.

'But even then these have had to make a pilgrimage to get here; we get very little passing trade. All this will change as we develop this place and the collection spreads across another two floors, something that will cost £500,000. At the moment we've only got about 60 per cent on show.'

Everett is the first curator not to have served in the Regiment. He is also the first to be paid, in his case out of regimental funds, the MOD picking up the tab for heating, lighting and the salary of one attendant. The Major, a TA officer for thirty-six years, spent his working life with computers in insurance offices and has brought these with him to the Museum, for there are many letters to write.

'Dear X, I am afraid I have been unable to find any record of your great-great-grandfather having been at Rorke's Drift.' Rorke's Drift is, after the film, in many people's minds. 'I don't think they sang "Men of Harlech" when the Zulus charged,' said Major Everett carefully. 'I may be wrong, but there are no records of this. Also the action took place almost entirely at night. But you can't shoot a feature film in the dark.'

Letters to elderly gentlemen trying to pinpoint the French crossroads at which they were wounded and which they have been unable to locate on any map, and so are anxious to be reassured that World War II was not just a private nightmare on their part. Letters of thanks, for almost every week families write, offering something some old soldier has treasured. 'You take the lot, just to save the families. So with the medals you get his watch-chain, perhaps even his wedding ring. I have drawers full of the strangest things,' said the Major, opening one. 'Just look at this, a pin-cushion with the inscription "From Jim to Bella". I've got an awful lot of embroidery done by bored soldiers on garrison duty in some far-off station. Look at these purple Chinese dragons, I think some Chinese bloke must have cashed in and gone round selling do-it-yourself sewing kits. And they end up here. Ten or fifteen years ago, museums like this would not have been popular. People thought of them as in some way promoting war. But they've come to see them as illustrating the life of soldiers who took part in events which had a profound effect on all of us.'

For most of the Regiment's history it was as though such men had never been. If they died, the state, until World War I, did not even pay for their headstones. If they saw active service, they were not given campaign medals until 1847, when the aged survivors of the Peninsular War were retrospectively awarded theirs. Fifty per cent of the Regiment were casualties at Talavera, but it was only the colonel, a man called Drummond, who got a medal, a gold one, for which the Museum recently paid £5800. As far as the authorities were concerned, the men who did the dying were just expendable extras, 'that article', as Wellington called the soldiers who won his wars.

But by the time of the Great War they had become men whose lives had to be accounted for in letters to their families. Frank Bradshaw, killed 26 September 1914, the war just over a month old. 'He had his senses for about half-an-hour after being hit, but the poor chap lost them after that.' Tact came late.

In Brecon I am walking through avenues of flags and guns, past a buckled cigarette case that saved the life of a Captain Lewis, past Turkish spoons and a piece of stained glass from a cathedral blown to bits, a Zulu knife thought to have killed the Emperor Napoleon III's son, the Prince Imperial, and spent bullets turned into cigarette lighters in the trenches in the quiet time. Things the soldiers brought home.

And I see on the wall the skin of a bass drum autographed by the great and good. This once belonged to the Rhodesian African Rifles, who had no wish to see it fall into the hands of the new regime and so sent it here, to Brecon, where it represents the final end of Empire, far away, in a museum to the men who propped that up in another time.

1999

THE VILLAGE AS WAS

First there was the tank. 'It was an armoured car,' said Owen Mathias. 'I should know, I was coming home from school. I heard the bang.' The driver, peering through the narrow slat, had seen something out of his dreams, two young women ringed by the afternoon sun, and was oblivious to the shouts from the turret about a bend in the road. So there went the bungalow, its furniture cascading out the other side and into the River Gwydderig, as though someone had hit the jackpot on a slot machine. 'The bed had been made,' said Bessie Morgan. 'Odd the things you remember.'

Then there was the crane, its long jib swinging wide as another driver, this time in the small hours, tried to take the bend. There went the pub, its eighteenth-century chimney breast bundled into the bar. 'And my mother didn't get up quick enough to take his number,' said Owen Mathias.

The council decided to widen the road after that, so there were another two houses gone. Finally there was the quarry, where the men could never quite get the quantity right when it came to blasting powder, erring on the generous side of things. 'I can see them now, the old rocks coming out of the sky,' said Margaret Morgan. 'They were just like flocks of birds.' And that was the chapel gone, first its porch and then the roof…

WELCOME TO HALFWAY. The new road signs are bright blue and breathless with bilingual invitation. CROESO I HALFWAY. The only thing is that nobody can remember when the signs came. It must have been like mushrooms in the night, for people who pass them every day have to have their attention drawn to them and to the invitation they extend.

They stand half a mile apart on the main A40 trunk road from Llandovery to Brecon, and are in Carmarthenshire. It is just that three years ago they would have been in the county of Powys, and thirty years before that in Breconshire, for these 440 yards of Wales, like Alsace-Lorraine, have long been the object of other men's geography. The signs, put up at the instigation of yet another local authority, Carmarthenshire County Council, are there to celebrate the council's successful drive to the east. Only in between them, in this disputed border area, there is…

'The falling down village,' said Owen Mathias, born in Halfway, now the proprietor of a garage 300 yards down the road, across the forecourt of which there careered a runaway articulated lorry. And that was Owen Mathias out of business for eighteen months. 'I should know that it's a falling down village, I'm trying to sell half of it.'

Two months ago he put the Halfway Inn on the market, the pub the crane hit and which he inherited from his father, who had inherited it from his mother. He also put the post office next door up for sale, which his mother kept for forty-seven years, and the building beyond that, still known as the Royal Oak, for it was a pub when this was a village of pubs. The Royal Oak was thatched then, and wisps of straw can be seen under its corrugated iron roof, like the thin hair under an old man's cap. But no one can remember the Royal Oak open, the Halfway Inn has been shut for twenty-two years and the post office for thirty.

'MAN TRIES TO REVIVE VILLAGE.' Owen Mathias was seeing the headlines form in the air. 'HE SEEKS YOUR HELP. Everyone send a pound.' He has had a large sign put up. THREE PROPERTIES WITH DEVELOPMENT POTENTIAL. Behind the three properties the gardens have run wild, but among the brambles their respective corrugated iron earth closets still stand sentinel on the hillside, and there is a batty grandeur to them up there. 'I was going to pull them down one day but a car stopped and this woman got out, said she was an artist and needed to paint them. I left her to it.'

A TV company once made a film about his pub. Though his family had moved out, they still had furniture there, and a couple of days after transmission a van came by night and effected the quietest house clearance. So that was the furniture gone. It probably parked on the little plateau he had cleared behind the pub, hoping that this would be the car park for the custom that would come. To do this he had demolished two small houses, which was another two gone. But the grass has grown back and in the middle of the plateau, a weird festal touch, a Christmas tree the size of a house grows.

'General Montgomery once spent an afternoon in that pub,' said Owen Mathias proudly.

'He was teetotal, for God's sake.'

'He still spent an afternoon in my pub. I can remember Canadian and American soldiers competing as to who would get to the top of those mountains first.' The mountains loomed above us, the sheep upon them so small they could have been moving punctuation. 'The Canadians won,' said Owen Mathias. 'Of course that was in the war, when everyone stopped in Halfway.'

You expect to find such places in the deserts of the American

Midwest, ghost towns when the gold ran out or the railway never came. Film has made images familiar, the saloon door ajar, the earth closet standing sentinel. It is when you find these beside the A40 that you sit up very straight in your car, and when you find new road signs welcoming you to them, you stop.

'Look.'

I am standing on a footbridge below the level of the road. The traffic is just a few feet away, but, to my amazement, I have stopped hearing it, for when something is a continuous band of sound, a point comes when it falls away. Where I am, there is birdsong and the sound of water.

'Look – a heron. There, under the trees…'

Upstream, just seven yards away, where the rocks have broken the flow of the river, an intent grey shape is peering into the white water, and it occurs to me, who has never been this close to such a bird before, that I could be watching a Victorian clerk hunched over his accounts.

'They say that when a heron moves upstream it's a sign of rain. Downstream, and it's going to be fine. But of course our heron doesn't look as though he's going anywhere,' says Mary Morgan, who, with her mother Bessie, lives across the road in the Forge. This is an immaculately limewashed house with a stream picking its way down through their garden, and they are the last of the old village families, just as the Forge is the last inhabited house in the centre of Halfway. Mary, a nurse, intends retiring here. She has worked away all her adult life, but she was born in this house and it is here that she will return.

And then she says it, the thing that stops me in my tracks. 'You know, I don't find anything funny about those signs. So long as I'm here, or my mother is here, there is a Halfway and there will be a welcome.' It is the matter of fact way she says this – without rhetoric or melodrama – that has me staring. I have been in Halfway for just 10 minutes, having driven 150 miles to make fun of this place and its people, and I have been invited into her house by someone I have never met before. And here I have collided with a statement of such dignity, I know at that moment that whatever I write, it will not be the story I intended to write about the bend in the road.

It is not the old road. For something like 1700 years the road crossed the mountains overhead, built by Roman soldiers whose camps are still up there. But the road being impassable in winter, the local gentry had another cut along the valley floor, in some places out of the solid rock. At the narrowest point of this, with just enough room for a road and a terrace of houses between the slope and the river, there was Halfway.

It was a good road – indeed, in the early 1800s the wonder of the age, for it enabled the London to Milford Mail to record, at 10 mph, the second-fastest average coaching speed in Britain (the London to Preston was a quarter of an hour faster). It is thus not surprising that a mile down the road there occurred the most bizarre of all accidents, when the Mail in 1835, driven by a drunken coachman, fell 121 feet into the river. Of the seven people and four horses, not one was injured, which prompted the belief that some of them, if not all, were in league with the Devil, and a local poet, invited to contribute some lines for the memorial, came up with: 'Then wait, Old Nick, have patience if you can. / And you shall surely gulp them one by one.'

These were not used, the organisers preferring instead the even crazier offering of one, and I kid you not, J. Bull, Inspector of Mail Coaches, who wrote, as may still be seen on the memorial: 'I have heard say, / Where there is a will / There is a way. / But many can assist a few / As this pillar will hew.' Which cleared up everything wonderfully.

How Halfway came by its name is a bit of a mystery. Some say it marks the halfway point between Milford and Gloucester, but it is more likely to have had to do with the usual explanation for such a place-name: that this was an overnight stop for drovers whose route from Llandovery passed through the village. These walking cheques (if you wanted to send money, you paid a drover, who then paid this into his local bank, paying whoever you wanted him to at the other end, having sold his herds) would have arrived in a hullabaloo that carried for miles, as they drove before them their cattle, pigs, sheep, geese and even turkeys. They would have put up for the night at the Halfway Inn, the Royal Oak, the Three Horseshoes.

'Come in, take a seat,' calls out Bessie Morgan, a merry eighty-five years old. 'Costs nothing to see the Fat Girl of Peckham.' She stops suddenly. 'Now where did I get that from? Oh, the things I've forgotten.'

Mrs Morgan is sitting in front of a black-leaded kitchen range that the drovers would not have found unfamiliar. Made, or assembled, by D.P. Davies, 'Ironmonger of Llandovery', its mantelpiece has been stripped by Mrs Morgan's daughter, who in the end got bored and used a sandblaster on it. Someday, said Mary Morgan, she would fill in the holes.

The door through which the horses were brought survives, as does the fireplace, but then this is not so long ago and they remember the last blacksmith, Morgan Gof, Morgan the Blacksmith. 'Though his real name was Augustus,' says Mrs Morgan. 'I think his son is still alive.' It was two houses when she came as a bride to a village that had a population of close on fifty. 'Oh, the old characters then. One man, Jones the Post, he delivered the mail, was a cobbler and, on top of all that, a preacher. And could he preach. When he was in full cry you could have heard him in London. And every time he said something important he gave this odd sound...'

I am to hear many renditions of Jones the Post's odd sound, part cough, part hiccup, delivered to give emphasis to what he was saying. Jones's house is a green hollow under the hill now, demolished when the council went about its road widening. Other houses survive as a few broken walls, and even the bungalow the tank went through is some asbestos boards above the river, but a house a man lived in whom people still imitate has gone as though it had never been.

It is one of the marvels of Halfway that nobody was ever run over, not even the man who, whenever he bought a new pram, would wheel this up and down the road just so his neighbours could see it was a new pram. 'Careful, his family still live in the area,' says her daughter.

'Go on with you, he's wheeled his last pram.'

And the shopkeeper who when in drink would be locked in his bedroom by his housekeeper and was thus obliged to watch, gibbering from his window, as others trooped into the pub. And the singing. And the odd adultery. 'It was a good place for couples to meet who didn't want to be seen together. I remember one night,' says Mary Morgan, 'this couple was there whom people had got to know, for someone said, "Good evening Mr Brown, Mrs Brown", and the woman was so startled she said, "I'm not Mrs Brown".'

'I played cricket in that road when I was a boy,' says Owen Mathias.

'You played cricket on the A40?'

Owen Mathias is a man in his early sixties. 'We had an oil drum for a wicket.'

'What do you think your life expectancy would be if you played cricket there now?'

'A few seconds, if I was lucky, that is.'

The children they played with left long ago, though they did not go far. Mary Morgan began to tick names off on her fingers. Betty Price, who became a teacher in London, now retired and living in Llandovery. Hywel Price, her brother, a haulage contractor, also retired and living in Llandovery.

'About twenty-five years ago the English came,' she says. 'Some were farmers, some bought holiday homes and did them up, so a cycle started when houses became holiday homes, then permanent homes, then holiday homes again. But the English don't stay long.' Across the road from the Forge, a house, its render immaculately stripped, is for sale at £90,000, its English owner having moved away. But behind this is a holiday home, the owner of which never did move away. Above the river under the trees is a tiny cottage that is one step away from being a ruin. The Englishman who has owned this for as long as anyone remembers is said to come down, book in at a local bed and breakfast, then turn up to listen to the birdsong and the sound of water in a place he has never moved into.

The much-blitzed Horeb is a ruin and every year the trees are thicker about it. 'My grandmother's buried there,' says Owen Mathias. 'Some bugger stole her cross.' But the tiny chapel Bethesda on the main road is still used. 'It's got a congregation of two, and they go just to keep the door open,' says Margaret Morgan. 'Me, I'm one of the two.' Mrs Morgan lives just outside the village.

'Every time I came home the village was smaller,' says Mary Morgan. 'The school closed, then another house had gone. "Oh, that's the council," they'd say, and I'd nod.' In west Wales the ways of the local council are as arbitrary and as implacable as those of the old KGB and are not to be questioned. 'I didn't see the decline really, but then suddenly there we were, bang, on our own.'

'We weren't the only village,' says Owen Mathias. 'There was another just up the mountain there. I went for a walk the other day and I could still see the walls and the damson trees.'

'What happened to that?'

'A flash flood. You know the stream that goes through Bessie Morgan's garden? My father saw a chest of drawers come down that.' And that was the neighbours gone.

'What do those signs say, WELCOME TO HALFWAY?' marvelled Gwyn Jones, a farmer who has lived in the hills above the village for 72 years and who as a boy was another who played cricket in the road. 'Oh, the council, too late as usual. I mean, what is Halfway?' A village as was, said his wife.

1999

THE GODS COME TO NEWPORT

Y ou and I, we are in a place of legend. Over the bridge from which the carved cherub heads get chipped, ever since the Stone Roses, a pop group, put them on an LP cover, to where, among kebab takeaways and balti restaurants, it is 6.00 in the evening in the nightclub called TJ's, an unreal time, before the amplifiers, and the young, get switched on. And we are where doomed pop icons meet and myths begin. In Asgard, which some call Newport.

Did Kurt Cobain really propose to Courtney Love here? 'Yes, over there.' Where? 'Behind that fruit machine…' It is an extraordinary voice, as though half a ton of gravel were being poured into a concrete mixer. John Siccolo, half Seychelleois, half Welsh ('it meant I missed out on the sun and got the rain'), once a sea cook ('like Long John Silver'), then a restaurateur and now to the young the Keeper of the Sacred Flame, owner of TJ's where, behind the fruit machine, on 10 December 1991, the gods met in Newport.

'I wonder when Steven Spielberg will ring me,' said Siccolo, a legend in waiting. He and I were drinking grog, to which he had just introduced me. 'Rum and lime, an old seaman's drink. Of course, to get the benefit it has to be doubles.' In between the benefits, we were discussing what might be about to happen to him. And to Newport.

Last year Neil Strauss of the *New York Times* materialised in the town like an interplanetary probe. How he found his way there is a mystery, for his newspaper had sent him to cover the National Eisteddfod, an event conducted entirely in Welsh, which nobody in living memory has spoken in Newport. But Mr Strauss had no doubts about where he was. He was, he told his readers breathlessly, in Seattle: 'When I was in Seattle just before Nirvana exploded, there was a feeling like this…'.

If you are over thirty, now is the moment for footnotes. Kurt Cobain was the singer-songwriter of the group Nirvana, who was to blow his head off with a shotgun in his garage in Seattle. Courtney Love, now his widow and the front woman of the group Hole, is the porn queen in Milos Forman's recent film, *The People vs. Larry Flynt*. John Siccolo, who was always over thirty, could have done with some footnotes the night they met in Newport. 'I was on the desk when this bloke came up. "That'll be three-fifty," I said. "I'm Kurt Cobain," he said. "It's still three-fifty…"'

Siccolo is a large man who looks as though he might be found waiting patiently under the pile of bodies after a riot. 'The next thing I knew, all these boys had come up to me. "Jesus, John, you shouldn't have charged him, d'you know who he is?" "Kurt Cobain," I said, for we had been introduced. And they shrank away from me as though I was Judas Iscariot. I mean, he just looked like your everyday hardcore grunge person.'

'What's that in English?'

'He was young and scruffy. Long hair a bit bedraggled. Designer-made holes in his jeans.'

Mr Siccolo is one of nature's grunge persons, whose appearance in various pubs that night attracted choruses of 'Good God, you're looking smart' and 'Hey, look, John's got a job…'. It meant he was wearing a jacket, growled Mr Siccolo. It was a lightweight jacket of the sort a man his age might wear in a summer garden, only he was wearing it in midwinter in the bleak streets of Newport. 'Somebody's got to be old,' he said.

'What was Courtney Love like?'

'Very nice girl, only I've got to be a bit careful here. What's the word? Ah, yes, decadently sexy.' He beamed, for he is after all the Keeper of the Sacred Flame. 'She was decadently sexy,' he said dreamily. 'And she was singing in my club in a backing group.'

Six years on he would need to mortgage most of Newport town centre to afford her, but in the early 1990s, touring American groups in their beginnings often used to call in on Newport. Nobody is quite sure why, though they were usually on their way to the Irish Ferry, so it must have had something to do with cut-price flights from Shannon to America. Whatever the reason, they stopped here in a place where nobody usually stops by choice, in a town stuck between the M4 and the mud flats of the Severn. And they played, the young listened, and it all began. Nobody knows for certain how many groups there are in Newport now, though estimates vary between sixty and twice that number. They can be very famous, like the Manic Street Preachers, from Blackheath just up the valley, or merely famous like 60ft Dolls from the town itself, and like comets their trail is vast, for these are groups in which the voices of the lead singers have yet to break. There are four Indie record labels, an equal number of fanzines, and every night somewhere the amplifiers are being turned up. It is probably possible to go deaf quicker here than on the Western Front.

Newport is a small town, frantically let out at the seams 100 years ago to take the coal exports from its industrial hinterland. But the market in steam coal collapsed and there was no way this could ever become a small town again. For a century it had only one public statue, and that was to Sir Charles Morgan, a landowner so hated that after ten years his statue was moved to a park that became known as 'the Old Man's Park'. They could not bear to say his name, remembering too well his role in the shooting of Chartist demonstrators. As Arthur Jones, the present leader of Newport Council, said, 'This was a place where people made money and then got out as quickly as they could. Newport had no benefactors.' It had no metropolitan veneer like Cardiff, for this was a workplace where suddenly there was no work, just 140,000 people marooned in the terraces of small houses, neither Welsh nor English, whose ancestors had flocked here in the boom time. Would-be saviours come and go. The great steelworks opened at Llanwern but in the early 1980s its workforce was cut from 9000 to 4000. The present saviour is a South Korean firm promising 6000 new jobs, whose arrival was enough to bring a prime minister to Newport to cut the turf for its new factory.

I met Jon Langford, founder of the rock group the Mekons and creator of the comic strip *Great Pop Things* in the *New Musical Express*, who had returned to his old hometown from Chicago for an exhibition of his paintings. Langford had spent much of his visit photographing the desolation in Newport docks. Wryly, without comment, he passed me a photograph of a boarded-up pub, its sign still brightly painted 'Welcome Home'.

It was into this landscape that a sea cook stepped when he came ashore in the late 1970s. 'It was in such a mess, the whole town seemed to be in a state of limbo,' said John Siccolo. 'I was trying to make up my mind whether to stay at sea for the rest of my life or to try something different, like the oil rigs in Alaska. It was then I met an old friend, another merchant seaman who had opened a taxi firm, and he told me about this place that was empty over the bridge. It had been a mini supermarket or something.' Thus Fate intervenes.

At first Siccolo opened a restaurant, one of those strange steak and seafood places, which became a fast-food American diner. He liked to put on a bit of music, a piano-accordionist wandering between the tables to remind the unemployed there had been better days. That Siccolo now has cult status in Newport ('The Prince, him') and that TJ's (named after him and Trilby, his late partner) is talked of as the Cavern Club in waiting, is a source of much amusement to those who remember him in the old days. 'I can remember when he first started putting groups on,' said Jon Langford. 'He'd be on stage arranging the bands and telling them where to stand. "Get the girl in front, always get the girl in front. That's it, that's lovely, that is."'

The age of a man who now lives by a canal, alone except for a dog and a parrot, is another source of amusement. 'Still alive, John?' asked a wit in a pub.

'Still rockin'. Excuse me, my public awaits.'

Over the grog, which by now seemed to be on some sort of assembly line, I asked how his hearing had stood up to ten years of rock.

'Pardon?'

Later he said he had practically lost the use of one ear and that he tried to keep as close to the door as he could in what the disc jockey John Peel calls 'the legendary TJ's'. On his answering machine he instructs callers to 'Speak as slowly as possible.'

But in those first days, when the accordionist circled and in the restaurant the battered face leant over the frying pan, he had no idea that these things would come. Then Simon called.

Simon Phillips runs Rockaway Records, a stall in Newport Market. 'It has always been my ambition to stock the most obscure records on earth, Japanese Noise Bands, just one step removed from white noise, and you couldn't get further away from the Beatles and Oasis. Mind you, I'd stock anyone who's into it in a decently enthusiastic way. I'd even sell…' He searched for the ultimate obscenity. 'I'd even sell Abba.'

A Gloucestershire man, with thinning hair and denims, he has run his stall for eighteen years ('And I'm poorer than if I'd been on a building site for that time'). But it meant that he knew the young who skived off school or hung around his stall, waiting to sign on. Thirteen years ago he formed Cheap Sweaty Fun and became a rock promoter. 'Newport's like a blank piece of paper. When you first come you think, "Omigod, what happens here?" But you soon realise you have been given the opportunity to draw something on it yourself.'

There are two Newports. There is the Newport of company shops, the Dixons, Lunn Polys, Halfords, in as anonymous a town centre as you will find anywhere, which comes to a dead stop when the sun goes down, just like social life in Transylvania. Then there is the other Newport, the Newport of the night, where the town's best Chinese restaurant only opens at 7 p.m. If you want to experience life after a nuclear holocaust, come to Newport at lunchtime on Sunday, any Sunday.

But in the weekdays there is a solitary bunker here, the market where, above the provisions stalls and the bright little cafés, humanity stands at bay. Here Simon Phillips dreams his dreams, and others, on stalls selling vintage comics, dream theirs. 'I think if Oasis had come along, we'd have said, "No, thank you." We like heavy noise in Newport. There's no Newport Sound or anything like that, but most bands that have come out of Newport are noisy.' The difficulty he found as a rock promoter was to find places to put them on. There had been years of working men's clubs, when one night he walked across the bridge and John Siccolo, to his alarm, found he had become a nightclub owner.

'Initially I thought, "Bloody hell, what have I let myself in for?" especially when I saw the way the young were dancing. You ever see Body Slamming? They just bumped into each other, and it looked so aggressive, except that after a few minutes you realise they're just having a good time. So from then on I just let everything build up.'

We had by now drunk so much grog it was clear that whatever

either of us was suffering from, it was certainly not scurvy. 'That's the lemon juice,' said Siccolo. 'Ensures you don't get visions on board ship.' On dry land he wasn't so sure, especially when in front of his eyes he saw the young change into the doomed icons of rock.

He remembered Richey Edwards of the Manic Street Preachers. 'Used to come into the club quite often. From Blackwood, he was, 14 miles away. Such an inoffensive chap, most of the time you didn't hear him.' Richey Edwards, who once advised all teenagers to kill themselves before the age of thirteen, disappeared two years ago when his Vauxhall Cavalier was found parked near the Severn Bridge and has not been heard from since. During his short professional life his pronouncements were taken down on stone tablets by the pop press, such as when he said having seventeen stitches for self-inflicted razor wounds had been a great help to him in his A-level revision. Further education in South Wales is usually hanging around somewhere.

The Manics, who only a few years ago were singing in TJ's, are the most famous local group. Even without Richey they were voted top group at this year's Brit Pop Awards. But there are others now, like 60ft Dolls, one member of which, Richard Parfitt, loftily informed me, 'I don't talk to the *Daily Telegraph*.' 'Him? He lives above my grandmother,' said Jon Langford. But then Newport, as everyone will tell you, is a place where everyone knows everyone else, where, as John Siccolo reflected, 'You're either in a band or you're getting drunk watching a band.'

Behind the door at TJ's is this notice: 'Play in a band? Then get your arse down to Disgracelands Rehearsal Rooms, close to Central Newport, £3.50 an hour…' The man responsible for this ribaldry is Dean Pool, who runs the rooms described to me as a couple of ramshackle sheds. 'I don't know how many bands there are in Newport, there must be close to a hundred, they come and go that fast. Most are just out of school, but you get the odd old-timer like me, aged thirty-one. How long do they last? Depends on the music. Some might last four years, but if they change their style, they could last longer. Some people just live for it. They form a band because they've heard some touring group or the Dolls have been in the paper again and they think, "Oh, we could do that." It becomes a lifestyle, drinking and playing music. If you want to know what Newport's like, listen to Maindee Run on the Dolls' LP. It's not about drugs, it just describes a pub crawl in Newport.

'You're in your mid-twenties, you live in a flat or with your parents. You're a student or unemployed, you're down the pubs most nights in jeans and T-shirt. You've got no ambitions about being famous, you play what you want to play and you couldn't care less if people don't want to hear it. Some give up, some never give up.'

But it all comes round to unemployment in the end. As one young man said, 'This place has got all the makings, just like Merseyside in the 1960s, and the main ingredient is not having a job. There isn't much to do in Newport except pick up a guitar.' They play in TJ's and in nearby pubs like Le Pub and the Riverside, to which, in the interests of research and Vitamin C, I was conducted by John Siccolo. From time to time we even met someone over thirty, like the scaffolder who that morning had slipped on ice and fallen on his head, building the new South Korean factory. We inspected his head. 'Forty pounds a day,' he said. 'I wouldn't build a house in this weather.'

'But you must try to imagine the effect on the lives of some of these young people,' said Siccolo. 'We put on a group called Darling Buds. All right, they only lasted eighteen months, but in that time they went to Europe, Japan and the West Coast, and I'll never forget this one boy, he had to be flown out as a replacement and was met at LA Airport by a stretch limo. He rang me, "Jesus, John, I was a tyre-fitter three days ago."' But why Newport?

'There's always been an interest in rock in the town,' said Paul Barrett, formerly the manager of Shakin' Stevens. He was peering into pre-history. 'The Sun label out of Memphis, which launched Carl

Perkins and Presley, had no UK releases in the 1950s, but I remember Danny Coffey, he lived in a caravan in Newport and went to the States and brought back these records in a knapsack. He progressed to importing them in boxes, it was a little cottage industry. If a rock explosion was going to happen anywhere, it would be here.'

'What's changed, though, is that until now you had to travel away to sign record deals,' said Simon Phillips. 'Now they come to Newport.'

'I wouldn't say there was a feeding frenzy yet, just a nibbling, a heavy nibbling,' said Jon Langford.

'I'm not really interested in local bands signing record deals,' said Phillips. 'What's important is that we put together the things that support good bands. We're not tin-pan alley, signing bands up only to kiss them goodbye in two years. We want them to be making music for ten to fifteen years, and if they get to be successful, great. We've got our own TJ label now, but if that happened to our bands, we'd tell them to sign on with someone bigger and we'd go back to square one. That's what interests me, the bottom of the ladder.'

Which is where John Standerwick finds himself at the moment. Aged twenty-eight and an unemployed butcher, he is bass guitarist with a group called Sweater and at the stage of playing as many gigs as possible and of sending tapes to record companies. From Glastonbury, he has been in groups since he was thirteen. 'I came to Newport because my brother was here and I knew there was a funky scene, but I'd no idea how many bands there'd be. It's ridiculous. The last band I was with, we had a vacancy so we auditioned. Know how many turned up? Fifty.'

Emily Wood, lead singer for the group Disco, is one rung higher. A month after we talked, the group's first single was due to be released, but now she is twenty-two and unemployed. 'Unemployed what? Unemployed cleaner, unemployed supermarket checkout girl, you name it, I've done it. There are four of us. Rohan on guitar, he's a student. Bob the drummer, he's unemployed. Ed on bass, I'm not sure what he is at the moment because he's broken his leg. Put him down as disabled. This is an extraordinary place to be. You go out and everybody you meet is in a band, even young kiddies, and it's so easy to get a gig, even if you start off playing in the toilets. There's all this… enthusiasm.'

It is 10.30 at night in TJ's. Siccolo introduced me to an enormous black bouncer. 'He tells me I'm his father,' said the bouncer, 'but I don't believe him.' A group of young rock musicians had been assembled for interview, only it had been a long night and all I could do was beam vaguely at Damian, guitarist and student, Dee of Hobgoblin ('the jobbing drummer of Newport, me'), Lee of Choketeens, John of Sweater, unemployed. The banks of sound closed in and the young were dancing, lithe of body, perfect of complexion, girls beautiful as the dawn that the *New York Times* assures us is rising on Newport. 'And I know all their fathers,' said John Siccolo glumly.

1997

THERE IS NO WORD FOR ORGASM...

Miss Mair Griffiths BA (Wales) took a much-thumbed copy of *The Happy Hooker* out of her handbag. She set it down very slowly on the table, as though frightened it could spill. 'I have read that with dark glasses,' she said sternly, 'because I am a Methodist.'

Once Welsh heroines stumbled barefoot over mountain passes to obtain translations of the Bible into their own language. Today they haunt the byways of their land like highwaymen, busily obscuring English place-names with aerosol paint sprays. But Miss Griffiths of Newcastle Emlyn in Carmarthenshire has braved more than geography or the law. To ensure the survival of the Welsh language she has waded into the swamps of English popular erotica. 'No, I don't think a Welsh word for orgasm has been invented.' She looked down her straight medieval nose. 'But I know a very good one for adulterer.'

It is an enterprise so bizarre that it runs the risk of being considered fantasy. At such times even Gulliver would stop his narrative to give readers a guarantee of truth. 'I could perhaps have astonished thee with strange improbable tales; but I have chosen rather to relate plain matter of fact in the simplest manner and style; because my principle design was to inform, and not to amuse thee.' Miss Griffiths and four young colleagues are reading their way through the entire range of English pulp fiction as an university research project. Their aim is to break down cowboy stories, romances, spy tales, science fiction and soft porn into recognisable formulae of narrative, style and characterisation. These will become do-it-yourself kits, which, it is hoped, will prompt a new range of pulp fiction in the Welsh language. Welsh cowboys will ride the ranges. Welsh astronauts will look on infinite space. Welsh spies will thwart international conspiracies. Suave Welsh lovers will sidle into boudoirs. These are heady prospects, especially the last.

Such books do not exist at present in the Welsh language, yet it is thought there is a potential readership for them. In the 1971 Census 400,000 people claimed to be able to read Welsh, though it was estimated that little more than a tenth of them did so regularly. So light reading could save the language from further decline (more than half the population of Wales spoke it at the beginning of the century but now less than a fifth do, and in wildly differing degrees of proficiency).

It has to be the most peculiar counterattack ever mounted on behalf of a beleaguered culture. Louis l'Amour, J.T. Edson, Barbara Cartland, Alistair Maclean and Xaviera Hollander may count their followings in millions, yet the books they write run counter to almost every criterion of taste a university department of literature has ever sought to establish. And now, unknown to them, they are being enlisted to save the language that has given Europe its oldest literature outside Classical Greek and Latin.

Islwyn Ffowc Elis, lecturer in Welsh at St David's College, Lampeter, and one of the most distinguished novelists in the language, has set up the Lampeter Research Project under the auspices of the Welsh Books Council and has recruited a research team of five under the Government's Job Creation Scheme. He is well aware of the reception he can expect initially, which explains the air of mild secrecy that surrounds the project. No mention of it at the time of writing had even appeared in the Welsh language press. 'People will probably say it's very silly,' said Ffowc Elis equably. 'That's why I prefer to do some things on the quiet; then when they're finished, people can say, "How marvellous!"'

He sat at a committee room table with his team, paperbacks piled before them, covers awash with guns, nipples and space monsters. They talked in Welsh, the name J.T. Edson rising like a benediction out of the soft vowels. The air of conspiracy was exaggerated by the jet fighters flying in and out of the trees outside, but in Lampeter they did not look up from the sagebrush and the six-guns.

Each had been given a speciality to research. A physics graduate concentrated on science fiction, a primary school teacher on Enid Blyton, while Miss Griffiths, who had lived in London, specialised in erotica. Their working pattern was to read eight books a week each, then meet up one day a week to compare notes, with blurbs dissected to identify the books' selling points, word counts estimated and narratives broken down to gauge the ratio of description to plot and dialogue. 'You have to know how long you can allow yourself with the moonlight on the water,' murmured Ffowc Elis.

Various types of heroine have been indexed, those of J.T. Edson prompting the most wonder. 'Their skirts keep coming off, and then they start fighting,' said Sylvia Williams, the primary school teacher. 'I didn't expect girls to behave like that.' Clichés have been listed with great care, the numbers of times mouths came firmly down on other mouths, also the different ways of death that Edson and l'Amour awarded the men in the black hats. Locations have been listed with the care of a tourist board, the cruise voyages, the country hotels, the small towns in the bad-lands, the worlds beyond the stars. At the end of the year Ffowc Elis plans to incorporate all this in an instruction manual for writers, far too many of whom, he smiled faintly, had tried to write the Great Novel in Welsh. For what was the point of writing such a book when there were no people to read it?

His own reasons for the lack of light fiction in Welsh were economic. A writer was lucky to clear £400 from a Welsh work of fiction, and then only when he had been able to sell television and radio rights. With such meagre returns, a man was prone to indulge himself more than his reading public. Ffowc Elis is hoping that his Welsh cowboys, spacemen and lovers will prompt a revolution among the 400,000 readers who at present lurk like some lost civilisation in the minds of Welsh writers.

That Welsh survives at all is something of a miracle. It has had to overcome military conquest, the steady hostility of an alien bureaucracy that is only just being relaxed, and, of course, the indifference of many of the Welsh themselves, who saw it as a brake on their own personal ambition. Mr Roy Jenkins, it was not generally recognised, was a very typical Welshman. So the language survived in an embattled state, closed to outside influences. English, by the nature of historical change, has remained fairly fluid, able to accommodate American slang and the various technological Latinisms. But a national competition was necessary in Wales to construct a word for television, and newsreaders live in terror of new English coinages like hijacking. Yet this very old, very stiff language is to be the speech of astronauts and lovers.

The lovers, this being Wales, could present the biggest problem of all. Nonconformity may be relaxing its hold after 200 years, but its taboos linger. 'I suppose you could get two Welsh people in bed,' said Mair Griffiths doubtfully. 'Together,' she added, almost as an afterthought.

Ffowc Elis is aware of the difficulties he is facing with his new literature. Translations of light fiction have always done badly in Wales because readers fail to identify with the characters. 'You can get round this. In one of my books I had a German prisoner-of-war who had learnt Welsh competing with the local minister for the girl. But then I had people writing in, "Pity the old Jerry got her." The Welsh have this great inferiority complex.'

Locations will pose another problem. The speaking of Welsh has shrunk to the Western seaboard, which means farms and villages and pubs. Mair Griffiths, who had just emerged from *Valley of the Dolls*, thought it would be difficult to interest hill farmers in such urban dilemmas as drugs.

'But where we will really be in trouble is the treatment of class,' said Ffowc Elis. 'The Welsh people have very little class consciousness. So it will be difficult for them to understand its tensions. Things like the romantic novel have a pronounced middle-class bias, with the heroine an orphan and usually poor, very much of an inferior social class to the hero. That is going to be difficult to get over.'

Nobody thought science fiction presented any problem. Technological terms were so fanciful anyway that it would be quite in order to throw in a few Welsh ones. Gwyndaf Rowlands, the physics graduate who has been reading his way across infinite space, felt there would be nothing bizarre in a Welsh-speaking Martian. 'I don't think English-speaking Martians are that common.'

All five have to find new jobs at the end of this academic year. But what has taken all of them by surprise so far is the enthusiasm the research has generated. 'At first I didn't like the idea of reading any of these books,' said Dylan Williams, a graduate in Welsh. 'My training had been quite against it. But they've been an eye-opener, especially the cowboy books: Louis l'Amour... Zane Grey... even some terrible man called Merle M. Funk.' He made them sound like a Congressional Roll of Honour. 'The cowboys are such poets. "I'll fill you so full of lead you'll be worth mining." How do you translate that?' Most said they would continue to read cowboy books. 'Louis l'Amour,' said Mair Griffiths dreamily, 'I love his little sentences. I've been reading all my life and yet I've never come across these books before.'

You felt they were catching up on their own childhoods, reading books they had always been told not to read. To die for your country would be painful. To read pulp fiction for it, and be paid, must be the finest play under the sun. But at Lampeter, Ffowc Ellis had a moment of doubt. 'I suppose I could be doing the language a disservice.' The stately volumes of the medieval *Mabinogion* on his shelves were in abrupt contrast to the covers of the paperbacks on his desk. 'Still, as one of our finest dramatists said the other day, "I prefer people to read anything in Welsh rather than nothing at all."'

So what if the Project succeeds? As the smoke clears in the Welsh pantheon, you will see the names cut in gold along the walls... Barbara Cartland... J.T. Edson... the incomparable Louis l'Amour. In time a small nation acquires strange allies, but never any like these before.

1977

DREAMERS AT BRIGADOON

T hree men stood among the dunes overlooking Carmarthen Bay. They had come to see something amazing, the thirteenth-century village of St Ishmael's, near Ferryside, which disappeared into the sand 400 years ago, but which the high tide, like a conjuror, uncovers perhaps once or twice in a man's lifetime, when for a few days or a week it is there again, in the sunlight, like Brigadoon. And all that is needed is for Cyd Charisse to come over the foreshore, exercising her unforgettable Scottish vowels and her even more unforgettable thighs. Instead it was a Mrs Sadler exercising her dog who saw the flagstones and the lintels protruding like broken teeth. 'I was really excited,' said Mrs Sadler, who phoned the newspapers.

It was a high blue morning, the light so clear that the three men could see, 20 miles away, the spires of Tenby on its headland rising in an immensity of sea and sky. And it was then that the first of the jets came in, turning lazily in the sun before it swooped: DUBADUBADUB. Cannon. 'Bloody Hell,' said one of them. That was me.

The jet peeled away, and there was a second plane coming in over the bay. DUBADUBADUB. 'See that caravan site?' A second man was pointing. That was Fred. 'When they opened that they put an advert in the papers. "Daily Aerial Displays." Which is true, only they forgot to mention that the displays involved live ammunition.'

'But it's only a mile away, we could be in a war zone,' said the third man incredulously. That was Geraint.

'They forgot to mention that too,' said Fred.

Fred Bevan is a local historian and a retired headmaster. Geraint Morgan is a university lecturer. We were at school together, when Owen Glyndwr was head boy. Geoffrey Chaucer topped the bestseller list and Fred was a rugby star, trailing clouds of teenage glory beside which everything that comes later in life – breakthroughs in medical science, marriage to Sharon Stone – is tired whimsy.

'Do you miss it?' said Geraint.

'It was a long time ago,' said Fred.

We talked about people we knew, like the crazed gym-master who kept boys behind when they couldn't do handstands. His reign of terror was interrupted only when he had an affair with the matron, who gassed herself in the school oven, otherwise I should still be there, aged fifty-eight, still trying to do handstands, my family, mortgage and dog waiting politely outside the gym.

'Remember when he introduced boxing?' That was Geraint. 'He staged this exhibition bout with Eddie Evans, the biggest boy in school, and he was clouting him all round the ring when Eddie got bored and knocked him down. Know what happened then? Oh, he had style. He reported Eddie to the headmaster.'

Nobody is sure what happened to the village of St Ishmael's. It disappeared even longer ago than when we were at school, when no records were kept of this remote place in the west, but there is a tradition of a tidal wave so vast that it is said a volcano had erupted deep in the Bristol Channel.

'Do you remember X?' I asked.

'I still see him, he sells insurance now. In fact, you could say he lives for insurance,' said Fred. 'I was at a funeral not long ago, he was handing out the order of service with one hand and tucking business cards into your top pocket with the other. He's beyond, he is.'

'He played rugby, didn't he?' said Geraint.

'Rugby's got a lot to answer for.'

When the village went, it went so completely that the old map-makers were not even sure where it had been, and made various wild guesses on the shoreline between Ferryside and Kidwelly. All that remains is the church, left high if not dry on the hillside, for it is so damp, the plaster green with lichen, you feel, even in high summer, as though you had come into one of those caves behind a waterfall that you find only in films. This is a church so old and far away that the Reformation passed it by: it still has the stoup for holy water.

'There was a vicarage, but that got bombed,' said Fred. 'Strange story. A London couple rented it, wanting to get as far away from the Blitz as it was possible to go. I think they were a mother and daughter. And then one night a German bomber, returning from a raid, decided to jettison its bombs before going out over the sea. They'd survived the Blitz, only for that to happen.'

History leans heavily on this estuary. Upstream are the ruins of Iscoed, that stately house from which General Picton, he who wore a top hat to the wars, left for Waterloo, bawling in his rough way to whoever would listen, 'A peerage or Westminster Abbey.' He was killed and got St Paul's Cathedral.

'God, he was a tough,' said Geraint. 'Did you see that face? But he needed to be, with the sort of blokes he commanded.'

DUBADUBADUB. The jets were coming in again, firing at Cefn Sidan sands, the sands of the Silken Back, a place of wrecks and wreckers, and a terror in living memory. The inhabitants were known as the Men with the Little Axes, who, signalling to ships with lanterns, enticed them on to the sands, and my grandmother talked of fingers severed from the dead for their rings, even of fingers severed from the living. Napoleon's niece was drowned here.

'My Mother,' began Fred.

'She wasn't a Wrecker, was she?'

'No, she wasn't a bloody Wrecker. She was one of the last cockle-women. She had her own donkey and a permit to gather two hundredweight of cockles at a time.'

'The Common Market forbids you to sell cockles in their shells now.'

'Not round here it doesn't,' said Fred.

It was always a place outside the law. When the *Brothers* bound for Liverpool from South America went down in 1833, *the third wreck in a week*, a local magistrate, a Mr Rees, was powerless to stop the locals from 20 miles around carrying away in carts her cargo of cotton and buffalo hides. In a letter to the Home Office, Mr Rees, who had been cuffed around the head when he tried to intervene, accused his fellow magistrates of being in on the plunder. But one of them, a Mr Morris, in a wonderful covering letter, said he and his colleagues had all been away from home at the time.

'The last ship to be wrecked was the *Paul* in 1925,' said Fred. 'She was a four-masted sailing ship carrying a cargo of timber out of Hamburg. They had just managed to get the crew off her when a little serving maid, a coloured girl, insisted they turn back to save the ship's canary. They did this, and a few minutes later she went down. I've got a photograph taken in Ferryside.' The girl, Pearl Ascae, is carrying the cage. She looks bedraggled but triumphant.

'We grew up with the *Paul*,' said Geraint. 'You could see this line of black oak across the bay from the beach at Llansteffan. Every year there was less and less of her.'

'And this year for the first time she disappeared completely,' said Fred. 'But she'll be back. Round here most things come back in time.'

They have their exits and their entrances... Ten years ago Fred saw the lost village briefly, just as others had done. Sir John Rhys, the great Oxford scholar who was investigating its folklore at the turn of the century, met a man who had actually seen whole streets between the dunes and the reef. John Lloyd Thomas, farming Tanlan Farm some three-quarters of a mile from St Ishmael's, used it as a quarry, which meant the lost village became even more lost. It was after the great storm of 1896, he said, when he saw rooms and unmistakable fireplaces in some 200 to 300 yards of building. He had, Mr Thomas confessed, carted fifty loads of stone away to build up his walls at Tanlan. And if he hadn't, he said defensively, others would have.

'Tanlan's the reason I'm here today,' said Fred. 'My father was a farm labourer out of Pembrokeshire, he came to work there and met my mother.'

'Going by on her donkey?'

'Perhaps,' said Fred.

We walked up the lane to St Ishmael's, where I wanted to see one gravestone I had never been able to find before. In the 1840s in West Wales there were the Rebecca Riots, when countrymen destroyed the tollgates, the charges of which were ruining them. Their faces blackened, and dressed as women, they rode through the night, terrifying the authorities and enacting bizarre charades as they went about their midnight work. It is one of the strangest episodes in the history of these islands, and the strangest aspect of all is that no ringleader was ever identified. *But there was a man...*

'This is it,' said Fred.

It is a large tomb, the lettering faded, to one Hugh Williams who died in Ferryside in 1874. There is no mention of his unique marital record, for this was a man who in early manhood married a

Kidwelly heiress twenty-five years his senior, then in his late sixties married a girl from Llansaint, two miles up the hill, who was thirty-nine years younger than him. There is no mention of his other interest either.

Williams was a lawyer, 'a man of large business till he lost favour by his defence of poor men', for whenever one of the rioters was arrested, he appeared for him in court. But there were, and are, suspicions that he may have been more than that. When Colonel James Love, at the head of a military force, was ordered into west Wales, he reported back to the Home Secretary about Williams. 'This man I shall recommend to the watchful eye of the Metropolitan Police when they arrive.' But nothing was ever proved and he died rich.

He was buried with his brother, a lieutenant in the Brazilian navy, which seems to have offered remarkable career prospects to the Welsh in the early nineteenth century. When the *Antiques Roadshow* visited Newcastle Emlyn recently, somebody produced the full-dress uniform of a Brazilian admiral, sword, epaulettes and all, the whole thing still with gold braid, which one of the programme's omniscient experts valued at £6000.

We drove to Tanlan Farm, into which the cartloads of submarine stone disappeared 100 years ago. It is a large, grand mansion, far grander than any farm, standing in bleak open land. There was, I noted, a great deal of stone walling. Mrs Dilys Evans, the matriarch of Tanlan and the great-niece of John Lloyd Thomas, he of the fifty cartloads, remembered how, as a girl of twelve in the 1920s, she saw what appeared to be flagstones and the outline of a room 300 yards out on the reef.

'Did you talk about this to anyone?'

'Not really, it's not the sort of thing that usually comes up in conversation.' Which seemed reasonable enough.

DUBADUBADUB. The jets were so near now they might have been flying in through one ear and out the other. Geraint sat in the car, making notes for a lecture on Democracy, while the farm dog peed dramatically on each hubcap in turn.

'It's an odd old place round here when you think about it,' said Fred in the pub at Llansaint. 'Just across the Bay is Pendine, where they test rockets. I was fishing in a boat when this powerboat came out of nowhere to warn us off. Just like in James Bond, except they don't have lost villages in James Bond.'

On the walls were photographs of rugby stars in their pomp, Gerald Davies among them, who had also been at school with us. Fred began to talk about the time he, Gerald, Max Boyce and their wives went to an international in Cardiff, then spent too long over lunch. By the time they got to the ground the gates were shut. 'We could hear the roar as the teams ran out, but old Max, he just climbed the gate and stuck his head over it. Suddenly someone shouted, "Look, there's Max," and suddenly everyone was shouting. I think they stopped the game. They opened the gates anyway.' He looked wistfully up at the massed photographs. 'If you really want to see history,' he said to me, 'I think my photograph's up there somewhere.'

In Brigadoon, where no one ages.

2001

PART SIX
VISITORS

THE TOWER AT THE END
OF THE WORLD

'Martin Borman's telephone directory,' said my host-ess, pointing to a small crumpled book with the Eagle and Swastika on the cover. We had paused by a glass-fronted cabinet on the fifth floor of the tower, or it might have been the sixth; I was beginning to lose count. 'And that's Hitler's lavatory handle.' To her they might both have been part of a house clearance. 'Loot,' she said, explaining that her hus-band had been one of the first English officers into the Bunker and had bought them from a Russian guard. I nodded, for by that stage nothing could have surprised me.

The Norman Tower stood in 300 acres of woodland, above a tidal inlet, and it was white, all of it dazzling white, being lime-washed. The drive had been through trees that touched over-head, one and a half miles of this, climbing all the time, until suddenly there was a plateau and sunlight and this thing against the sky like a Saturn V. I knew then where I was: I was in Nutwood. A tower like this, surrounded by trees, was in all the endpapers of the Rupert books. It was lived in by the Professor and the Dwarf, his servant. At this point I should add that everything that follows is true. I was there to have tea.

And it was a wonderful tea, of buns and biscuits all baked by my hostess, a lady in her seventies, who, as we sat down, said casually she had limewashed the tower herself, working off 50-foot ladders. For the tower is not a ruin, it is her home. Mind you, on Ordnance Survey maps it is a ruin, which it had been for 300 years, when in the 1930s a hermit bought it and proceeded to restore it. His name was Pegge, his family having changed their name from Pigge, who made their money from the Briton Ferry Lunatic Asylum, which they owned. This, alas, is again true.

Pegge did not bother to inform the mapmakers that the tower was no longer a ruin, nor did my hostess and her late husband when they bought it. Both were from old military families and had the sort of toughness needed to live in such a place. 'See those stairs? Feller fell off 'em, having not turned backwards as he'd been told. You never heard such a fuss, he was screaming before he even hit the ground.' She buttered a tea cake. 'Blighter claimed £10,000 off my house insurance.'

Inside, the tower was straight out of the nightmares of *Guardian* readers, being stuffed full of weapons and animal heads. 'That tiger, she'd done for six people 'fore they got her. Pregnant, too, I've got the skin of one of her unborn pups somewhere.' On the wall were three swords. 'All from Trafalgar, all *used*.' There were lavatories gouged out of the stone, so their doors closed in your head, like doors sealing off the priests prepared to accompany their Pharaoh into the afterlife. And on every floor the objects were more bizarre.

What if I was to ring the numbers in Borman's phone book? More to the point, what if someone answered? But we were at the top now, peering down on a maze she had had built. This was on a lower terrace between the tower and the river, and from the battlements it looked like one of the puzzles in Rupert which I could never solve.

But close to, it looked scary, for she had had it built out of stone slabs and it looked as though it had come out of some terrible moment in pre-history. The mutual friend who had introduced us had said she had felt it necessary to have this blessed at long range by the Dalai Lama.

All this time my hostess was talking. She talked for two hours about her family, about her son, the Gulf War general, but mostly she talked about dowsing. Her speciality is dowsing, not for water but for dead bodies, for which she is sometimes called in by police forces. I'm afraid this is also true. She uses the largest scale maps available, dangling a pendulum over them, and can make mistakes (once a police dig revealed a pack of shot foxhounds in a wood) but is still accurate enough to be taken seriously. I said at the outset that I felt nothing could have surprised me again that afternoon. But it did.

For she began to talk about bodies being found from which all internal organs had been removed. 'Spare part surgery,' she said breezily. 'The human body, you know, is worth approximately £94,000 on the open market.' We then had scones in the tower at the end of the world.

THE KAISER TAKES THE WATERS

The handwriting does not disappoint. In the hotel visitors' book it looks much as you hoped it would look, big and impatient, a signature for films. You can see a hand dashing it off on the mobilisation order, then the screech of a whistle as the first night train bursts through the paper, then another and another, as millions of men hurtle westward. Good God, can this be the hand which launched the…? But all that is two years into the future, for it is September 1912 at the Lake Hotel in Llangammarch Wells in Mid Wales.

'Why should he sign himself Prince Münster?' I asked Jean-Pierre Mifsud, the hotel owner.

'Must have been one of his titles,' said Mr Mifsud. 'That was how royalty travelled – incognito.'

'Ah,' I said.

In Mid Wales there is a tradition that in 1912 the German Kaiser Wilhelm II took the waters at Llangammarch Wells. David Baird-

Murray, the fourth generation of his family to own the Metropole Hotel in Llandrindod Wells, the biggest hotel in the area, grew up with this tradition. 'The spas of Mid Wales had close links then with Baden-Baden, and my father always said he knew when the Great War was starting from the way the German band began to disappear from the Pump Room.' As a boy, he met Lindbergh, also incognito, at the Metropole in the days when the world came to Mid Wales.

Its spas have fascinated me ever since the night twenty-five years ago when I stayed at the Metropole, where there were 135 bedrooms, only three of which were occupied. Three men sat in the lounge watching *Softly Softly* on the television, sitting close together, as men do when the past is overwhelming; we might have been round a campfire in the Valley of the Kings. The past was all around us, in the corridors which together stretched to infinity, in the brown photographs of the fashionable dead (in one year before the Great War, 80,000 people came to Llandrindod), in the emptiness.

'You should have been here before the Great War, boy,' said a man who clearly had been. 'We had a lavatory every ten yards.' Of course, they drank the stuff as well and the water was a potent laxative. My father used to say that had a film been made then of the spas from a hundred feet up, people would be puzzled by all the sudden frantic departures from the streets, the agitation of long skirts, the bowlers falling.

A few months ago we were in Llandrindod. It was the holiday season, a time that brings the modern equivalent of the Spanish treasure fleets – conferences – to the spa hotels. You know the sort of thing: long morning lectures and hangovers and the wistful possibility of adultery (which at least would be a re-run of the old days, when this was somehow fitted in between the eight-course meals and the terrifying evacuations). In the Metropole, delegates from the Crown Prosecution Service and the British Jacob's Sheep Society came and went, thinking only of punishment and wool. But what if they mistook their lecture halls?

How soon before the solicitors woke up to the fact that castration was not a sanction open to them in their war against drink drivers?

There were four spas: Llandrindod, where the grandees went; Llanwrtyd, beloved of Nonconformist ministers; and Builth, where Welsh farmers stayed with their sisters. But the fourth spa, Llangammarch, was mysterious, being off all main roads. Its waters were also different, for at the Lake Hotel there was a barium spring, one of only two in Europe. The exotics went to Llangammarch.

Now gourmets do when the hotel holds one of its periodic beanos that are booked up weeks in advance. Some come early, to glide between the padded leather chairs and the cake trolley, for the teas at the Lake Hotel are as grand as they were before the Great War. Grander, for now you can look down over the terraces of lawns and rhododendrons to the satisfyingly ruined pump house. The cycles of excess and purge have been broken; there is just excess now.

I fell into conversation with Mr Mifsud, the owner, as he sat among the guests in the lounge. His wife was sewing in the window. I said it was sad that the world before the Great War had disappeared so completely, it would have been fascinating to write about it, except that now this would be melancholy. 'Then you haven't read our visitors' book,' he said.

The visitors' book is a small, dark ledger kept in a drawer where anyone might read it. I started reading it thinking it would be a boring roster of names, but it wasn't that at all, for our ancestors were never content just to write their names: out of the pages came people making jokes and little asides. There were addresses I recognised, and in one case the surname of a family I knew. The past was walking and talking.

Here were Sir James Hills-Johnes VC and Lady Hills-Johnes of Dolaucothi, where the family butler had murdered her father. Dolaucothi is in ruins, as is that fantastic house Bronwydd, with its minarets and Biblical mottoes over every fireplace. And here was Miss Nesta

Lloyd of Bronwydd, from a time when trains brought the now long-vanished Welsh squirearchy north.

'I am delighted with the place and grateful for its health-giving properties,' wrote a London doctor. There were many doctors, and they all recorded their gratitude. Even the grandest of them, Lord Lister, wrote in 1898, 'Much invigorated.' Nobody was specific about what the waters did for them, though they were agreed as to its effect.

Whole families came, children, maids and all, some of the children recording their own impressions, which were later corrected by their mamas, a hand crossing out the second 'i' in 'minuite'. It was a fairly international clientele, which included German nobility, a Mr Morgan of Madras and Sir Spencer Wells Bt from Jamaica. In 1898 a spidery hand recorded a link with a remoter past, 'W Bird, late 8th Hussars, and one of the 600…' Some names recurred, among them a Mr Gwyn Lewis of Briton Ferry who in April 1898 wrote, 'This is like Home.' So much like home that Mr Lewis underlined the last two words for emphasis and in June was back again. He came every year after that, twice in one month in 1903. There were others who also didn't seem to spend much time in the Pump Room, one preferring the hotel, which gave him 'that family feeling so conductive to the life of an Irishman…' One man, after a staid entry for 15 September 1912, 'Mr and Mrs Blofeld of Portman Square', wrote in a wild hand, 'That's me, Ernest Blofeld…'

The impression is of a privileged little world out of time altogether. The first sign of change comes in 1912 when military ranks appear: a colonel and two captains gave their address as The Camp, Rhayader; the two captains were back again the following month. And then I came on the entry I had been looking for. On 24 August a Princess Münster of Derneburg booked in, staying until 28 September. On 10 September she was joined by her husband Prince Münster and by a Count Münster.

'When I came here this was the first story I was told,' said Mr

Mifsud. 'They said he'd practically taken over the whole place. And it made me so curious I had the waters tested, to see what could have brought him such a long way. D'you know, those springs are toxic? The people who stayed to take the waters were actually being poisoned.'

Could the Kaiser have stayed here? I went to the biographies and found that between the spring of 1912, when he was in his Corfu villa, and October, when he was in Berlin, there was a curious haziness about the Kaiser's whereabouts. Moreover, he did go for bizarre holidays, as when the English tutor to his children recorded that for three weeks in 1907 the Kaiser rented Highcliffe Castle in Sussex, bombarding the aged Florence Nightingale with carnations and his own wife with requests to join him there. 'Poor Papa,' wrote one of his daughters, 'he's quite broken-hearted about leaving his dear Highcliffe…' Five years later he was pestering his general staff to produce plans for an invasion of Britain 'on the grand scale'. What had happened in the interval?

Of course, the poisoned waters of Llangammarch. Any man who spends a fortnight on the lavatory would bear a grudge to the end of his days. But Prince Münster? I found the *Almanach de Gotha*, the greatest Bible of snobbery ever compiled, and there in its tiny French print found his list of titles… King of Prussia, Margrave of Branden-burg, Duke of Silesia… My finger traced them line after line. Prince of Rugen, of East Frisia… And then there it was, Prince Münster.

Now I had heard of Count Münster, his ambassador to France, an old friend of his and already a confirmed Anglophobe. Why shouldn't these old friends have got poisoned together? It would explain a lot, with the two, pale and determined, plotting among the rhododendrons.

Last year I met a very old gentleman who had survived the Great War. He said, 'One thing's always puzzled me, what was it all about? Why did it start? D'you know?' I didn't then, but now in my mind's eye I can see a small, angry man with a withered arm, a man with his posterior red as a gas-ring.

1992

THE GREAT ESCAPE... IN WALES

The Great Escape is the most forgotten story of World War II. Who among you knows that on the night of 10 March 1945 67 prisoners of war, using a tunnel 15 feet down, 60 feet long and just 3 feet high, made a successful mass bid for freedom? Very few, if any. But around Bridgend in South Wales they do, which is perhaps not that surprising. It happened in Bridgend. The escapees were German.

It is now 56 years later and I am one of two men who have travelled 180 miles to see what remains of the old camp at Island Farm at the side of the A48 on the Porthcawl road, just before the turn to Merthyr Mawr. Now owned by Bridgend County Borough Council, it consists of undergrowth into which, at one point, mysterious stone steps disappear, as though leading to some lost temple. The council has put up a large hopeful sign: 'To Let, Modern Business Space'. With this in mind, it has razed the old prison huts, with a single exception – the one from which the tunnel started. I have heard strange stories about this hut.

That the tunnel is still there, being last used in the 1970s by some cavers. That the entrance to it in the hut survives, under some wall-paintings of half-naked women put up to distract the guards. That its exit is where it always was, hidden by undergrowth in a nearby field. Even more bizarre, the excavated earth is still in the hut. Everything, with the exception of the guards and the escapees, is still there. You just imagine what a tourist trap anyone with half a brain could make of this frozen moment beside an arterial road.

I know all this from Herbert Williams, the author of *Come Out Wherever You Are* (Quartet 1976), the one account of the Great Escape. Herbert, who has come to meet my friend Geraint Morgan and me, has arranged for a council official to open up. For Bridgend council has erected a metal palisade 12 feet high around the hut, which, along with the hut itself, it now keeps locked. The only thing is, when the official turns up, brandishing a huge bunch of keys, the relevant key is not among them. Sixty-seven Germans got out, two of whom got 150 miles away. We have come a similar distance and we cannot get in.

The sudden embarrassed silence is broken by Geraint. 'You still in touch with those Germans, Herbert?'

'I may have the odd address, yes. They must be in their late seventies and eighties now.'

'But fit?'

'I'm sure some of them are very fit.'

'Herbert, if you asked them nicely, d'you think one of them might come over and let us in?'

That is the trouble with this story, the comedy will intrude.

When 1600 German prisoners, most of them officers, were brought to Bridgend after D-Day, they came by rail, *and the old GWR had forgotten to remove the holiday maps of the British coastline from its compartments.* As the trains crossed England, the Wehrmacht and the SS did not pose a problem to their guards: they were too busy copying maps on to their handkerchiefs and their shirt-tails.

Mrs Joan Knights, daughter of Superintendent William May, the policeman in charge of their recapture, still has the shirt-tail her father kept as a souvenir. Mrs Knights is keeping it to convince her grand-children that all this did indeed take place. As she had been unable to wash it, she said, it had gone a bit grey.

But there was nothing remotely comic about the arrival of the pris-oners of war in Bridgend. 'It was snowing, and our family was watch-ing from an upstairs room when they came by,' said Mrs Knights. 'But it was the *way* they came. They towered over their little Scottish guards, bayonets and all, they were stamping their feet and singing a marching song at the tops of their voices. They didn't look a bit depressed, it was terrifying. And when they passed our house, we all dodged behind the curtain. One of them had looked up.'

They were going to a barracks built for munitions workers and hurriedly converted into prison camp 198 for the masses of men now falling into Allied hands. This had no towers, no raised catwalks and no searchlights. What was more, one hut was within 60 feet of the outer ring of barbed wire, beyond which the guards patrolled, bemused by acetylene flares which made it difficult for them to see into the camp, and unnerved by hundreds of sheep which in the dark-ness coughed like men. The guards rarely went into the camp, their commandant, his men outnumbered by eight to one, having leapt at the thoughtful German offer to take over its administration for him. In any case, his were not fighting troops. They were in France. These were men from the depots, older men, the sick and the wounded, who patrolled the wire, wistful for the pubs of Bridgend that were a refuge from the inmates bellowing 'Horst Wessel' and the coughing sheep.

One story will tell you as much as you need to know about camp 198. When all 1600 prisoners decided to send Christmas cards to their Führer, some having made these themselves, some having bought them through the camp purchasing scheme, their guards, in the middle of a world war, duly sent them, posting them to a Germany their own planes were bombing to bits every night.

The tunnel started from Hut 9, the one nearest the wire, and its occupants cleverly solved the greatest problem of tunnelling: the disposal of the displaced earth. It was some time after the escape before the guards found out how. They had built a whole false wall in the shower room and put the earth, compressed into clay, behind this. Paintings of remarkable quality were going up all over the camp, nostalgic paintings of German landscapes and even more nostalgic ones of German women in their underwear. These paintings were particularly remarkable in Hut 9; no one in an art gallery looks at the floor or at the walls.

Work at the face was terrifying, the air so bad that no one could stick it down there for more than two minutes at a time. This became a quarter of an hour when they managed to construct an air line from condensed milk cans. Their ingenuity was limitless: they laid an electric cable so they had light below ground; they sawed through the legs of bunk beds throughout the camp, reducing them by exactly the same amount, so they had timber for shoring up the tunnel. They saved rations, built compasses, circulated the geographical shirt-tails, for the Britain into which they would emerge was one without signposts.

'Their motives varied,' said Herbert Williams, who thirty years later was to meet the stately company directors and professional men those prisoners had become. 'The youngest were the most fanatical. They wanted to get back into the war, one of them telling the men who captured him on Margam Mountain that he hoped one day to return as governor of an occupied Wales. Amazing bloke, he asked them for Aneurin Bevan's address, whom he thought might help him. Some did it out of pride, some for a laugh. And there were some who were just fed up with the bloody place. But there was one little group who planned to steal a plane and fly it home through all the anti-aircraft barrages. They thought all they had to do to alert their countrymen, who were having the daylights bombed out of them, was to waggle their wings.'

It was this group which at 10.00 at night had a freakish stroke of luck. Having got through the tunnel and crossed the field, they came on the one car in Bridgend, petrol rationing being what it was, with a full tank. It belonged to the local doctor, Dr Baird Milne, who was expecting a confinement that night and so had parked it outside his house. The only thing was, the keys were not in the ignition. There are various versions of what happened next. One has four guards, on their way back from the pubs, helping them jump-start it. The Milne family disputes this, pointing out that no doctor awaiting a confinement would have had a flat battery. But all are agreed on one thing. When the POWs were recaptured, they wrote to the doctor, offering to pay for any damage and for the petrol they had used. As Dr Valerie Milne, the doctor's daughter, said, 'Long after the war my mother's car was stolen and when found it had been vandalised. Unlike the Germans, nobody offered to pay for that.'

The doctor's stolen car was to run out of petrol near Lydney and was found abandoned. Long before that, by 2.15 a.m., sixty-five men had gone through the tunnel and were away. But for the last two their luck ran out. The sixty-seventh, carrying, of all things, a white kitbag, was shot and wounded by a guard, and the sixty-sixth, in hiding, was caught when he burst out laughing as he saw a guard fall into the open tunnel. At that point the solids should have hit the fan.

But the camp commandant, having done a check on numbers, at first refused to believe that anyone except the last two had escaped. He changed his mind when Germans, like mushrooms, began to turn up all over Glamorgan. The first two were captured by an incredulous village bobby, who found they had packed their *slippers*, in addition to shaving kits, fags, food and maps. But the Germans, however good they were at getting out, were very bad at getting away. Some made for the coast, others went inland, hoping to make for Ireland. Most just got lost, in spite of their maps. The arrests began.

Some had blacked their faces, hoping to be mistaken for miners, one man in a thick German accent hopefully informing a policeman at midnight, 'I'm only a poor Welsh miner out looking for food for my children.' One little group just gave up, wandering into a cowshed the following morning where they stood watching a farmer milk, as though this was the most exciting spectacle on earth. But the funniest moment came when three of them boarded a bus near Neath *and did not talk*. The other passengers, being Welsh and unused to silence, had a word with the driver, who did a quick detour and stopped his bus outside the local police station.

Many of the escapers appeared not to have their hearts in it, but then the war in Europe had only eight weeks to go. By the seventh day the Great Escape was over. The four who stole the car had actually got to Birmingham Airport, where one of them, posing as a Norwegian engineer, had spent an interesting afternoon, his comrades awaiting night and his return in some nearby undergrowth. All were picked up by five farm-workers armed with shotguns. But the prize for distance went to the 150 miles covered by two prisoners who, jumping goods trucks, made it to the outskirts of Southampton. Unfortunately for them, the last truck they had jumped was one full of cement powder, from which they emerged looking like Laurel and Hardy in one of their escapades.

All 1600 prisoners were dispersed within a fortnight of the escape, but the authorities had not yet done with Island Farm. Its most bizarre years were still ahead as, the war over, No. 198 became No. 11 (Special) Camp, when the people of Bridgend found they knew many of its new inmates by name, for they had been reading about them for long enough. Here the paladins of the Third Reich were brought – at least those not facing war crimes charges.

There were four German field marshals in the camp at one time: Gerd von Rundstedt, who had been C-in-C West; Erich von Manstein, architect of the blitzkrieg, which broke France; Walther von Brauchitsch, formerly commander in chief of the army; and Ewald von Kleist. There were generals and admirals, and among them was Walter Dornberger, who had directed the rocket research programme.

It was a strange time. Wehrmacht generals delivered milk in Bridgend, others taught their guards how to read and write, and in the case of Dornberger, lectured them on rockets, so that for some years conversations in the pubs of Bridgend were very strange. Von Rundstedt walked along the country lanes with a small girl who later remembered that he had taught her the names of wild flowers. Men who had presided over the most terrible war machine the world had seen since Genghis Khan, men who had shut their eyes to genocide and massacre, now picked flowers to make dandelion tea. And then by 1948 they, too, were gone.

And it is a Sunday morning three days after my first visit and I am entering Hut 9, for even Bridgend council in time finds the key. It is just as Herbert Williams told me it would be, the fading pictures on the walls, the great mound of earth from the tunnel still in the shower room. Long passageways, rooms on either side. Dust and damp. Nothing at all has changed. The council, fearing vandals, has put shutters on the windows, and I am standing there, peering in the poor light, as Carter and Carnarvon peered into a Pharaoh's tomb. This is an amazing place.

2001

THE JOKER WHO KILLED HIS KING

He died on 9 September 1680 in Chepstow Castle. It had become his Spandau, its garrison guarding one old man of seventy-eight. They would never have released him; the event he had been part of over thirty years before cast too long a shadow for that. He had already written his own epitaph, for, as he acknowledges in the course of it, he had had the time. 'Here / Was buried a True Englishman / Who in Berkshire was well known…' Even then he could not resist the wintry little joke at what must have seemed like another life. 'But living immured full twenty year / Had time to write as doth appear / His epitaph.' You will find it under the mat just inside the front door; that, too, would have appealed to his sense of humour.

St Mary's Church, Chepstow, has a startled look. It is under the bypass now, which, by ripping through the town, has left the church in a wasteground of car parks and bright arcades. That his tombstone survives is even more surprising, given its travels. The present incumbent hurries over it in his guidebook before explaining, as though to visitors from another planet, the purpose of the font that stands above it ('A person starts his life with Baptism by water, and this takes place at the Font…'). He always did worry vicars.

One in the eighteenth century, shocked to find him buried in the chancel, had him moved to his present place where the feet of the generations might tread him down. In death men still thought him dangerous who in life so worried them that a vast medieval castle was brought back into service to keep just one man inside. The feet of generations have done their work, so the present gravestone is the third, and no attempts have been made to chalk in the blurred inscription. All you can make out for sure is the acrostic in the epitaph, the first letters of each line spelling out his name. Henry Marten, a man who killed his King.

The men who voted for the death of Charles I were extraordinary even to their contemporaries. 'I hear they all die defending what they did to the King to be just, which is very strange,' wrote Pepys. Kings had been killed before, but not like this, in plain day ('It was not a thing done in a corner,' said Cromwell). They would be killed again, but never under a warrant which used the title: Charles was killed as 'King of England', a reigning king and not plain Charles Stuart, as the French would kill their king.

To us the regicides seem more than men: old General Harrison going to his dreadful execution and answering the jeers of the crowd as to where his Good Old Cause was now, 'Here in my bosom, and I shall seal it with my blood'; the elderly General Goffe emerging from his cave on the American Frontier where he had hidden for years to take charge of a town under Indian attack; Alderman Scott on the scaffold not being allowed to address the crowd. 'Surely it must be a very bad cause which cannot suffer the words of dying men.' They are fenced off from us by their calm and their unshakeable belief in

God's will, so everything they did and said seems unreal. But there was one man.

A small, laughing man who loved women and fun, jokes and horseplay, a man who scandalised both sides by his behaviour, being in and out of gaol all his life, yet was there at the centre of events, being once well known in Berkshire. Amongst them he is a curiously modern figure, the only one who did not have God as a pen-pal, 'an indomitable little Roman pagan,' wrote Carlyle. 'Sir Edward Baynton was wont to say that his company was incomparable,' said Aubrey, 'but that he would be drunk too soon.' What on earth was Henry Marten doing in the seventeenth century?

First, he scandalised his father. 'He was a great lover of pretty girls,' sniggered Aubrey, spending so much money on them (according to Aubrey again, he even employed talent spotters) that he was in debt for much of his life. In the end Marten senior, a judge, found him a rich widow ('whom he married something unwillingly'), who after being led a dog's life came to live with him in his Chepstow gaol; it was a life full of ironies. A short man, 'his face not good,' brooded Aubrey.

But what is so remarkable is that two successive heads of state, in the midst of all their troubles, found time to be scandalised by Marten's private life, both Charles and Cromwell calling him a 'whore-master'. Long before Marten rose to any political prominence, Charles caught sight of him on his way to the races in Hyde Park, and the prim little King, usually so circumspect, burst out: 'Let that ugly rascal be gone out of the park, that whore-master, or else I will not see the sport.' That, wrote Aubrey, raised all Berkshire against the King.

Yet this was the man who emerged as leader of the extremists, who in 1643 scandalised even Parliament but this time with his opinions, remarking that it might be a good thing if the whole royal family were done away with. His fellow MPs expelled him for that, even though by then they were at war with the King, and he spent some days in gaol, his first stretch. But his opinions were genuinely held.

When the House of Lords was agonising about what to do with the King's private property, Marten seized his horses and refused to return them and is said to have also seized the regalia in Westminster Abbey, declaring 'there would be no further use of these toys and trifles'. Mr Marten, MP for Berkshire, was beginning to enjoy his Civil War.

He stunned the Presbyterian party, which itself had stunned the established order by its plans to do away with bishops, by saying that toleration should be extended to include Roman Catholics. Again, when the Commons was trying to work out what to do with the crowds who were flocking to be cured by the touch of the imprisoned King, Marten remarked that Parliament's Great Seal might do just as well. By the standards of his time this was a very rum character indeed.

Yet they liked him. In all the passion that was let loose in those years in the House of Commons, this was the man who made jokes. When one of those with a hot-line to God moved that all profane people should be expelled, Marten moved that the fools go as well, when there would be 'a thin House'. He slept a lot in the House, and when someone moved that all sleepers should be expelled, exclaimed, 'Mr Speaker, a motion has been made to turn out the Nodders, I desire the Noodles should also be turned out.' His jokes, like his epitaph, may have been blurred by the centuries but at the time men laughed.

Just as they laughed when they debated whether to sentence the royalist poet Sir William Davenant to death. The talk had been that a sacrifice should be made, but Marten remarked that traditionally sacrifices were of the pure and unblemished. In Davenant's case it would be the sacrifice of an old rotten rascal. Men laughed again and forgot their desire for vengeance, but the extraordinary thing is that in the atmosphere of the Civil Wars, things like that just did not occur. Honour surfaced, and occasionally justice, but not humour.

Yet in one matter there was no humour and no tolerance. As early as 1643 Marten was demanding that Parliament should not enter into negotiation with the King, and when he suspected Cromwell of such negotiations later, is said to have plotted his murder, carrying a pistol and dagger about with him for that purpose. The second Civil War, brought about by the King's prevarication and plotting, incensed him and he raised a cavalry regiment in case Parliament came to terms with Charles. He got the horses for this by stopping travellers on the highway. Just as he was straightforward in his speech (unlike Cromwell, for whom God was always hanging around somewhere), so he was straightforward in his actions once the laughing had to stop.

He was one of the main movers in bringing the King to trial, and when the judges, of whom he was one, worried over what answer they should give if the King demanded by what authority they brought him to judgement, said promptly: 'In the name of the Commons in Parliament assembled and all the good people of England.'

At the signing of the death warrant there occurred that bizarre scene when Henry Marten and Cromwell inked each other's faces like schoolboys, and later it was Marten who designed the new Great Seal and had the King's statues pulled down. But the men of the Army who had made use of his talents had other plans that did not include him, as he was to write at the Restoration: 'Had I suspected that the axe which took off the King's head should have made a stirrup for our first false general, I should sooner have consented to my own death than his.'

When Cromwell dissolved the Long Parliament, he is said to have attacked Marten personally for immorality, who, losing his Parliamentary immunity, spent part of the Protectorate in gaol on account of his debts, being outlawed in 1655. He was released with the restoration of the Long Parliament in 1659, and then, so it was said, only to make up a quorum.

On the return of Charles II he surrendered himself as a regicide, making no attempt to flee abroad. For a while, despite Parliament's fine promises, he was under a sort of suspended death sentence. He put his faith in the King's original proclamation that those regicides who surrendered would have this taken into account, observing in his usual way that 'since he has never obeyed any royal proclamation before, he hoped that he should not be hanged for taking the King's word now'. Men laughed at that, just as they laughed when Lord Falkland repeated his old joke that they should not make a sacrifice of this old Rotten Rascal. The Commons voted for his execution but the Lords spared him.

But he could not keep his mouth shut. 'That honourable House of Commons, that he did so idolise, had given him up to death, and this honourable House of Peers, which he had so much opposed, especially in their power of judicature, was made the sanctuary for him to fly to for his life.' He had done his best to talk his way to the disembowelling knife. 'I think his majesty that now is, is king upon the best title under heaven, for he was called in by the representative body of England.' If you examine that, it is a denial of the hereditary right of monarchy.

At first he was in the Tower, then at Windsor, being 'removed from thence because he was an eye-sore to his Majesty'. Around this time someone came upon his letters to his mistress Mary Ward and printed them, thinking to blacken his reputation, 'but 'tis not to his disgrace; there is wit and good nature in them,' wrote Aubrey. And so he came to Chepstow, his 'old cage' as he was to call it in his epitaph. He was there so long that a tower in this medieval castle above the Wye is now named after him; you can see the elegant windows that were cut in its walls and the fireplaces that were installed, for the curious thing is that his imprisonment was not at all what you might expect. His wife and he occupied a first floor apartment and their servants the one above.

He seems to have been well off, for an eighteenth-century

antiquarian met someone who had known his two maids and heard that they had saved money in his service. He was also allowed to receive guests and to walk the town, even being permitted to be a guest in neighbouring mansions, accompanied by a guard. It was during one of these visits that his host asked whether, had he his time over again and the opportunity to make things good, he would still have killed the King. Marten said, 'Yes.' And that was one house less in his social round.

His presence in the castle, and the consequent maintenance, ensured that this lingered on beyond its allotted span, being in turn an eighteenth-century glass-factory, wareshop, smithy, until the roof of Marten's Tower fell in about 1803. The subsequent history of the castle is as fascinating, and far more mysterious, than its heyday. In 1914 a man called Lysaght bought it from the Duke of Beaufort and a year later bought the town wall as well. In 1953 the Ministry of Works came.

As I pushed open the door to the town library, I saw two notices, one put up by the town council. 'Chepstow Town Council are your eyes, ears and the corporate voice of the town. Defend your right to the above.' The other might have interested him even more. 'Fresh Horizons, for women who want to meet new people…' He would certainly have accommodated them. I was thinking that as I copied down the jaunty epitaph he must have had such fun writing. God, as usual, is absent.

> Here or elsewhere, all's one to you, or me,
> Earth, air or water gripes my ghostless dust,
> None knows how soon to be by fire set free,
> Reader, if you an oft tried rule will trust,
> You'll gladly do and suffer what you must.
> My life was spent with serving you and you,
> And death's my pay, it seems, and welcome too,

Revenge destroying but itself, while I
To birds of prey leave my old cage and fly,
Examples preach to the eye; care then (mine says)
Not how you send but how you spend your days.

I think I should have liked him, this one who laughed.

1993

THE SERGEANT AT CHRISTMAS

They are preparing to put up a war memorial in the village church, even though few of them are old enough to remember the event it commemorates. It will take the form of a wooden plaque. 'To the memory of Sgt. T.C. Jones, who died in this parish, Christmas 1944.' Nothing more. But then they do not need more, for it is something the village will never forget. This is their Christmas story.

There are already two war memorials in the village of Myddfai in Carmarthenshire, and they do not have many names, just four on that for World War I, three on that for World War II. You have to know how small the village is, in the foothills of the Black Mountain, how removed from all main roads, to realise the intrusion those wars represented and the overwhelming tragedy of those seven deaths. But there was an eighth death.

It was different from the others in that it did not take place on any far-off battlefield. It happened here. But nobody in the village met the man, even though for three weeks it might be said he was part of their community, and he could see them, at least he could see their lights far below him, for the wartime blackout had been lifted. He might have heard them, too, calling to their sheep and their dogs, as he crawled towards them. He had a broken leg and, when they found him, had almost reached safety. It was the morning of Christmas Day. He was nineteen. This is the Stranger's story.

But it is also the story of another man fifty years on who heard it as it was passing into folklore, when people were beginning to add details of their own. Alun Evans, now in his early forties and a mature student reading for a history degree, was the local pest-control officer ('rat-catcher, if you like') and had heard many versions of the Stranger's story. The man had been on the run. He was an Army deserter. He had bailed out of an aircraft, though no one knew why, for, so it was said, the aircraft landed safely. But certain details were never questioned. He was very young and it was Christmas when his body with the leather elbows of a flying suit worn through from crawling was brought down, carried on a gate by farmers and laid, draped in the Union Flag, in Myddfai Church. It was just that everything else had become a mystery.

Who was he, this man who had tumbled into their small world? Where had he come from? Was there a family still living which remembered him? Alun Evans had asked such questions before and, through his researches, had answered them, for he was a man fascinated by two things: by flight and by the Black Mountain where so many flights had ended above his home town of Ammanford. For him it had started when he read that 350 planes had crashed during the war in north and Mid Wales. But it wasn't that, it was the fact that in popular folklore most had become German bombers, when almost every one was an RAF training flight, young crews just out of school let loose in Lancaster bombers, which, as he says, were then considered workaday vehicles, little more than the equivalent of Ford Transit vans

today. It was later he found out that their families knew little, beyond
the bald official announcement of death and letters of condolence
from commanding officers, of what had happened to their sons or
husbands or brothers. Alun Evans decided to make it his life's work to
change this.

I already knew something of this man. My cousin, a hill farmer
who had on occasion called Alun Evans in to deal with wasps' nests,
talked with awe about someone he seemed to consider the modern
equivalent of the Ancient Mariner. 'A nice man, but you might as
well forget the rest of the day if you get him on to the Second World
War.'

It was twenty years ago that Alun Evans heard about his first
wrecked plane on the Black Mountain. A hill walker himself, he met
others who talked of finding craters up there with twisted bits of
metal in them and of scattered ammunition lying around. But finding these, at 1800 feet, in that terrifying expanse where Carmarthenshire and Breconshire meet, was something else. Stray from its
sheep-tracks at any time outside the brief window of summer and
there is the very real possibility you may never come down from the
bogs and the sink holes. The weather changes abruptly up there.
Members of the SAS have died on the Black Mountain, and even
now Alun Evans, who knows it as well as any man living, never goes
up without leaving a large-scale map at home, with instructions to
his wife as to when she should phone the police. The map is in their
front parlour, a small room his wife abandoned long ago to what he
calls his obsession. A large propeller stands behind the door, and
there are models of planes, bits of metal and a whole wall given over
to his books and files.

That first wreck of his came when he found a long ditch with
four deep gouges torn into the mountainside, which indicated a
four-engined bomber, and the fact that nothing grew there was a
measure of the fireball in which eight young men had died. This was

when he discovered that the Black Mountain was a graveyard for planes, six having come down within a radius of five miles. Remoteness and danger have deterred souvenir hunters, so he knows of the complete tail section of a Wellington in a place where even he dares not go.

Having found that first plane was a beginning, for it was not just bombers that had crashed. 'My two children were small, and I wondered whether these men had had children, whether they had been married, and it was then that I decided to trace their families. It seemed to me that if there were any of these still alive, they must often have wondered where it took place, this event which changed their lives. I looked around me at that desolate place where I found my first wreckage and there was nothing at all to say what had happened there. I remember thinking, I will see to it these men are remembered.'

And this is what he did. His researches produced a date. The date produced a list of names from the Ministry of Defence, which in turn produced the names of the next of kin from the War Graves Commission, also of the towns where the dead airmen had lived. There the trail ran cold, but he advertised in the local papers of those towns, which was when the first letter he had waited for, and dreaded, came. For how would the families react to his intrusion? He need not have worried. The letters, at first formal ('Dear Mr Evans, I am the brother…'), changed as soon as contact was established. 'Dear Alun, May I thank you…' In the end there was a memorial to that first plane on the mountain, and he met them, these people he felt he knew already and who felt they knew him. He stood there with them and felt things were at last complete. But there was another death he could not put out of his head, the death at Christmas.

It is now 1998 and a bleak winter's day of wind and rain as he and I begin our climb. At this height farmhouses have been abandoned, some in living memory, others long ago. There are still sheep in the fields but their owners have moved down, for the winters are terrible, as they were that December in 1944 when for three weeks fog and torrential rain closed in over Europe and made possible the German breakthrough in the Ardennes. Conditions this day are much as they were then, and from where we are, heads bent against the rain, we can see the weather changing beneath us as the gale blots out the valley. It occurs to me that I would not last a night out in the open here. 'What would he have eaten in those three weeks?'

'We don't know. He'd got down to the fields, there might have been kale, but he must also have had emergency rations.'

The constant rain had flooded the valleys and up here now streams had become rivers, brooks had become streams, so the whole hillside moved with red water. The rest was mud and broken gates. We waded through a stream and suddenly there were walls indicating an approach to somewhere, but walls so thick with lichen it might have been above the clouds, then more walls and stunted trees. 'This is it, this was where they found him.'

On the afternoon of 9 December 1944 a Lancaster with a largely Canadian crew was making a training flight, when at 2 p.m., 24,500 feet above Carmarthenshire, flying in cloud, it entered severe turbulence and went out of control. This plane already had a record. Just three days earlier it had suffered engine failure in a raid on the Ruhr and five members of another crew bailed out over the Continent, though the pilot later managed an emergency landing at RAF Manston. This time it went into an uncontrollable, screaming dive.

It is thought that they had flown straight into the centre of a huge cumulus nimbus cloud when a powerful updraught threw the Lancaster on to its back. The RAF records at Hendon record only that the pilot managed to regain control at 8000 feet, but that by then, 'through a misunderstanding four of the crew had bailed out'. The plane, with three still onboard, made an emergency landing on Fairwind Common, an airfield near Swansea.

You have to rely on your imagination for what really happened up there, the crew being thrown about so that one of them, the wireless operator, hurled against the main spar, was bringing up blood even before he jumped. Alun Evans found this out from 166 Squadron Association, of which the plane had been part, for facts were beginning to emerge. He had names now, that of the Canadian pilot R.H. Chittim, who had stayed on board, and that of the flight engineer, Trevor Jones, one of the four who had jumped.

He had also discovered that the plane itself, with the surviving members of the crew, was lost the following month in a raid on Germany, and this is one of the grim ironies that surrounds this story. But as to what happened on the Mountain, the mysteries persisted. Alun Evans contacted the War Graves Commission and was told that Sgt Jones had died on 9 December, even though the village knew he had lived for up to three weeks after that. But the Commission also informed him that Sgt Jones had come from Hucclecote near Gloucester and was buried there. Alun Evans wrote to the Mayor of Gloucester, asking him to suggest the local paper with the widest circulation in the Hucclecote area, which was how the story appeared in the *Gloucestershire Citizen*. The result was a letter that began, 'I have read your story of my brother Trevor in the local paper…'.

Ivor Jones, a retired aeronautical engineer, had been in Burma when his brother died, but his wife Edna, who had sung in concert parties with Trevor, remembered those terrible weeks when he had merely been reported missing. The other three airmen had been found safe and well the same day. All that had been found of Trevor was his neatly folded parachute, which was when the family ordeal had begun. For though it was said that he might have lost his memory, the RAF police were openly searching for a deserter. The result was that when the family first heard about Alun Evans's search, they were upset, as an old wound was being opened.

So what had happened? There were search parties out on the Mountain, so why had he not revealed himself to them? Why had he crawled 3 miles from where his parachute had been found? What follows is Alun Evans's theory. Trevor Jones, disorientated in that dive, was in great pain, having broken his leg on landing, but he had also come down in a landscape where a massive ground exercise had taken place before D-Day.

'Where he was, there would have been spent ammunition and wrecked vehicles which had been used for target practice. Until the 1950s there was even an old Churchill tank up there. He must have thought he was on a battlefield. And the searchers who were out would have been calling to each other in Welsh, which must have sounded foreign to him. It is possible that in his state of mind he thought he was in Occupied Europe.'

It is also possible that the incessant rain blocked out all sounds altogether, for he was making his way down towards the lights below him. This is the more poignant explanation, for below him was safety and Christmas, and he had almost made it – when he was found he was off the mountain and among fields, at the gate of Pentregronw Farm, deserted when the Army moved in for its exercises. The fact that he had managed to survive so long was a tribute to his fitness. Trevor Jones, Alun Evans discovered, had been an athlete.

He began to find out more, for the Vice-Chairman of the Gloucester King's School Society, where Trevor had been a chorister, wrote to him. There were photographs now of a good-looking young man. People who had known him began to write, remembering a cricketer and a mathematician. One old friend mentioned a bride who had her bouquet put on Trevor's grave. At Christmas, a half century on, another Trevor Jones, a schoolmaster named after his uncle, attended a candlelit midnight mass in Myddfai church.

'It was very moving,' said Judith McSwiney of the parochial church council. 'The story itself was moving enough, the way they carried him down the mountain and then, when they might have put him in some morgue, chose to lay him out like some great hero in the church. And on our Christmas Eve the priest took one of the poppies from the Remembrance Day wreath and put it in the crib, for now we had someone else to remember.' By an overwhelming majority the council voted to put up a plaque.

'My husband and I came down to meet Alun Evans,' said Edna Jones. 'At first we'd been a bit upset, but that was before we realised what a wonderful man he is. We went up the mountain with him. It was a terrible day. When we saw the landscape through which Trevor had come we couldn't believe it. I had some yellow roses with me, for it was a song he had loved singing, "The Yellow Rose of Texas". When we got to the place where he was found, Alun and the farmer whose father found Trevor, they went away and left us. I was glad his father and mother hadn't seen where he died. But there was something very moving about it, we knew so little, we'd just tended the grave and thought it such a waste. So we just stood there. And it was an ending.'

1998

PART SEVEN
PEMBROKE

THE CHILD SNATCHERS

They are a symbol of lost childhood, these swings, hanging in a deserted park at the end of Wales. Usually it is time that takes the children away, but not here. If I were to name the street where the swings hang, or reveal anything that would make it possible to identify the children who played on them, I should find myself in the High Court. For not only do the terms of the Children's Act apply, there are also injunctions in force here. This is a story without names.

That it is a tragedy no one would doubt. What is at issue is whether what happened four years ago in the small town of Pembroke is one of the greatest, and the most bizarre, miscarriages of justice in our time. The story that began in Cleveland years earlier, then moved on to Rochdale and the Orkneys, ended here. For the first time the case against an alleged paedophile ring employing satanic rituals had reached a criminal court – and there were convictions. Six men were sent down for a total of fifty-three years. This was the big one. It did not matter that only half of those who originally stood in the dock, six of the twelve, were convicted. The inquiry, said Ray White, chief constable of Dyfed–Powys, had been 'a model of perfection', involving 1200 police actions.

At its outset it had everything: cloaked figures, mass orgies in barns and caves, small, terrified children being transported around the countryside in trailers pulled by tractors. All the horrific scenarios that had been publicised for seven years by social workers were here on charge sheets in court; not in case histories or in care orders, but in a criminal court.

Yet, apart from a brief statement of those charges on the first day and an equally brief account of the convictions, it went unreported in the national press. It was hard to report on a case that went on for so long, in which no one, neither the accused nor the alleged victims, could be named.

The columnist Christopher Booker alone mentioned his doubts, referring to a case 'which will one day be looked on as a turning point in a singularly murky chapter in the history of English law'. Like many others, Booker thought everything would come right at the Court of Appeal. Only it didn't. The Court dismissed appeals by five of the accused and today Booker regards this case as the greatest single injustice he has encountered in recent years. He is not the only one. A defence barrister told me this had been the most worrying case of his career. Four years on, a solicitor said he still woke in the middle of the night thinking about Pembroke.

Then there is me. I was brought up in a small Welsh town of roughly the same size as Pembroke, just 20 miles away. It was the last time I was part of a *large* community. To live in a city is to live in a village of your friends and colleagues. To live in a town in west Wales is to know more people, and to know more about them, than you ever will again, because this is the noisiest, and most censorious, society on earth. If you stole a wheelbarrow, the whole town would know. Yet here I was expected to believe that for four years a conspiracy was in progress to abuse children and to practise satanic rites in just such a town.

'There is something very odd about this one. Like everyone else I was shocked when I heard the charges, but then they said an orgy had taken place in a garage in a nearby hamlet. I know the people who live there. I talked to them, and they said nothing could have bloody happened there.' This is David Allen, a man who spent his working life as a local journalist.

It all began in May 1991. A local boy of nine, already in care for a year, suddenly accused his father of sexually abusing him. The boy, subsequently the main accuser in the case, was a disturbed child from a broken home, and had been put into voluntary care by his mother, who felt unable to cope with him. Nobody had ever paid the child much heed. But then, after prolonged counselling by social workers, he was the centre of attention. The social workers were to set up a Child Sexual Abuse Therapy Group, which, to one defence solicitor, was 'a combine harvester awaiting its first harvest'.

The boy described orgies in barns, in which men in gowns fired shotguns into the roof to ensure the silence of the children who were being abused. Goats were ritually slaughtered in the local cemetery. The boy went on to accuse his mother, then other local adults, and how many he eventually named is not known, for the judge was to tell the jury, 'If everyone named had been charged, the case would have gone on forever.'

In August 1991 the boy's father was arrested. A well-known local man, who drove around the town in a tractor and trailer, he was notorious for his affairs with women, and, to those who knew him, would have been the last man on earth to find it necessary to prey on children. One of his fellow defendants is convinced he still does not know what has happened to him. 'He kept telling me when we were on remand that he thought Jeremy Beadle had something to do with it and that we would be out by the end of the month. He is doing fifteen years in Dartmoor now.'

But at the time of that first arrest the woman the tractor driver lived with was also interviewed and her three children taken into care. But a month later all charges were dropped and the man freed. The children, however, were not returned, being made wards of court. No charges were brought against the other adults, some of whom lived on the same council estate as their nine-year-old accuser. But a year later something happened in one of these families that was to change everything.

It was June 1992. A fourteen-year-old girl ran away from home, then accused her father of rape. The man was arrested, pleaded guilty and was sent down for seven years. This would have a considerable effect on the trial because, brought out of gaol, he was placed in the middle of the dock among defendants some of whom said they had never seen him before. He pleaded his innocence of being part of any paedophile ring, but the jury saw every day in court a self-confessed child abuser and the prosecution made much of his being there.

His presence also affected the prosecution team's outlook. 'On that housing estate, I heard someone say it was the culture that when a mother got to a certain age she handed her sexual duties over to her daughter,' said a barrister who had managed to convince himself that these were not people like us.

The daughter, interviewed for the second case by social workers, now began to talk about orgies and named adults; but her orgies – unlike those described by the boy – had a marine setting. She mentioned beaches and caves, even on a February night. In Swansea the one defendant credited with practical experience of *al fresco* sexual activity would later say, 'February in west Wales? Don't they know that would freeze the...'. In the midst of his troubles he went on to say what it would freeze. There were no jokes at the time.

December 1992 saw the first arrests after other children made similar statements. Eighteen children from nine families were taken into care. Eleven men and two women were arrested, of whom all but one of the women would stand in the dock. Some said they met for the first time there.

Who were they? They included two farmers, one of them an Englishman newly moved to the area, another aged eighty, who had to buy a new hearing aid just to hear the charges against him. 'That cost him £500,' said a fellow defendant. One man ran a scrapyard, one was a seaman, two unemployed. They were not formidable men. 'They got the blind, the halt and the weak,' said a local solicitor. They also got the child abuser out of gaol.

January 1994: the trial started. Within four months, the twelve in the dock had dwindled to seven, as the judge directed the jury that some defendants had no case to answer. The two adults expected to be prosecution witnesses, the former wife and the girlfriend of the man first accused, also recanted statements in which they had named people. The girlfriend said she had only named them because social workers had said she would otherwise never see her children again. 'I knew what they wanted me to say – I just added on and on, but none of it was true.'

A teenage boy also recanted, claiming he, too, had been pressured into giving a version of events by social workers. The prosecution case thus rested on the evidence of six children speaking over a videolink, and it was hard for the defendants to establish an alibi, for no dates or times were given. There was much medical evidence, bitterly contested, but there was no corroborative evidence, no forensic testimony.

Week after week, month after month, the jury (one of them with a T-shirt inscribed 'I'm Only Here For The Beer') heard all of this.

'I kept waiting for someone to say, "Hang on…", but nobody did,' said one defendant. 'I think I'd have found myself guilty if I'd heard all that stuff.' A defence barrister said: 'We were lucky, the judge let our man go at half time. Had he been standing there at the end, there is no doubt in my mind that he'd have been convicted.'

Which the others, with one exception, were. Then something very odd happened. The Social Services had not applied for a permanent care order on the children before the criminal trial but they did so after it was over, and one of the families, the wife acquitted, the husband sent down for seven years, decided to oppose this. And Mr Justice Connell, sitting in the Family Division of the High Court, refused to grant the care order, even though he heard the evidence the jury had heard. He said of one social worker, 'I attach very little weight to the conclusions she had formed from the interviews she had conducted.' This judgement created the extraordinary situation of a man found guilty in a criminal court, who had now, in effect, been found not guilty by a judge in a civil court, sitting without a jury.

The defence in the Pembroke case had to move heaven and earth to get the findings of the Civil Court admitted when the case went to Appeal. But it was admitted, and it was the first time this had happened in English legal history. When he was released, this man had served three years in gaol and was branded a child abuser. The appeals of the other five – who had no civil judgement to fall back on – were dismissed. What follows is the direct experience of two men caught up in the case, told as far as possible in their own words. First, there is the father's story.

'Right then, let's go sightseeing…'

He would like you to know his name. He would love you to know his name, and also the names of his children, because this is the man released by the Court of Appeal after three years in gaol. He is home again in Pembroke now, in the old house, picking up the pieces of his life. But his marriage has broken up. The two older children have moved away to live with their mother, and he lives with his youngest, whom he was accused of abusing. 'People need to know this story,' he said. 'I was thirty-four when this started, thirty-seven at the end. Three years went out of my life, during which, for eighteen months, I did not see my youngest child. Why us? In the process I got crushed. Come on then…'

He is a stocky, fair-haired man with the open face of a boy, and he was giving me a guided tour of the barns and sheds where the nine-year-old had said the ritual abuse had occurred. One of the most extraordinary features of the trial was that the jury was merely shown a video of these. Some years later, during a war crimes trial, a High Court judge took a British jury to their alleged location in Belorussia, but, despite defence requests, a jury sitting in Swansea was not brought to Pembroke.

'Right, this is the first one.' It is 50 yards from his house and is a small, corrugated-iron shed in the grounds of a small-holding. The shed is full of rusting machinery and old clothes, a mess that had built up over many years. 'They said there were thirty people in there shouting and squealing and letting off guns. Can you see any holes in the roof? It was supposed to be like a colander, the boy said, but they crawled all over it and didn't find a single hole. Now look at that house on the corner. How far away would you say that is? Ten yards? And there's a window at the side. Didn't they hear what was going on?'

He drove me through a town to a council estate. There was a graveyard on our left. 'That's where they were pouring goats' blood on the gravestones, but they never found any.' We turned into the council estate. 'That's the garage where they were supposed to be spinning a bottle to see who would go with who. See the size of it? If you dropped a hammer, the neighbours would hear.'

We were driving through the lanes. 'See those mud flats? They were doing something down there… Ah, here we are.' It was another shed that, like most of those I was shown, looked as though it was about to fall down. 'They're supposed to have brought a Land Rover full of kids to that. But see how close that house is? Did nobody hear anything? And these lanes were supposed to have had thirty or forty people walking along them. Nobody saw them. If you or I saw forty people in a lane, we would never forget it.'

We drove out of Pembroke to the farm that was mentioned in some scenarios. 'There were forty children screaming in a trailer pulled by a tractor. Now wait…' He had slowed, for on the Cleddau Bridge there is a tollbooth where you pay to cross. 'Odd nobody in that noticed forty screaming children.'

He began to describe his arrest. 'On 8 December 1992 I was turning into my workplace, which I'd had since November 1990 (though they said things had been going on there since *May* 1990), when these police cars blocked my way. I was told I was being arrested for being part of a paedophile ring. I didn't even know what the word meant. They took me into the Portakabin I used as an office and the phone rang. A policeman pulled the wires out. "You're not going to need this again."

'There were three days of being treated as the scum of the earth in Carmarthen police station. I wasn't told what had become of my wife – who was, I found out later, just one cell away. Then there was the court and running into court with a blanket over my head. They had searched my yard, I found out, and my house, for gowns, wigs, cloaks and guns. They took away one thing, a clown's wig I had bought my little daughter at a street market for 50p. I still have not had it back.

'For me the first moment of sanity was in Swansea gaol. The prison officers treated me as though I was not guilty, they let me use the phone as often as I wanted and did not lock me in. There was one odd incident. This chap asked me what was I was in for. I said I'd been charged with being part of a paedophile ring. "Whereabouts?" he asked. "Pembroke," I said. "Good God," he said. "And me." I'd never met him before.

'When the trial came, I just sat there, letting it all pass over me. If I had listened, I might well have been driven crazy. That is why I turned on Gerard Elias, the Crown prosecutor. I couldn't understand. I wanted to know why he was accusing me of those things. As I told him, he knew I was innocent… The odd thing was there was no despair. If you have not done something, you cannot despair.

'Then the Appeal. Can you imagine it? Someone gives the word, you walk over a line and you are a person again. That was in London and I had two guards I had never met before. One said to me after a day in court, "You know, pal, there's something strange somewhere…".

'When I came home I said to a neighbour, "I expect I'll move," but he said, "Oh, no you won't, d'you hear me?" One or two of the others have also been let out now and they have come back. And the boy who made all the allegations, he is also in town. One day we will all be back.'

Then there is the lawyer's story. He has kept one memento of the trial. This is an invitation to a party when it was over, and he has had it framed. A cartoon shows one of the defendants, with the Devil's horns and fork added, driving the tractor mentioned in evidence, though this time the trailer is full of happy, laughing lawyers. 'No cloaks or masks' insists the invitation.

'I kept that because it summed up the farce of the case and the attitudes of the men who took part. At the end they just walked away. I have never walked away and never will so long as I draw breath.' Michael O'Connell – and, for the first time, there is a name – is thirty-eight.

'I was horrified when I read the allegations. My firm came late to the case, when an accused husband and wife switched solicitors six months after their arrest. I read the papers at home, and when I started on the prosecution summary I said to my wife, "Bloody hell, this is really serious." Half an hour later, I went to find her. "You know half an hour ago I said we were in real trouble? I now think none of this is true." Nothing since then has made me change my mind.

'I read about a barn at harvest time in which twenty to thirty people, in capes and balaclavas, were having an orgy, with children in a pit being made to eat excrement and a fire blazing on the floor. I was brought up on a farm, they were terrified of fires in barns. Where was the smoke going? And how could a barn be empty in the middle of harvest?

'I was being expected to take seriously the idea that convoys of cars had rushed through the countryside and that all those children had just gone off to school on Monday morning. Had nobody noticed anything, no teachers, no GPs? At the end of the first file I thought the prosecution were insane. As for the social workers, I thought they needed help.

'And that was just the beginning. In a serious fraud case, which is about as big as you can get, there might be six folders of evidence. This had ten, and it took me three weeks to read my way through. The amount of paperwork in this case really would fill a barn, and it would take a pantechnicon to get it there. There were boxes of unused material. An old lady walking her dog at night said she had seen a huge fire with naked people dancing round it but when she got there they had vanished. But the police did not ask what had happened to the fire or if she had seen cars drive away. Yet they had taken this statement down.

'There was also one thing nobody mentioned. They talked about orgies on beaches in summer. In Pembroke in summer every bed and breakfast is full. For God's sake, where were all the tourists when all this was going on? When the trial judge refused to let the jury see the locations, one of the defence solicitors made a video of them. Do you know the greatest problem he faced? It was that wherever he filmed, whenever he did so, people kept straying into shot.

'If only someone had said, "This is not a case for a jury to decide." They were lost by day three. By the end they didn't know what was going on. They had heard months of evidence so complicated that, as far as they were concerned, they might have been asked to decide on whether there were black holes in space.

'Mr Justice Connell [the judge in the subsequent civil case] sat without a jury, he looked at the evidence and he said in effect, "This is rubbish." But the trial judge, Mr Justice Kay, took everything so seriously. It was probably his first case of this nature, and he lacked the experience a Family Court judge could bring. Unfortunately, the defendants paid dearly for this.

'Some children had genuinely come to believe that they had been abused. I don't know. What I do know is that vulnerable children suddenly found all this interest being taken in them. As for the nine-year-old boy, he was out on his own, a highly manipulative boy, capable of telling a QC to "F---off" when he did not like a line of questioning.

'But I also remember a twelve-year-old insisting that nothing at all had happened. The prosecuting counsel, Gerard Elias QC, grilled him for two hours, to the point where the boy could not remember his own age, but he could not be shaken. Elias kept asking him about naughty videos and, in the end, he said yes, he had seen one. It had the comedian Chubby Brown in it. So I had to sit there, and it was like watching a Beckett play, except that when the curtain came down, people were ruined.

'I remember two incidents. One chap owned a council garage in which, it was said, an orgy had taken place. Do you know the size of a council house garage? The Crown didn't. And this chap said no, he didn't think there could have been twenty people in his garage; the old Skoda was in there at the time. Well, they would have wheeled that out. No. Why not? The old Skoda was on bricks. It was such a moment of black humour.

'The other incident was quite different. My client, being cross-examined by Gerard Elias, suddenly said, "Mr Elias, you know all this is untrue." For a moment all the rules were disregarded, and he spoke so quietly and with such sincerity that there was total silence. This

QC, this clever man, he had no answer, he just stood there with his mouth open, but then the judge intervened. It was the one moment when commonsense broke in.'

And now accusers and accused pass each other in the streets of Pembroke. It is just that the circus has left town and the swings hang limp and abandoned.

COMING HOME

It was just a few weeks to the prisoner's release, and the guard was curious. Where, he asked, was he thinking of going? Home, said the prisoner. The guard shook his head. Surely it would be better to go to a hostel or somewhere away. He meant well. In the circumstances, said the guard, it would not be normal to go home.

'This was not a normal case,' said the prisoner.

And so a convicted paedophile came home.

Such an event may be familiar to you, given the television news coverage of similar homecomings. There should have been people with placards picketing a house, the police hustling a man away to a secret address and then, as this in turn became known, moving him on. A homecoming in Pembroke was not like that.

'All I've got to say is that he's back in the darts team,' said a man who had worked with him for fourteen years. 'Now I don't know whether you or your readers realise the significance of that. Pub darts teams are made up of big, hairy-arsed drinkers. Something like this would be guaranteed to rile them up, especially after a shed-full of beer. *And nobody has ever said anything to him.*

'Nobody to my knowledge, and I play in the same team, has even asked him what it was like inside. It's just "How's it going then?" Something stinks about this case, mate, and people know it.'

Again there are no names. These are well known now in the town of Pembroke, but because of the law I may not even give the darts player's name, in case, through him, someone could identify a released prisoner and through him the children involved.

A seaman, he was one of twelve defendants who in 1994 stood in the dock accused of being part of an alleged paedophile ring employing satanic rituals, his two sons, one sixteen, the other eleven, having testified that, with other members of the ring, he had abused them in public. But the jury, despite the boys' evidence against their father, found him not guilty of this. Instead, and inexplicably, they went on to find him guilty of abusing them in private, within the family. He was given eight years, the third longest sentence in the fifty-three years handed down to six of the accused. The others were released.

Like all those sent down, the seaman subsequently refused to acknowledge his alleged guilt. Apart from anything else, he dryly justified this on practical grounds. 'Do you understand, if you haven't done any of those things, you would have to memorise whole pages of evidence to say you had.' He thus did not qualify for parole, and when he came home he had served five years four months, the two-thirds of a sentence after which it is customary to release on licence.

'It was a hot day and I walked out into the garden. Suddenly there was a roar and one of my neighbours, a very large man, was stepping over the fences. To be honest, I wasn't sure what was about to happen, for in spite of all I'd said about coming home, I was still a bit nervous about how people would react. The next thing was this man was shaking me by the hand.'

Consider these facts. He came home, not to the anonymity of a city, but to a small Welsh town where news spreads quickly. He should have found himself a pariah. 'In the past seven years I've only ever heard one man say anything derogatory about him, and that was a bloke who said something to the effect that there was no smoke without fire,' said a friend. 'Anyway, he came out and the next thing he was at this man's sister's fiftieth birthday party and they were chatting away. Around here everyone believes it's a load of bollocks.'

Not everyone. To members of the county's Social Services department the accused 'were formidable and frightening, even in the dock'. To the chief constable of the investigating police force the inquiry was 'a model of perfection'. But the local MP has 'serious reservations' about the case and wants to see it referred to the Criminal Cases Review Commission.

For odd things keep surfacing. In gaol with the seaman was a man, also convicted of being part of the ring, whose son, then eleven, initially testified against him but then in court denied there had been any abuse. He said he had been pressurised into giving evidence by social workers. Nevertheless, a condition of his subsequent care order was that he should not see his father. This year the boy went to court to get the condition overturned and now visits his father who is still serving an eleven-year sentence. 'That was an eye-opener,' said the seaman.

He remembers as though it were yesterday the circumstances of his own arrest. 'It was Tuesday, 8 December when a dockyard policeman and two detectives came and said they had some questions to ask. "Fire away," I said. They said it was a buggery charge. Now I had been married just eleven weeks and my first wife, who had a record of mental illness, had been making things awkward for us. But then the detective said "Of children", and I just burst out laughing.'

Because of his wife's confinement in a mental hospital, and work which in his case meant he was away at sea, he had been obliged to put their two boys into care in 1989. Both, but in particular the elder boy, found this break-up of their family very painful. Then in 1992 there came to their foster home the boy who subsequently became the main accuser in the trial. His allegations made him the centre of attention.

It was now that the seaman's sons began to make allegations, initially against their father, then against other adults. The elder boy, who had been receiving psychiatric treatment from the age of seven but had never made such allegations before, named thirty-seven adults, not one of whom was arrested. Among those he named was a serving police officer.

'The police ransacked my house. They said they were looking for pornography, that I had photographs developed by some gypsies living in a quarry. They didn't find anything, there was nothing for them to find. They then took me away and I never came back for seven years. I sat in court and heard my son say there had been forty of us running round naked in a barn. I hate farms. I hate farm animals, they frighten me. He was asked about the road that ran by, hadn't people seen us? We all hid behind bales, he said. But when he was asked whether he and the boy who made most of the accusations might have made up some of these together, he said this: "There has been no collusion for any fraudulent or deviant purpose." A boy of sixteen said that. When the girl spoke, whose father in an earlier case had pleaded guilty to raping her, she was in distress and used simple words.

'The prosecution was worried about me. I had heard of one of the men who was accused with me, but that was all; I didn't know any of the others, having been at sea most of the time. So I was slipping out of the frame. But the charges on which I was convicted, "offences occurring between 6 February 1978 and 8 December 1992", do you know what those dates are? The first was when my son was born, the second the day on which he made his allegations. There was no way in which I could establish an alibi. Yet that jury found me guilty.

'When I went to gaol they wanted to put me through therapy, which is what they do with all sex offenders. I refused, as did the man who had been convicted with me. So there was no home leave, no open prison, no parole. But I talked about it to anyone who would listen and those who did said, "What the Hell is going on?" A lot of prisoners say they're innocent but they say this in an odd way. "I did touch her", that sort of stuff. I think they believed me.

'I remember one of the prison officers shaking my hand before I left. "Good luck, a few of us know. And remember, we didn't convict you." And this woman officer said, "There's something strange about this."

'There *is* something so strange it has to come out. I understand my elder boy is a policeman now, so he must have liked the courts. But I haven't seen him or my younger boy, nor do I want to ever again. I go to see my parole officer every Friday and I used to be asked about my offending behaviour. They've stopped doing that now. I just get asked, "Everything all right, any problems, how do you feel?" How do I feel? I've no job, I'm skint, and I have a record.'

And every Friday night, said a man who has all the time in the world on his hands, he played darts.

1999

PART EIGHT
DEPARTURES

BEHEMOTH CALLED, WITH ROSES

It happens once or twice in a man's life, rarely more, that he encounters a newspaper story so extraordinary he afterwards keeps the cutting in his wallet, the way an ancestor might have kept a holy relic. From time to time he shows this to others, but mostly he takes it out to read himself or to finger dreamily. This is mine.

The story appeared in the weekly *Carmarthen Journal*. It didn't make the nationals, and even the *Journal* did not think it worthy of the space it gave that week to the proprietor of a bus company who announced his retirement because 'he was tired of thinking'. The setting is Nott Square, called after a local general who invaded, then retreated from, Afghanistan. In our time a Soviet re-run of this prompted the world's outrage, but 150 years ago it got Nott a square, the townsfolk pulling down houses to accommodate his statue, the plinth of which he shares with the bishop burnt, amongst other things, for whistling to a seal.

And it was here, in Carmarthen's Civic Hall, that a Psychic Fair was held, something which so startled the *Journal* that it described it as a Physic Fair, not quite the same thing. To it came an astrologer, Raymond Castrogiavanni, a name redolent of eighteenth-century alchemy. The last time an astrologer came to Carmarthen was in 1403, when the Welsh leader Owen Glyndwr, having taken the town, summoned one. Since then the supernatural has fallen into disuse here.

But Mr Castrogiavanni, aged forty-one and a father of four, came, and did not come alone, being followed by his personal stalker, Linda Jane Miller, also aged forty-one, from Fife in Scotland. It is more than 400 miles from Fife to Carmarthen, but distance is apparently no obstacle to Linda Jane Miller who, according to Mr Castrogiavanni, has been stalking him for two years. So the fact that the events took place here is pure chance. Like Sarajevo in 1914, the town was merely a backdrop for the obsession of others, who lingered here for a day in summer.

Linda Jane Miller bought roses from Stems, the florist in Nott Square, which she intended to give to Mr Castrogiavanni. He, interestingly enough, had not seen her arrival in the stars. The first thing he knew was when he saw her coming through the doors, and he immediately sent out an alarm call to the local police on his mobile phone.

This is a feature that fascinates me. Why should an astrologer, a savant of the old world, have a mobile phone? Either he was a big-league stargazer with clients like the late

Princess of Wales, or he was frightened out of his wits by Linda Jane Miller, about whom the *Journal* threw in a little detail two-thirds of the way through the story. She weighs 18 stone.

I have never seen, let alone met, an 18-stone woman. Lady Hamilton weighed 14 stone at the time of Trafalgar, Nelson 6½ stone, which lends an element of awe, even geography, to their relationship. But 18 stone…? Behemoth had called, with roses.

Picture them for a moment, the father of four retreating and frantically dialling, she coming on through the foyer like a battle tank. How things might have resolved themselves is anyone's guess, except that rescue came in the form of WPC Sharon Davies. The only thing was, Carmarthen police, not short of 18-stone male constables, had despatched a nymph. WPC Davies is just 8 stone.

In trying to prevent Ms Miller from approaching the astrologer, she jumped on her back and found herself being carried irresistibly along. Ms Miller kept on advancing down the steps of the hall and into the fair, the policewoman clinging like Captain Ahab to the Great White Whale.

Did Ms Miller trip among the green baize and the astral charts or did the heavy mob arrive at last? All we know is that somehow she was stopped, for, as WPC Davies said proudly afterwards, 'On every other occasion police have just moved her on. This is the first time she has been arrested, and Mr Castrogiavanni was quite impressed with Carmarthen's police.'

Perhaps not so with the town magistrates. In spite of the fact that stalking is now a national issue, when Ms Miller appeared before them they merely bound her over to keep the peace for twelve months, so the scene shifts to other towns, other halls. But it has left me with a hopeless longing.

Two things I have always wanted to see: a Roman Legion on the march and a tea clipper under full sail. To these I now add Ms Miller at full gallop through Carmarthen Psychic Fair, WPC Sharon Davies up. We that are young shall never see so much, nor live so long.

THE WELSH GODDESS

A very old lady died last week in west Wales, dying in the house where she was born at the turn of the century and to which, in her last years, she had returned as a paying guest – to Coomb, now a Cheshire home. And that must be the end of it now. You can draw red lines under the Welsh squirearchy, the social class to which she belonged. Her name was Nesta Donne Philipps, later the Countess of Coventry.

My grandmother, to my father's irritation, curtsied to her, as her mother might have done and her mother before her, yet for the past forty years this lady went unrecognised in the streets of the local town. It is the speed with which the squirearchy have disappeared that is so remarkable, this class that dominated Welsh life for 1000 years – or more, in the case of the Rhyses of Dynevor, who claimed to have been at the court of King Arthur and had a family tree to prove it. Some went long ago. Kilvert met the last Gwynne of Glanbran, a hackney carriage driver in Liverpool. One of the Pryses of Gogerddan, once lords of 30,000 acres, became a barman in Shanghai, another a tramp, while a third fled abroad with the proceeds of a Talybont Flower Show. But somehow, mortgaged into infinity, the family lingered on, and, as I said in the Foreword, I met the last of them, a ghost from a past before feudalism.

When his grandfather, old Sir Pryse Pryse, of immense size even as a boy, turned up at Eton, it was in a suit of wool from his father's sheep, spun for him and then run up by the local tailor. It must have been like the arrival of Gareth at Arthur's court.

One or two squires in Victorian times still exercised the *droit de seigneur*. Thomas Lloyd of Coedmore, a Lord Lieutenant, driving to the Assizes with a judge, broke the silence by remarking affably that both the coachman and the footman were his bastards. He set the women up in houses all round his estate but boarded out his legitimate sons, like foxhound puppies, to quote his biographer, on neighbouring farms to save himself the trouble of rearing them.

Their estates were mostly small, their preoccupations local; one old squire, homesick in Italy on some Grand Tour, groaned aloud, 'Give me Narberth on a wet Sunday afternoon.' But at the end they were isolated, fenced off by their inability to speak the Welsh language they had neglected, by their Tory politics and by their championing of the Church in a nonconformist country.

Nesta alone lived on and on, twice widowed, with her portrait by De Laszlo to remind her of her beauty in that Georgian mansion at Llansteffan. Old men remembered seeing her ride, straight-backed and side-saddle, and marvelled that they should have seen such a thing. But a film of her wedding seventy-five years ago survives, in which it will forever be a September morning with the wind blowing as she comes, a head taller than her bridesmaids, Athene in the streets of Carmarthen.

1998

THE CHAPELS ARE CLOSING

The chapels of Wales are closing at the rate of one a week. *One a week.* Some, a few, are being converted, but the size of most of them rules out conversion by anyone sane. By the year 2000 the townscape of an entire country will be dominated by blackened teeth as, boarded up and abandoned, the chapels stampede out of history.

Where I live in Middle England, a man has for the past three years been converting the village Baptist Chapel; I went by last week and the work was almost done. A place built when things were still touch and go in the war against Napoleon is now a brand-new five-bedroom house, with only the varnished pine double doors and the rows of gravestones to remind people of what this was. It had been his second chapel, he volunteered, and soon he would be gone. He was not sure where, but probably it would be westward, where the big game was. The village chapels of England were always small, kept that way by the opposition of squire and parson, so they lend themselves to house conversion. But to the west lie the great temples of non-conformity, the Horebs and Smyrnas, Canas and Bethels. The Welsh called their chapels after place-names in the Bible, which is why every flashpoint of the Middle East has the puzzling suggestion of a domestic incident to people like me.

There are more than 5000 chapels in Wales, more than in all England and Scotland put together. Of these, at least 1000, according to Anthony Jones, Rector of the Royal College of Art, are currently under threat of demolition, and the process is just hitting its stride. But what is so curious is that Mr Jones, whose *Welsh Chapels* has just been published, is about the only man to show any interest in their fate.

Since 1993 there has been a Historic Chapels Trust in England, which takes into ownership 'chapels… of outstanding architectural or historic interest'. Nothing like this exists in Wales, where the Trust has been reluctant to intervene. 'We didn't want to take on more than we could chew,' said the director, Jennifer Freeman. There is a group called Chapel, but its function is to salvage chapel records and to photograph the building in its last throes. There is also the Welsh Heritage body, CADW, which can apply planning restrictions to the more bizarre conversions.

So what *have* the chapels become? 'A lingerie factory,' said Anthony Jones, 'furniture showrooms, a strip-club, agriculture feed stores, bingo halls, recording studios, a boxing club, squash clubs, climbing centres, a Women's Institute, the headquarters of the Welsh National Opera. And mosques.'

You have to have been brought up in this society to appreciate the shock of the tiny news item earlier this month in the *Daily Telegraph*. 'A chapel in Rhyl, Clwyd, where generations of Baptists worshipped, has become an Islamic Centre.' The most bizarre chapel of all, Crwys Road, Cardiff ('grotesque, but loveable… it stands like a toy castle in front of the railway station') has long been a mosque.

From the mid-nineteenth century on, there were always too many chapels. At one stage, following the religious revival of 1857, one chapel a week was being built and others extended. 'Built 1850. Extended 1855.' How often have I seen such proud plaques. Anthony Jones, who went through the 1906 Census, found there was a chapel for every 106 people in Wales, not all of whom were non-conformist anyway. They could never have been filled, not then, not ever. The early chapels of the seventeenth and eighteenth century, the little whitewashed rooms of the countryside where a man might talk to his God, were humble and beautiful so as not to draw attention to themselves. The fields where persecution forced them to worship were then still a living memory to their congregations.

By the mid-nineteenth century chapels were going up in the booming industrial towns, on which the shadow of the architect had fallen. For such men, these public buildings were a heaven-sent opportunity to ape every building style they had ever read about, with the possible exception of the pagoda and the igloo. And they were *huge*. A Wesleyan minister in Merthyr Tydfil was in the habit of creeping on to the site in the dark to move the builders' markers and thus increase the size of his chapel. Chapels Gothic. Chapels Byzantine. Chapels Doric. Chapels Corinthian. Chapels Romanesque. Chapels Doric *and* Corinthian *and* Romanesque. Chapels that were a complete anthology of 2000 years, culminating in Crwys Road, which has Dutch gables, some baroque, some classicism and also some art nouveau touches.

I grew up among them, passed them every day on the way to school, and it did not occur to me how odd they were, crouched between shops and houses, these temples that could have been built for Cecil B. De Mille. And they were odd, they were very odd, especially the frontages:

> The Trellwyn Methodists have built a church
> The front looks like an abbey

But thinking they can fool the Lord
They've built the back part shabby…

But, inside, they were all the same. They were designed so that attention was focused on the pulpit; not the little pulpits of the established Church, but vast structures floating in air, in which stood a man who seemed more than man. And the preacher could also see all of you below him in the rustling quiet of coughs and sweets being unwrapped. Never such authority again. Never such guilt.

When the chapels began to compete over the grandeur of their organs, they installed these behind the pulpit, so when the preacher rose, the pipes streamed from his head in a crown of polished metal, and Caesar stood in Bethel. And Smyrna. And Horeb. Where now the converters are coming, for the most part solitary, like the Mountain Men of the Old West, to camp out for two years or more in these great barns, the last hunting-grounds of their kind, and then to move deeper into the west. And all I can record is a bewilderment that all this has happened in one man's lifetime. Mine.

1996

A SCHOOL CLOSES

The children were playing with sand, which was fascinating them, small fists closing round it until it became a trickle falling but a tornado that moved across their world, burying cars and toy soldiers. They looked up when they saw the two men standing there.

'They've got more sand than we had,' one of these said to the other, genuinely indignant. For that had been the oddest thing about the evening: men in their forties forgot families and careers, forgot everything except that there was now more sand in a wooden tray, and it mattered. He must have felt he owed the three wary faces some explanation. 'We were here,' he said, 'in this school.'

They stared at him. It was their school; that it had ever contained creatures like this, out of pre-history, was too fantastic even to be entertained. But still they stared, for grown-ups were capable of anything, and perhaps these two had once sat, huge and hunched, inside their Wendy House.

That was new. But some things were familiar, and the man who had spoken had earlier picked up a reading book that had been used in his time, forty years before; he remembered one of the goblins. The man with him, a civil servant, was tugging on a coat-peg. He had not forgotten that peg, for one autumn morning he clung to it, kicking and screaming until his mother who had brought him took him home. That was his first day at school.

But there was something else, something so suddenly poignant it was like the skull painted into a Renaissance portrait. The three sheep-crooks, the ends bound in silver paper, were stacked against the cupboard as they always had been, awaiting the next generation of shepherds in the Christmas play. But the next Christmas would also be the last. My school is closing.

They, in this case the Church in Wales and the local education authorities, have decided it is too old. And it is old, it is 140 years old, though not a spot of damp appears inside the 20-inch-thick walls, not a window needs replacing, not a stone repointing. Small things like this, and the certainty that it will still be standing as the rain blows into the new brick barn, have not deterred them from closing my school, forty years to the month after I entered it. After all, it is just a primary school. It has no old boys' association, no roll of honour, no grand anniversaries. The grammar school that had stood in the town since Elizabethan times had all these and has gone as though it had never been, disappearing in a bagwash of educational change.

It had been thought that nothing would mark the passing of the Model School in Carmarthen, until one of its old pupils, Sian Morris, decided to hold her own ceremony, got together a small exhibition at her own expense and invited the exiles home. The response took her aback. The young came, who had just left, and men came who had been there during World War I. Middle-aged women stood round their old teacher and many talked of headmasters few of the others had even heard about. Mrs Morris had bought a buttonhole for the oldest pupil, only to find someone even older; and at the very last, like the Green Knight, an old lady appeared who had been there in Queen Victoria's time.

It was a wonderful evening. For days afterwards you came on little groups in the town talking about the event and the people they had met there. In a working-class childhood there were always faces that, because of the 11-plus, disappeared as abruptly as in any totalitarian state, so if you met them afterwards, either you or they were embarrassed, not knowing how to react. And now for this one evening they were together again in the rooms they had once shared. An eerie familiarity tugged at them, for they all knew where everything was and the only thing that was strange was themselves, those awkward bodies that could no longer fit into the chairs.

They looked at old photographs, remembering the days when they were taken and who had stood next to them. Buried selves, like much-loved heroes in fiction, were scrambling into the light, as they recalled old nicknames, old jokes, old bullies. Among the exhibits was a school report that had clearly been treasured over the decades, for there never was afterwards a triumph like this: 'No. of children in class, 26. Position in class, 1st.'

It was such a lovely little school. I remember its chestnut tree and the apple orchard that provided the prizes in the spelling tests; the smell of disinfectant on the wooden floors in summer; the smell of the wet coats in the lobby, which for one morning in 1948 had been sanctuary to Alan Jones, clinging to his peg.

The headmaster in my time was an old athlete called T.H. Jenkins, whose university career had ended gloriously when he lowered a chamber pot on a rope until it clinked on the bars outside the dean's room; the dean grasped it, only to find he could not bring it in, at which point Jenkins let the rope go. The reverend gentleman stood all morning in his window, chamber pot in hand, watched by the curious passers-by in the street below.

As a headmaster, Jenkins had two interests, music and the school sports; his year turned on the carol service, during which he brandished a baton, and on the sports, when he brandished a revolver. The rest of the time he would vanish into a shed, where I was always under the impression that he was making something. But his greatest impression on the school was his genuine belief that all his pupils were part of an elect, a belief he never lost. When my father died I was left with two 12-bore shotguns, which I had to license in the town, the difficulty being that I was no longer a resident. The police were awkward about it and I went to see T.H., then old and a retired magistrate. He picked up the telephone and rang an inspector who must have argued with him, for he suddenly growled into the speaker, 'Listen, you don't understand. This is an old Model School boy.' I think I could have had a licence for a field-gun, as an old Model School boy.

What we were taught at the school I cannot remember, except for the Bible, it being a church school, and fractions, which came one day and never went away. But Mrs Thomas, who taught the second form, opened an enchanted door. She lent me her collection of the old Welsh prose tales, the *Mabinogion*, and there was a forest on the sea, and a mountain above it, and only Branwen knew that it was her brother, whom no boat could hold, and his fleet, moving on Ireland.

One teacher was unmarried, and one break, bringing in the empty milk crates, I came on her and a male student teacher singing a duet, 'Sweet Lass of Richmond Hill', and standing close, too close, together; I quietly closed the door on them. Another woman wore tweeds and had her hair cut in the 1920s style, in an Eton crop. She threatened us with a leather tawse and one day went round the class asking the children what they called their parents. If you said 'Mummy and Daddy', you were ridiculed; I said 'Mum and Dad', and like Simon Peter heard the cock crow.

From time to time we had people come to lecture us. There was a wonderful gaunt man, all in black, who came with diagrams to address us on the evils of drink, and eight-year-old eyes opened in awe. From a suitcase he produced a jar with something green bobbing in it; it was, he said, a drunkard's liver. We thought it beautiful.

Because it was a church school the children were taken to all the major Anglican festivals. My parents, being Nonconformist, for some reason took a stand on this at first, so I had a series of guilty little half-day holidays, walking across the fields to my aunt's farm, firing my pop-gun at the spiders' webs in the dew. But later I was abandoned to the 39 Articles and sat through Ascension Day after Ascension Day, listening to the cold little voices singing. God, like fractions, was always hanging about somewhere. We had religious instruction every day and enacted scenes from the Bible. Once I was made to play Goliath.

There was an unchanging quality about the school. Adolescence was another country, except for the head boy whose voice broke in the last year. He fell in love with one of the girls in a bewildering, practical way, and we used to come on him hanging round her door at night. He would not play with us.

The rest of us were only just emerging from a long-running battle with our bodily functions. One boy kept suffering defeat. I was sharing a desk with him when one of these defeats occurred, and we stared together at the terrible puddle on the floor. But he was possessed of an imagination: he poured ink into the puddle and told the teacher it had been spilt. I saw him a few years back in a pub and he told me tales of North Sea rigs and the money he was earning. Later I found out he had been on the dole for years.

Another boy was what is now called dyslexic, but not then. One of the teachers used to read out the papers he had covered with reams of writing during exams: 'Emergi, ramscona yargo.' Everyone laughed, but I remember turning and seeing a pale face that had closed on itself like a fist. Then the trap doors of the eleven-plus opened and both boys were gone.

Whatever is said about comprehensive schools now, remember this: the eleven-plus was a terrifying thing. You heard the sound of it, forms away, like weirs on a summer river, and however much you tried to forget, there was no way round. For two years we were in daily training for it, with even God elsewhere for once, and when it was over, two-thirds of the children I had grown up with had gone. The headmaster read out the names of the successful in front of the school, and for most there was no failure to run it close afterwards, for this was failure in front of an entire community.

Someone had kept the eleven-plus papers dating back to World War I and I came on the arithmetic paper I had sat. 'A soldier's step measures 2ft 7½in. How many miles will he travel in 1hr 20 mins if he takes 132 steps a minute?' In 1987 it took me close on an hour to work it out; in 1953 it was one of eight questions in an exam lasting an hour. And the question I still dream about was there, involving weeks in a year, which I worked out on the basis of fifty weeks in a year, so all roads led to two-thirds of a man. But the early papers were incredible. The rainfall in Port Said, and this: 'What were the Crusades? In what ways did they affect the life of the people of this country?' That had been set in 1916. I looked at the faces of the older people who must have attempted such questions.

One face I did not see. She was in my class; she was six years old, and when we had gym she would tie my shoe-laces for me. Welsh mothers do this for their sons (the historian Gwyn Williams once spoke of his gratitude to the British Army, which had taught him to tie his shoe-laces on the eve of D-Day). I had not asked her to: I must have been sitting there blank with misery until she knelt down. Her hands had little cracks in them, and I can see them now. I only met her once in later years, and she was married and pregnant; when I got out of my car she asked brightly how many miles it did to the gallon, and I did not know.

When the reunion was over I met a man the same night who had not gone. He was out on bail on a fraud charge that involved so much money, the news report of it had forced the resignation of the Swansea Town manager off the front page of the local evening paper. There was a flash of gold as he lifted his drink. There was gold on his wrists, gold at his throat; during a break in the conversation he told me the price of gold that day in dollars.

He had always, he said, hated the school. It was all to do with the spelling and the apples. Because he had never learnt to spell, he had never been given any apples, and he was bitter. It had turned him against apples, he said. It had turned him against spelling, too, and he had managed, he said proudly, to spell one of his aliases wrong on one of his three cheque-books. His ambition, he said, was to have his case postponed again; he hoped to see the bulldozers go into the school.

1987

AFTER 800 YEARS, THE ESTATE AGENTS CLOSE IN

She came as a bride, arriving at night. It was only in the morning that she saw the scale of it, the passages and paintings, and the damp. She leaves it a widow, and next week, for the first time in 800 years, a house on this site is for sale.

In the valley where I was born there were three great houses, one of which became an agricultural college, another passing into the possession of the National Trust. But in the third – until now – the old family lived on. Think for a moment: a house where no estate agent ever came, one without deeds or conveyance of any kind, a house so old the prospectus bewilderedly records that it has been in the possession of one family 'for all time'. A huge roll of parchment the size of a carpet hangs on a wall. Fully extended, the roll is 28 feet long and is as close to a title deed as they will ever get, being marked, simply, 'Pedigree'. This, too, is up for sale, for it is all over, and she, this small, elderly lady, is the last of them in the great house.

For weeks hers has been a world of strangers. They came and went, the smart young men from Sotheby's who knew the price of everything and the journalists who published these prices – which so terrified her that she hired a security guard, something she had never thought of doing before. In between these, the men from the national collections came, who asked few questions but talked apart among themselves. All were enchanted, seeing Tudor friezes and furniture, incredibly, from the late Middle Ages on which the carved battle scenes did not feature a single gun.

But a few may have been caught by the human drama of an old couple who chose to live on alone here in fewer and fewer rooms, the beetle tapping, the damp spreading every year. The small, elderly lady hovered and smiled, and tried to forget that these people were walking through her life.

'When we moved in, we would lie in bed, my husband and I, hearing these crashes in the night. At one point we came to think the place was haunted, but I told him, "Don't worry, it's only another ceiling gone."' She and her husband were a remarkably handsome couple, their young faces looking out of the many framed photographs that will not be sold. But it was her humour that caught me, for then her face lit up and it was the face of the photograph. 'I suppose if we'd had children, we might have tried to do something about some of the rooms. But where do you start when you have forty-four of them? We turned the key in another door and the holidays got longer.'

The warlords had become squires; the squires, Justices of the Peace. But it was only in 1887, when the County Council Act put local administration in the hands of popularly elected bodies, that their influence began to wane. At first we did not notice, for they were still there in houses few of us had seen, at which death duties began to nibble. This estate, which once stretched for almost 16 miles, is just 240 acres in the sales prospectus now. In the last quarter of the twentieth century the great houses died.

The servants who once posed dutifully on the lawns are long gone. Two chainsaws hang in the conservatory, because keeping warm represented a major effort in this family's last years. But the hard-faced men of the seventeenth century and the pop-eyed heiresses of the eighteenth still line the walls. 'We used to have such trouble finding a birthday present for my husband's cousin who lived here before us. I suggested giving her a print one year. He just smiled. It was only when we moved in that I found out why. There were so many things hanging up, it was impossible to see the colour of the walls.'

The husband died this year. By then they had moved downstairs into the one room with portraits and the pedigree. Old tenants, their farms sold off to them long ago, rang daily to check how she was. One young man had called that morning to leave a packet of Mr Kipling's cakes at her door.

She had no self-pity, such people rarely do. They rehearse this moment, knowing there is absolutely nothing they can do about it. In the great hall at Derwydd an old lady talked about bungalows, which appeared to interest her very much.

1998

EPILOGUE:
THE BANK MANAGER AND
THE HOLY GRAIL

It was late in the afternoon when I almost found the Holy Grail. Hah, you don't often get to read a sentence like that. It had taken me the best part of two days, the almost finding, but then I had an edge on the Knights of the Round Table: I had a reference library on my side. Sir Lancelot almost found the Grail in the Castle Carbonek, guarded by two lions. I almost found it in Lloyds Bank in Aberystwyth, guarded by Mr Jack Jones, the manager – at least the memory of it, for the Grail had been moved. The Grail was always being moved.

'I have seen so many great marvels that no tongue may tell, and more than any heart can think,' reflected Lancelot. 'And had not my sin been before time I had seen much more.'

That must have been it, the sin. For two days I had had a bit too much fun confusing a whole line of bank managers' secretaries across Cardiganshire. You must imagine the bright, hard little voices. 'I'm sorry, Mr Humphreys is in a meet-ing. Anything I can do? I'm his PA, can you tell me what you want to speak to him about?'

'The Holy Grail.'

A long pause, after which there was nothing bright or hard about the little voice. 'How are you spelling that?'

I had just one clue. I had heard that at some point in the 1950s the Holy Grail, or what many people devoutly believe to be the Holy Grail, had been in the strong room of a bank somewhere in Cardigan-shire, so with a list of numbers from Cardigan to Aberystwyth, I began to phone. And late on the second afternoon there was this.

'That was before my time but, yes, it was here,' said Mr Jack Jones. 'I found in the records that we had a package deposited here then. Nobody saw it, for it wasn't entered as the Holy Grail, but as the Nan-teos Cup. I assumed it was something to do with horse racing.' Of course, the unopened package. 'And he saw a table of silver, and the holy vessel covered with red samite…'

The trail went cold for a bit, but then I was told of a family which, inheriting the old house in Cardiganshire where for centuries the Grail was kept, became its hereditary keepers. But they had moved, taking it with them, and the present Guardian, an unmarried lady in her fifties studying for an Open University degree, was under such pressure from people wanting water the Grail had held, a request she could not refuse, that no one would give me her address.

> But there is always a thing forgotten
> When all the world goes well,
> As the gods forgot the mistletoe,
> And softly as an arrow of snow
> The arrow of anguish fell.

The thing that people forget is the stacked telephone directories in all reference libraries. Directory Enquiries, now these have been comput-erised, will give you a number only if you have a specific address, but the books, provided you have a name, allow you to hunt, area by area, across an entire region. Which was how I came to a little house in a lane. Lions greeted Lancelot. Lion dogs greeted me, five little Pekinese leaping in welcome, only too eager to see this latest pilgrim.

'Y Graal Sanctaidd' in Welsh. The 'Saint Graal' in Old French. From the Latin *cratella*, a small bowl. It was this that spelt the end of the Round Table when it appeared in a sunbeam at Camelot, for then the quest of Arthur's knights began. 'He took the Cup and when he had given thanks, he gave it to them, saying, "Drink ye all of this, for this is my blood of the new testament, which is shed for you and for many for the remission of sins."' They were seeking the Holy Grail from which Jesus drank at the Last Supper.

It enters European tradition in the early medieval French romances of the Round Table, in which details vary. At times it provides food, which suggests a link with Celtic legends of the replenishable cauldron. At other times it is a reliquary made of gold, out of which such brightness shines that it puts the candles out. This is the Grail of health, offering perennial youth. But other details are shared. The Grail, it was said, was brought to Britain, and to Glastonbury, by Joseph of Arimathea. But the odd thing is that the monks of Glastonbury, who laid claim to so many marvels, the Holy Thorn and the grave of Arthur among them, never once claimed they had the Holy Grail.

Glastonbury even said it had the tomb of St Joseph of Arimathea, though the monks were a bit vague as to where this was. But in 1345 someone called John Blome, a man with his eye on the main chance (like his namesake who sold washing machines in the twentieth century), applied to the King for permission to conduct a dig there for the saint's bones. Not only did he get this, but Edward III himself also replied, 'hoping for ourselves and our realm a wealth of grace from the revelation aforesaid'. Yet about the Grail itself, the supreme relic… nothing. But then, as Professor R.F. Treharne noted in his book *The*

Glastonbury Legends, the Church itself had never given formal recognition to the Grail story. There was too much magic involved: the Grail, even at a time when two Italian monasteries laid claim to the foreskin of Jesus, was a bit too dodgy.

Even so, it is in Glastonbury that there starts what John Matthews, author of *The Grail, Quest for the Eternal*, has called 'a very fragmented history, but still the best, most connected Grail story'. It starts on the eve of the Dissolution of the Monasteries, with Henry VIII's Commissioners closing in on all the holy relics, when the last abbot of Glastonbury (later to be hanged on the great hill above his Abbey) entrusted his most holy, and most secret, relic to seven monks. They fled westward with the Grail to one of the most inaccessible of monasteries, Strata Florida in the hills of Mid Wales. From there, as the hunt again closed implacably in, the Grail passed into the keeping of the squires of even more inaccessible Nanteos.

There is nothing too bizarre about this. The gentry, particularly those living in the more far-flung corners of his realm, could defy Henry in their championship of the old religion. Nor should we read too much into the fact that for centuries nothing was heard about the Grail, or at least nothing that reached the ears of men recording historical events. All this was taking place in the far west, where the culture was monoglot Welsh. It was only in the nineteenth century that it became known that a family of Welsh squires, the Powells of Nanteos, had in their possession a little bowl 4 inches in diameter and made of olive wood. This, according to tradition, was the Holy Grail.

It looked then much as it looks now, like part of a coconut shell with teeth marks on it. Deike Begg, author of *In Search of the Holy Grail and the Precious Blood*, said, 'I met someone whose aunt had been to tea there in the 1930s, and the Cup was just sitting there in the parlour, much chewed, for they used to send it out to local people when they were ill, and they would take bites out of it. To the Powells it was no great deal, they had the Holy Grail and that was that.'

Their butlers' receipts survive, recording to whom it was lent and what sureties were left against its return; '3rd August 1862, the Cup lent to Wm Jones, Llanbadarn. Left a silver watch; returned 4th September 1862. Case cured.' The more you hear about whatever it was they had at Nanteos the more you realise that the Middle Ages, and their beliefs, are not over, nor will they be over in our time. Supplicants and Guardians alike had a matter of fact attitude to the miraculous, though the fact that the Welsh had started to eat, not out of the Grail, but the Grail itself, was something quite new to the myth.

Nanteos, in the hills behind the town of Aberystwyth, would have seemed like the end of the world, even to nineteenth-century travellers. Its present owners, intent on transforming it into a country hotel, are wary of its long association with the Grail, fearing the sort of visitors this might attract. But to the Powells, a line of hard-drinking countrymen, the Grail was just part of the inventory of the house.

Its national fame may be said to have come at the end of the nineteenth century, when the Bishop of St Davids said that not only had it come from Strata Florida, but that he also thought it a piece of the True Cross. At some point the tradition came that Wagner stayed at Nanteos when he was working on his *Parsifal*. But the odd thing is that the poet Swinburne did stay yet nowhere mentions the Grail, even though other features of his visit, like his experiences in the pubs of Aberystwyth, remained vividly with him. 'Give my remembrances to my sailors,' he wrote to his friend George Powell. Old Squire Powell of Nanteos had such doubts about his son George's masculinity (he wrote poetry), he once gave him a loaded shotgun and sent him out into the park, telling him not to come back until he had shot something. George shot a bullock.

The Powells died out in 1956, at which point the present family of Guardians inherited both the house and the Grail. During their five years there they claimed to have experienced its power when in 1959 a ladder fell on the youngest child. She was taken to Aberystwyth Hospital with a fractured skull and it was reported that her case was hopeless on account of the bleeding. It was then that her mother took the Grail from its box and prayed. Ten minutes later the hospital phoned to say the bleeding had stopped.

At first they had been prepared to show the Cup, even putting it on exhibition in the National Library of Wales, but growing public interest, especially when the Fundamentalist churches of America became involved, was one of the reasons behind the move from Nanteos in 1961. By then the Grail had had some strange adventures. On one occasion it was loaned to an American millionaire, and it was only the intervention of the late Bob Danvers-Walker, who used to announce the prizes on the old TV programme *Take Your Pick*, which secured its release. American Baptist ministers, with television crews, have since wandered the Welsh Border trying to find it, and various vicars of Glastonbury have demanded its return.

You may get an idea of its effect from the testimony of one man, himself not a believer. By sheer doggedness on his part he managed to track the family down. 'I had been talking about the Cup to the present Guardian's mother when she said, "Would you like to see it?" Now, not for a moment do I believe it to be the Cup from which Jesus drank, but when she said that... It is a mere fragment now, riveted together. She held it, and I looked at it. It is very dark with a deep grain in what is said to be olive wood. Then she passed it to me and for a moment I held it in my hands. *And it was very cold*. I was, I must admit...'. He paused, searching for the word. 'Impressed.'

Whatever it is, this cup is very old. The Dean of St Davids, a historian who saw it when it was on show in the National Library, thinks it is a treen, a wooden drinking vessel from the Middle Ages. And the man I have quoted, who held it in his hands and felt the coldness, received some water from it some years ago when he suffered a slight stroke. 'I may not believe that it is from the Last Supper, but when so many people have believed in something for so long, that thing acquires power.'

I also have water from it. This is in a small, brown plastic bottle on the top shelf of a bookcase, which once contained a vet's prescription and still has the label 'For Animal Treatment Only'. What I believe, or do not believe, is of no account. All I know is that I treat a small, brown plastic bottle with the wariness I reserve for fuse boxes.

The Cup is in another bank now, the manager this time left in no doubts, for it is in their records as the Holy Grail. The present Guardian takes it out once a month to supply water from it to those who ask for this. I promised not to use her name or to give this to anyone who asked. There is just a little house, smelling of dogs, in a lane where one afternoon I called and am not sure as to what I found.

2000